THE

CENSUS OF IOWA

AS RETURNED IN THE YEAR 1867,

SHOWING, IN DETAIL, THE POPULATION, AGRICULTURAL STATISTICS, DOMESTIC AND GENERAL MANUFACTURES, AND OTHER ITEMS OF INTEREST.

PUBLISHED UNDER DIRECTION OF THE CENSUS BOARD.

WILLIAM M. STONE, GOVERNOR,
ED WRIGHT, SECRETARY OF STATE,
JOHN A. ELLIOTT, AUDITOR OF STATE,
SAMUEL E. RANKIN, TREASURER OF STATE,
} CENSUS BOARD.

DES MOINES:
F. W. PALMER, STATE PRINTER.
1867.

THE

CENSUS OF IOWA,

AS RETURNED IN THE YEAR 1867.

SHOWING, IN DETAIL, THE POPULATION, AGRICULTURAL STATISTICS, DOMESTIC AND GENERAL MANUFACTURES, AND OTHER ITEMS OF INTEREST.

PUBLISHED UNDER DIRECTION OF THE CENSUS BOARD.

WILLIAM M. STONE, Governor,
ED WRIGHT, Secretary of State,
JOHN A. ELLIOTT, Auditor of State,
SAMUEL E. RANKIN, Treasurer of State,
} Census Board.

DES MOINES:
F. W. PALMER, STATE PRINTER.
1867.

CENSUS RETURNS,

SHOWING THE POPULATION OF THE SEVERAL COUNTIES OF IOWA FOR THE YEAR 1867.

ADAIR COUNTY.

No. of Township.	Range.	Names of Townships, Towns, and Cities.	Names of Post-Offices.	No. of Dwelling Houses	No. of White Males.	No. of White Females.	Total White Population.	No. of Colored Males.	No. of Colored Females.	Total Colored Population.	No. entitled to Vote.	No. of Militia.	No. of Foreigners not Naturalized.	No. between the ages of 5 and 21 years.	No. of Blind.	No. of Deaf and Dumb.	No. of Insane.
74 75	30	Grand River	Hebron (T. 75)	29	88	85	173	....	....	....	31	13	8	66	..	..	..
74 75	31	Greenfield	Greenfield (T. 75)	18	60	51	111	....	....	....	27	27	....	45	..	..	..
76	31	Grove	....	7	20	18	38	....	....	....	10	8	....	10	..	..	..
76	30	Harrison	Arbor Hill	47	133	125	258	....	....	....	52	47	....	111	..	..	..
75 76	33	Jackson	....	37	115	75	190	....	....	....	50	38	....	72	..	..	..
77	31	Jefferson	Holiday	23	63	60	123	....	....	....	28	24	1	48	..	..	..
74	32	Richland	....	17	58	52	110	....	....	....	20	20	....	52	..	..	..
75 76	32	Summerset	Fontanelle (T. 75)	26	97	87	184	....	....	....	48	37	....	66	..	..	..
77	32 33	Walnut	....	11	26	29	55	....	....	....	12	10	....	18	..	..	..
74	33	Washington	....	47	179	173	352	....	....	....	61	40	5	150	..	..	1
....	....	Total	....	262	839	755	1594	....	....	....	339	264	14	638	..	..	1

ADAMS COUNTY.

No. of Township.	Range.	Names of Townships, Towns, and Cities.	Names of Post-Offices.	No. of Dwelling-Houses.	No. of White Males.	No. of White Females.	Total White Population.	No. of Colored Males.	No. of Colored Females.	Total Colored Population.	No. entitled to Vote.	No. of Militia.	No. of Foreigners not Naturalized.	No. between the ages of 5 and 21 years.	No. of Blind.	No. of Deaf and Dumb.	No. of Insane.
73	33	Carl	Carl	23	75	57	132	...	...	...	27	17	...	59	..	..	..
73	32	Colony	Nevinville	13	35	37	72	...	...	...	16	13	...	23	..	..	..
72 73	35	Douglass	...	37	138	119	257	...	...	...	56	35	2	114	..	..	..
71	34	Jasper	Simpson	30	100	103	203	...	...	...	38	31	...	78	..		..
71	35	Nodaway	East Nodaway	57	191	182	373	2	6	8	76	59	4	171	..	..	..
71	33	Queen City	...														
72	33	" "	...	51	152	111	263	...	...	...	63	43	2	104	..	..	..
pt 72	34	" "	Queen City														
pt 72	34	Quincy	Quincy	101	270	266	536	...	1	1	112	91	1	223	..	..	
71 72	32	Union	...	22	78	53	131	...	...	...	30	26	...	42	..	..	1
73	34	Washington	...	56	176	165	341	...	...	...	65	54	...	165	..	..	..
...	...	Total	...	390	1215	1093	2308	2	7	9	483	369	9	979	..	..	1

ALLAMAKEE COUNTY.

No. of Township.	Range.	Names of Townships, Towns, and Cities.	Names of Post-Offices.	No. of Dwelling-Houses.	No. of White Males.	No. of White Females.	Total White Population.	No. of Colored Males.	No. of Colored Females.	Total Colored Population.	No. entitled to Vote.	No. of Militia.	No. of Foreigners not Naturalized.	No. between the ages of 5 and 21 years.	No. of Blind.	No. of Deaf and Dumb.	No. of Insane.
98	4	Center	Elon	154	472	420	892	...	...	...	149	83	47	355		..	3
96	3	Fairview	Allamakee	92	306	280	586	...	...	...	117	44	11	260	..	..	..
96	5	Franklin	Volney, Hardin	132	395	398	793	1	...	1	162	127	4	351	..	2	..
99	5	French Creek	French Creek	125	346	322	668	...	...	...	113	55	18	278	..	..	..
99	6	Hanover	...	73	240	202	442	...	...	...	71	46	18	161	2	..	2
100	3 4	Iowa	...	55	166	118	284	...	...	...	65	38	3	123	2	..	..
97	5	Jefferson	Rossville	176	560	493	1053	...	...	...	184	162	4	414	..	1	..
98	2 3	Lafayette	Village Creek (R. 3)	170	529	495	1024	...	...	...	193	107	106	402	..	1	..

99	3 4	Lansing, excl. of town		164	483	413	896	5	4	9	171	96	19	326	..	1	..
In 99	3 4	Lansing, town of	Lansing (R. 4)	196	812	725	1537	1	....	1	351	333	35	444	..	..	1
96	4	Linton	Ion	92	257	219	476	....	....	...	97	64	7	176	..	..	1
97	6	Ludlow	Ludlow	159	391	382	773	....	....	...	153	112	9	297	..	..	..
98	5	Makee	Waukon, Lycurgus	282	832	792	1624	....	....	....	354	193	80	596	..	..	1
97	4	Paint Creek	Waterville	176	560	548	1108	....	....	...	171	99	50	437	..	2	..
96	6	Post	Postville, Lybrand	210	504	503	1007	....	....	...	222	148	5	351	..	1	..
97	2 3	Taylor	Harper's Ferry (R. 3)	151	452	463	915	....	....	....	171	103	1	415	2	..	..
100	5	Union City	Clear Creek	77	216	209	425	....	...	....	75	52	16	127	1	..	..
98	6	Union Prairie	Union Prairie	163	441	424	865	....	....	....	161	73	25	341	1	..	..
100	6	Waterloo	Dorchester	115	306	303	609	8	7	15	101	63	35	229	..	..	..
		Total		2762	8268	7709	15977	15	11	26	3081	1998	493	6083	9	8	8

APPANOOSE COUNTY.

pt 68 69	18	Bellair	Numa (T. 68)	102	316	271	587	1	....	1	116	84	....	267	..	..	1
pt 67	16	Caldwell															
pt 67	17	"	Caldwell	163	493	463	956	1	....	1	192	138	....	429	1	2	..
pt 68	17	"															
pt 68	17	Center															
pt 68	18	"	Centerville	201	738	703	1441	2	5	7	295	228	1	584	..	2	..
pt 69	17 18	"	Dennis (R. 17)														
pt 70	18	Chariton	Iconium	120	337	322	659	....	...	.	136	80	....	290	..	..	1
pt 69 70	17	Douglas		67	227	247	474	...	....	....	97	59	....	185	..	..	..
pt 67	19	Franklin	Livingston	126	345	341	686	2	5	7	137	102	....	315	..	1	..
pt 68	19	"	Hibbsville														
70	19	Independence	Milledgeville	129	474	438	912	....	....	..	173	128	1	413	..	2	..
69	19	Johns	Memphis	109	359	318	677	....	....	....	130	104	....	316	..	1	..
pt 68	19	Lincoln	Jerome	83	253	220	473	....	....	....	80	59	....	175	..	..	..
pt 67	17 18	Pleasant	Cincinnati (R. 18)	147	402	386	788	5	3	8	181	117	8	341	..	..	..
pt 68 69	17	Sharon		59	251	225	476	....	....	...	88	61	1	201	1	..	..
pt 70	17	Taylor	Moravia	149	526	468	994	1	....	1	216	167	....	408	3	4	..
pt 70	16	Union		92	340	310	659	....	....	....	125	96	....	313	..	..	2
pt 69 70	16	Udell	Unionville (T. 69)	150	445	422	867	....	....	....	166	128	....	389	..	..	..
pt 69 70	18	Walnut	Walnut City	101	338	328	666	....	....	....	143	108	....	288	1	1	..
pt 68 69	16	Washington	Orleans (68), Beetrace (69)	149	479	498	977	5	2	7	174	140	1	417	..	2	..
pt 67 68	16	Wells	Wells Mills (T. 67)	125	380	351	731	5	3	8	143	92	....	318	2	1	1
		Total		2072	6703	6321	13024	22	18	40	2592	1891	12	5649	8	16	5

AUDUBON COUNTY.

No. of Township.	Range.	Names of Townships, Towns, and Cities.	Names of Post-Offices.	No. of Dwelling-Houses.	No. of White Males.	No. of White Females.	Total White Population.	No. of Colored Males.	No. of Colored Females	Total Colored Population.	No. entitled to Vote.	No. of Militia.	No. of Foreigners not Naturalized.	No. between the ages of 5 and 21 years.	No. of Blind.	No. of Deaf and Dumb.	No. of Insane.
		Audubon	Hamlin's Grove	34	86	98	184				41	32		70			
		Exira	Exira	52	158	154	312				74	54		120			
		Oakfield	Oakfield	53	156	138	294				63	41		98			
		Total		139	400	390	790				177	127		288			

BENTON COUNTY.

No. of Township.	Range.	Names of Townships, Towns, and Cities.	Names of Post-Offices.	No. of Dwelling-Houses.	No. of White Males.	No. of White Females.	Total White Population.	No. of Colored Males.	No. of Colored Females	Total Colored Population.	No. entitled to Vote.	No. of Militia.	No. of Foreigners not Naturalized.	No. between the ages of 5 and 21 years.	No. of Blind.	No. of Deaf and Dumb.	No. of Insane.
85	9	Benton		129	369	362	731				127	101	1	256			
84	11	Big Grove		95	295	253	548		1	1	126	99		223			
86	12	Bruce		50	140	131	271				58	41	1	120			
84	9	Canton	Shellsburgh	222	699	601	1300	1		1	297	235	4	510			
86	11	Cedar	Mount Auburn	132	425	362	787	1		1	175	141	4	340			2
84	10	Eden	Unity	92	315	250	565				126	99	7	202			
83	10	Eldorado		31	118	89	207				44	33	3	76			
82	9	Florence	Florence	141	437	399	836				124	119	56	319			
83	9	Fremont	Robin	74	212	188	400				67	50	10	131			
86	10	Harrison	Burke	92	270	239	509				103	84		219			
84	12	Homer		38	99	84	183				44	32	1	56			
82	12	Iowa	Belle Plaine	283	970	876	1846				418	339	47	655	1		1
85	11	Jackson		117	393	347	740				144	80	8	324			
83	12	Kane		59	184	170	354				76	57	14	125			
82	11	Leroy	Blairstown	179	576	545	1121				245	181	13	437			
85	12	Monroe		63	204	191	395				75	57	5	164	1		

86	9	Polk	Urbana	173	563	523	1086				225	155	6	436			
82	10	St. Clair		80	238	195	433				88	66	5	168			
85	10	Taylor	Vinton	352	1004	1035	2039	2	2	4	437	269		844	*43	1	
83	11	Union		62	239	175	414				65	44	6	169			
		Total		2464	7750	7015	14765	4	3	7	3064	2282	191	5774	*45	1	3

* Including the inmates of the State Asylum for the Blind.

BLACKHAWK COUNTY.

89	11	Barclay	Barclay	122	356	343	699				137	55	20	288			
90	12	Bennington	Nantrille	61	188	164	352				56	44	15	129			
pt 87	11 12	Big Creek	La Porte City (R. 12)	131	357	312	669				150	115	2	227			
88	14	Black Hawk	Hudson	70	232	182	414				86	64	26	173			
pts87 88	12	Cedar	Cedar Valley (T. 87)	90	284	247	531				102	54	56	208			
pt 89	14	*Cedar Falls, city of	Cedar Falls	554	1709	1676	*3385	4	2	6	621	497	46	1251			1
pt 89	13 14	Cedar Falls, ex. of city		143	379	378	757	1		1	141	97	13	267			
87	13	Eagle		40	133	107	240				39	39	4	93	1		
pt 88	12	East Waterloo		332	933	946	1879				405	177	21	623	1	1	
pt 89	12	" "															
pt 89	13	" "															
88	11	Fox		76	223	210	433				90	66	6	158			
90	11	Lester	Lester	124	335	318	653				149	115	6	250		3	
87	14	Lincoln		26	61	66	127	1		1	24	21	9	41			
90	13	Mount Vernon		147	392	357	749				163	99	8	253			
88	13	Orange		110	352	296	648				161	113	4	227			
pts 87-'9	12	Poyner	Gilbertsville (T. 88)	115	325	328	653				135	99	10	261			
pt 87	11	Spring Creek	Enterprise	102	369	312	681				140	104		253		7	
w. ½ 90	14	Union		68	168	173	341				67	57	1	105			
e ½ 90	14	Washington		83	252	231	483				106	66	5	205			1
pt 89	12 13	Waterloo	Waterloo (R. 13)	348	1172	1158	2330	3	1	4	578	394	14	879			
		Total		2742	8220	7804	*16024	9	3	12	3350	2276	266	5891	2	11	2

* The returns for the city of Cedar Falls include, in the population, 300 children at the State Soldiers' Orphans' Home.—[Clerk District Court.

BOONE COUNTY.

In 84	26	Boonsboro	Boonsboro	264	813	811	1624				340	238		550			
82	27pt26	Cass	Prairie Hill (R. 27)	84	259	238	497				105	88		174			

BOONE COUNTY—Continued.

No. of Township.	Range.	Names of Townships, Towns, and Cities.	Names of Post-Offices.	No. of Dwelling-Houses.	No. of White Males.	No. of White Females.	Total White Population.	No. of Colored Males.	No. of Colored Females.	Total Colored Population.	No. entitled to Vote.	No. of Militia.	No of Foreigners not Naturalized.	No. between the ages of 5 and 21 years.	No. of Blind.	No. of Deaf and Dumb.	No. of Insane.
pts 83–'5	.25–27	Des Moines, excl. of Boonsboro & Montana	....	152	846	735	1581	....	....	..	360	248	97	583	1	..	..
...pt 85	.26 27	Dodge............	Mineral Ridge (R. 26)....	148	505	434	939	....	....	....	181	129	13	405	..	..	..
...pt 82	.25 26	Douglas......... ...	Swede P't, Rapids, (R. 26)	140	447	432	879	....	....	...	171	136	33	281	..	..	..
85 pt 84	25.[28	Jackson	....	56	162	168	330	....	....	....	65	40	3	133	1	..	..
......83	27pt26	Marcy	Moingona (R. 27)........	193	570	489	1059	....	....	....	215	200	....	395	..	..	..
...In 84	26	Montana, town of...	Montana	139	602	502	1104	3	...	3	315	281	4	301	..	..	..
......85	28pt27	Pilot Mound	Cassady's Corner (R. 27)														
......85	27	" "	Pilot Mound..........	28	162	155	317	....	....	....	47	45	18	136	..	..	..
......85	27	" "	Carson's Point........														
82 pt 83	28	Union	....	43	129	114	243	....	....	...	55	45	....	101	..	..	..
pts 82 83	.25 26	Worth.............	Worth (T. 82, R. 26).....	102	311	295	606	....	....	....	111	79	8	284	..	..	..
......84	28	Yell	....														
......84	.pt 27	"	Yough..............	133	368	316	679	....	....	....	153	126	7	281	1	1	..
......84	.pt 27	"	Riverside														
....	......	Total...... ...	....	1482	5169	4689	9858	3	...	3	2118	1655	183	3624	3	1	..

BREMER COUNTY.

No. of Township.	Range.	Names of Townships, Towns, and Cities.	Names of Post-Offices.	No. of Dwelling-Houses.	No. of White Males.	No. of White Females.	Total White Population.	No. of Colored Males.	No. of Colored Females.	Total Colored Population.	No. entitled to Vote.	No. of Militia.	No of Foreigners not Naturalized.	No. between the ages of 5 and 21 years.	No. of Blind.	No. of Deaf and Dumb.	No. of Insane.
......92	11	Dayton............	Grove Hill	49	146	131	277	....	....	....	53	27	....	106	..	..	..
......93	13	Douglas	Frederika	55	156	141	297	....	....	....	65	55	3	86	..	..	..
......91	11	Franklin	Eagle	90	231	205	436	....	....	....	96	71	9	156	..	1	..
......93	12	Frederika	Tripoli	46	132	129	261	....	....	....	50	93	2	105	..	..	..
..... 92	12	Fremont..........	....	81	231	203	434	1	....	1	83	64	11	168	..	..	..

......91	.13 14	Jackson	Janesville (R. 14).	139	505	469	974	2	5	7	216	164	....	363	..	..	..
......91	13	Jefferson	Bremer..............	109	349	297	646	....	....	....	146	104	6	242	..	..	..
......92	14	Lafayette	....	86	257	215	472	....	....	....	109	69	2	216	..	..	..
......93	.11 12	Le Roy..........	Mentor..............	59	185	173	358	....	....	....	65	36	8	140	..	..	1
......91	12	Maxfield	Maxfield	91	285	237	522	....	....	....	74	39	33	187	..	..	..
......93	14	Polk	Horton..............	162	498	441	939	2	....	2	209	132	....	350	..	..	..
......93	11	Sumner..........	Sumner	55	178	145	323	....	....	....	74	51	2	117	..	..	..
......92	13	Warren	....	85	261	229	490	....	....	....	70	46	25	194	..	..	..
......91 / 92	.13 14 / 14	Washington, excl. of Waverly..........	....	118	411	367	778	....	....	....	158	101	9	297	..	1	1
......91	14	Waverly, town of....	Waverly	361	1102	1018	2120	....	....	....	483	349	19	678	1	..	..
......	......	Total..........	....	1586	4927	4400	9327	5	5	10	1947	1330	129	3405	1	2	2

BUCHANAN COUNTY.

......90	8	Buffalo..........	Buffalo Grove, Castleville	54	162	146	308	....	....	....	64	43	....	112	..	..	..
......89	8	Byron	Winthrop..............	129	380	329	709	3	....	3	161	114	3	265	..	..	..
......87	8	Cono..........	....	59	187	138	325	....	....	....	71	52	....	127	..	..	..
......90	10	Fairbank	Fairbank, Kier........	175	501	461	962	....	....	....	198	110	8	379	1	1	..
......89	7	Fremont..........	....	53	182	155	337	....	....	....	63	45	6	135	..	..	..
......90	9	Hazelton	....	133	373	334	707	....	....	....	145	89	18	244	.	5	..
......87	9	Homer..........	....	49	161	155	316	....	....	....	61	40	3	138	..	1	..
...In 89	9	Independence, city of.	Independence..........	375	1254	1213	2467	1	....	1	549	375	17	777	..	..	..
......87	10	Jefferson..........	Brandon, Sunnyside....	141	392	362	754	....	....	....	157	128	10	291	..	..	..
......88	8	Liberty..........	Quasqueton	225	630	627	1257	....	....	....	270	194	3	56	..	1	1
......90	7	Madison	Ward's Corners........	96	245	245	490	....	....	....	103	52	4	206	..	..	..
......88	7	Middlefield	....	61	211	195	406	....	....	....	73	55	5	178	..	..	..
......87	7	Newton..........	Atlanta	127	401	393	794	....	....	....	142	94	8	367	..	..	..
......89	10	Perry	Jessup, Chatham.......	178	534	484	1018	1	....	1	240	152	17	372	..	..	..
......88	9	Sumner	....	41	163	139	302	....	....	....	65	39	2	106	..	..	..
......89	9	Washington, excl. of Independence.....	Otterville............	153	422	441	863	1	....	1	180	115	1	344	..	..	..
......88	10	Westburg..........	....	41	111	98	209	....	1	1	47	37	1	77	..	..	..
......	.....	Total..........	....	2090	6309	5915	12224	6	1	7	2589	1734	114	4174	1	8	1

BUENA VISTA COUNTY.

....	......	Barnes	....	29	87	64	151	....	....	....	38	28	6	49	..	..	1

BUTLER COUNTY.

No. of Township.	Range.	Names of Townships, Towns, and Cities.	Names of Post-Offices.	No. of Dwelling-Houses.	No. of White Males.	No. of White Females.	Total White Population.	No of Colored Males.	No. of Colored Females.	Total Colored Population.	No. entitled to Vote.	No. of Militia.	No. of Foreigners not Naturalized.	No. between the ages of 5 and 21 years.	No. of Blind.	No. of Deaf and Dumb.	No. of Insane.
90	16	Albion	Swanton, Parkersburg	106	321	294	615				133	101	10	230			
90	15	Beaver	New Hartf'd, Willoughby	160	428	440	868				193	130	12	263		2	
93	18	Bennezett	Belgrove	20	65	45	110				20	15	5	43			
92	15	Butler	Clarksville	145	478	460	938	1	2	3	202	139	6	593	2		
93	17	Coldwater	Elm Springs	50	163	170	333				65	42	2	144			
93	16	Dayton		46	137	138	275				60	38		121			
93	15	Fremont		36	129	121	250				50	35	2	116			
92	16	Jackson		52	165	165	330				71	46	2	148			
91	16	Jefferson	Butler Center	74	224	230	454				104	68	4	177			
91	18	Madison		22	78	79	157				35	17		63			
90	17	Monroe	Aplington	72	221	186	407				80	56		190			
92	18	Pittsford		68	193	156	349				81	62		139			
91	17	Ripley		34	115	85	200				40	21	3	75			
91	15	Shellrock	Shellrock	204	487	465	952				248	182	3	327			
90	18	Washington		26	81	65	146				32	19		59			
92	17	West Point	Boylan's Grove	29	79	76	155				34	18	4	95			
		Total		1144	3364	3175	6539	1	2	3	1448	989	53	2783	2	2	1

CALHOUN COUNTY.

No. of Township.	Range.	Names of Townships, Towns, and Cities.	Names of Post-Offices.	No. of Dwelling-Houses.	No. of White Males.	No. of White Females.	Total White Population.	No of Colored Males.	No. of Colored Females.	Total Colored Population.	No. entitled to Vote.	No. of Militia.	No. of Foreigners not Naturalized.	No. between the ages of 5 and 21 years.	No. of Blind.	No. of Deaf and Dumb.	No. of Insane.
86 87	31–34	Calhoun		62	149	128	277				73	51	12	135	1		
88 89	34	"															
In 86	33	" Lake City	Lake City	12	35	30	65										

..88 89	.31–33	Lincoln	Yatesville	40	114	90	204	....	....	....	62		1	57	..	..	..
....	......	Total	....	114	298	248	546	....	....	....	135	99	13	192	1	..	..

CARROLL COUNTY.

...84 85	.33–36	Jasper	Glidden	48	134	141	275	....	....	....	49	34	....	136	..	..	..
...82 83	.34–36	Newton	Carrollton (83, 34)	50	107	95	202	....	....	....	45	33	...	85	..	..	..
...82 83	33	Union	Coon Rapids (82, 33)	34	109	102	211	....	....	....	44	45	...	86	..	..	..
....	......	Total	....	132	350	338	688	....	....	....	138	112	....	307	..	..	..

CASS COUNTY.

pts 76 77	37	Brighton	....	19	73	56	129	....	....	....	28	25	1	54	..	..	..
......74	37	Cass	.... }														
......75	37	"	Lewis }	132	471	437	908	1	....	1	213	168	1	348	1	..	..
pts 74–'6	...36 37	"	.... }														
......74	34'5 pt36	Edna	Edna (R. 35)	39	117	109	226	1	...	1	42	42	15	94	1	..	1
pts 76 77	...34 35	Grant	....	33	87	91	178	....	....	...	36	29	....	73	..	..	..
pts 76 77	...35–37	Pymosa	Gurley (77, 36)	51	200	165	365	....	....	....	77	55	....	180	..	..	..
pts 76 77	...35 36	Turkey Grove	Grove City (76, 36)	102	318	293	611	....	...	....	107	103	2	259	1	..	..
......75	...34 35	Union	Whitneyville	12	33	27	60	...	....	....	16	9	....	17	..	..	..
....	....	Total	....	388	1299	1178	2477	2	....	2	519	431	19	1025	3	..	1

CEDAR COUNTY.

pts 80 81	...3 4	Cass	Cedar Bluffs (81, 4)	87	290	260	550	...	....	....	128	72	2	220	..	..	4
......80	...2 3	Center, excl. Tipton	York Prairie (R. 2) }														
...pt 81	2	"	Cessford }	302	868	834	1702	2	2	4	356	238	4	696	..	2	..
...pt 81	3	"	Woodbridge }														
......82	2	Clarence, town of	Clarence	82	260	227	487	....	1	1	86	72	7	179	..	..	..
......82	2	Dayton, exc. Clarence	....	95	286	242	528	....	....	....	105	88	17	207	..	..	..
......79	1	Farmington	Durant	124	450	386	826	2	....	2	194	140	18	294	..	..	1
......82	3	Fremont	....	94	308	290	598	....	....	....	107	70	1	266	14	..	..
...pt 80	...3 4	Gower	o a r (R. 4)	156	425	392	817	3	1	4	177	134	13	306	..	..	4
......80	1	Inland	Inland	121	337	325	662	1	....	1	156	90	8	232	1	..	..
79 pt 80	3	Iowa	Pedee (T. 79)	185	539	525	1064	1	....	1	237	159	9	428	..	1	..
...pt 81	...3 4	Linn	....	73	214	184	398	...	...	....	100	75	....	152	..	..	..
......82	1	Massillon	Massillon	153	461	399	860	....	....	...	172	115	90	295	..	..	..

CEDAR COUNTY—CONTINUED.

No. of Township.	Range.	Names of Townships, Towns, and Cities.	Names of Post-Offices.	No. of Dwelling-Houses.	No. of White Males.	No. of White Females.	Total White Population.	No. of Colored Males.	No. of Colored Females.	Total Colored Population.	No. entitled to Vote.	No. of Militia.	No. of Foreigners not Naturalized.	No. between the ages of 5 and 21 years.	No. of Blind.	No. of Deaf and Dumb.	No. of Insane.
82	4	Pioneer	Mechanicsville	221	689	650	1339	1	....	1	325	190	5	512	..	..	..
pt 81	2 3	Red Oak	Red Oak (R. 3)	118	408	370	778	....	....	....	163	121	7	324	..	..	..
pt 79 80	2 3	Rochester	Rochester (T. 79, R. 3)	132	416	395	811	1	....	1	166	119	2	311	2	3	2
79	4	Springdale	Springdale														
79	4	"	West Branch	210	623	618	1241	3	4	7	280	156	36	353	1	..	..
79	4	"	Downey														
81	1	Springfield	Louden, Rosette	202	671	592	1263	3	....	3	245	166	38	459	..	1	1
pt 79	2	Sugar Creek	Pleasant Hill	117	379	360	739	1	1	2	153	116	10	295	..	..	..
In 80 81	2 3	Tipton, town of	Tipton (T. 80, R. 2)	275	675	687	1362	6	8	14	265	181	2	543	2	..	1
		Total		2747	8299	7736	16035	24	17	41	3415	2302	269	2072	20	7	14

CERRO GORDO COUNTY.

No. of Township.	Range.	Names of Townships, Towns, and Cities.	Names of Post-Offices.	No. of Dwelling-Houses.	No. of White Males.	No. of White Females.	Total White Population.	No. of Colored Males.	No. of Colored Females.	Total Colored Population.	No. entitled to Vote.	No. of Militia.	No. of Foreigners not Naturalized.	No. between the ages of 5 and 21 years.	No. of Blind.	No. of Deaf and Dumb.	No. of Insane.
97	19	Falls	Plym'th, Shellrock Falls														
pt 97	20	"		80	212	227	439	....	....	....	92	59	4	164	..	..	1
pt 96	19	"															
pt 94	19	Geneseo															
94	20	"	Geneseo	23	63	71	134	....	....	....	27	23	1	59	..	..	..
pt 94 95	21	"															
pt 94 97	22	Lake															
95 96	22	"	Clear Lake (T. 96)	66	206	206	412	....	....	....	98	67	....	155	1	..	..
pt 95 96	21	"															
pt 97	21 22	Lincoln	Rock (R. 21)	36	110	115	225	....	....	....	50	31	....	100	..	..	..

96	20	Mason	Mason City														
pt 96	21	"															
pt 94	21 22	"		89	310	281	591				136	80	2	220	1		
pt 95	20 21	"															
pt 97	20 21	"	Lime Creek [R. 20]														
pt 94 96	19	Owen															
95	20	"	Owen's Grove	32	99	88	187				41	32	1	88			
pt 96	19 20	"															
		Total		326	1000	988	1988				444	292	8	782	2		1

CHEROKEE COUNTY.

		Cherokee	Cherokee [T. 92, R. 40]	18	54	48	102				24	8		35			
		Pilot	Pilot Rock [T. 91, R. 40]	22	59	48	107				29	16		47			
		Total		40	113	96	209				53	24		82			

CHICKASAW COUNTY.

94	14	Bradford	Bradford, Nashua	179	592	548	1140	2		2	259	140	1	448			1
95	14	Chickasaw	Chickasaw	148	398	370	768				161	108	3	303			1
95	13	Dayton	Dayton Center	53	176	153	329				64	25	1	122			
96 97	14	Deerfield	Deerfield [T. 96]	29	96	73	169	1		1	34	25	1	66			
94	12	Dresden		60	169	160	329				70	51	2	136			
94	11	Fredericksburg	Fredericksburg	78	257	247	504	1		1	122	60		174			
96 97	12	Jacksonville	Jacksonville [T. 96]	103	344	316	660				131	88	6	281	1	1	
95	12	New Hampton	New Hampton	82	214	210	424				89	61		158			
94	13	Richland	Williamston	62	199	198	397				79	45		163			1
95	11	Stapleton	Stapleton	63	196	173	369				70	42		161			
96 97	11	Utica	Little Turkey	113	354	334	688				101	70	81	239			
96 97	13	Washington	North Washington [T. 96]	78	238	201	439				95	55	2	169		1	
		Total		1048	3233	2983	6216	4		4	1275	770	97	2420	1	2	3

CLARKE COUNTY.

71	27	Doyle	Hopeville	123	388	397	785				158	111		395			
71	24	Franklin	Smyrna	103	316	277	593				125	91		247	1		
73	25	Fremont		63	195	189	384				79	67		172			

CLARKE COUNTY—Continued.

No. of Township.	Range.	Names of Townships, Towns, and Cities.	Names of Post-Offices.	No. of Dwelling-Houses.	No. of White Males.	No. of White Females.	Total White Population.	No. of Colored Males.	No. of Colored Females.	Total Colored Population.	No. entitled to Vote.	No. of Militia.	No. of Foreigners not Naturalized.	No. between the ages of 5 and 21 years.	No. of Blind.	No. of Deaf and Dumb.	No. of Insane.
71	25	Green Bay	Green Bay	77	238	211	449	...	...	..	99	53	...	203	..	..	..
72	24	Jackson	Ottawa	90	282	283	565	1	...	1	115	97	...	254	1	.	1
71	26	Knox	Lacelle	110	328	337	665	5	3	8	127	103	...	297	..	1	1
73	24	Liberty	Liberty	113	313	319	632	1	1	2	137	96	...	249	..	..	..
73	27	Madison	La Porte	37	114	108	222	...	...	...	45	36	1	81	..	1	1
72	25	Osceola	Osceola	162	493	499	992	12	13	25	203	148	...	398	..	..	..
72	27	Troy	Riley	22	70	60	130	...	...	...	31	17	1	44	..	..	..
72	26	Ward	...	43	143	145	288	...	...	...	53	41	1	180	..	2	..
73	26	Washington	Prairie Grove	82	241	262	503		...	...	94	58	...	233	..	1	..
...	...	Total	...	1025	3121	3087	6208	19	17	36	1266	918	3	2753	2	5	4

CLAY COUNTY.

No. of Township.	Range.	Names of Townships, Towns, and Cities.	Names of Post-Offices.	No. of Dwelling-Houses.	No. of White Males.	No. of White Females.	Total White Population.	No. of Colored Males.	No. of Colored Females.	Total Colored Population.	No. entitled to Vote.	No. of Militia.	No. of Foreigners not Naturalized.	No. between the ages of 5 and 21 years.	No. of Blind.	No. of Deaf and Dumb.	No. of Insane.
...	...	...	...	58	204	165	369	...	...	...	98	60	...	128	..	1	..

CLAYTON COUNTY.

No. of Township.	Range.	Names of Townships, Towns, and Cities.	Names of Post-Offices.	No. of Dwelling-Houses.	No. of White Males.	No. of White Females.	Total White Population.	No. of Colored Males.	No. of Colored Females.	Total Colored Population.	No. entitled to Vote.	No. of Militia.	No. of Foreigners not Naturalized.	No. between the ages of 5 and 21 years.	No. of Blind.	No. of Deaf and Dumb.	No. of Insane.
93	5	Boardman	Elkader	230	805	695	1500	3	...	3	350	210	26	540	.	..	1
91	1	Buena Vista	...	69	189	180	369	...	...	...	79	69	10	138	..	..	..
91	6	Cass	Strawberry Point	192	490	462	952	...	...	...	201	103	7	372	..	1	..
93	2	Clayton	...														
pt 93	3	"	Clayton	136	423	381	804	1	...	1	154	100	13	344	..	..	..
pt 94	3	"	...														
92	5	Cox Creek	Communia, Cox Creek	162	474	417	891	...	...	...	163	113	15	263	..	..	..

......91	4	Elk...............	....	111	329	314	643	....	....	....	123	88	10	275	..	..	..
......94	4	Farmersburg.......	Farmersburg, National..	196	626	575	1201	...	...	...	243	169	13	451	1	..	..
...pt 93	3	Garnavillo.........	Ceres .... }														
...pt 93	3	"	Garnavillo........... }	182	611	555	1166	1	...	1	232	153	11	451	..	..	..
...pt 93	4	"	.... }														
......95	4	Giard	Council Hill, Giard......	208	377	345	722	1	1	2	171	85	38	514	2	..	..
......95	6	Grand Meadow......	....	146	452	395	847	....	....	....	182	129	38	322	3	..	..
...In 92	2	Guttenberg, city of..	Guttenberg	119	428	407	835	1	....	1	189	101	10	347	..	..	..
......93	6	Highland	Highland...............	116	359	317	676	....	....	....	114	76	15	297	..	..	..
pt 92 93	...2 3	Jefferson, excl. of Guttenberg..........	....	223	645	609	1254	1	....	1	223	125	44	482	1	..	1
......91	5	Lodomillo..........	Yankee Settlement......	136	406	417	823	....	....	....	170	117	2	360	..	..	3
...In 95	3	McGregor	McGregor	264	1058	983	2041	2	3	5	520	480	30	706	..	..	..
......91	3	Mallory	....	127	382	347	729	....	....	....	153	90	....	304	..	..	..
......94	6	Marion	Gem	60	200	201	401	....	....	....	60	39	7	170	..	..	..
95 pt 94	3	Mendon, excl. McGr.	North McGregor [T. 95].	198	563	532	1095	....	....	....	197	107	29	362	..	..	..
......91	2	Millville..........	Millville...............	141	412	402	814	....	....	....	185	89	10	330	..	..	..
......95	5	Monona............	Monona, Sawana........	257	684	681	1365	....	....	....	297	219	19	513	1	..	..
...pt 93	4	Read	Clayton Center, Sigel ..	156	522	428	950	....	....	....	176	131	45	364	2	3	5
......92	6	Sperry	Volga City	156	473	474	947	....	1	1	194	110	10	385	1	1	..
......92	4 pt 3	Volga	Elkport [R. 4]..........	185	516	488	1004	....	....	....	269	105	34	360	..	..	..
......94	5	Wagner............	Wagner................	148	417	418	835	....	....	....	128	83	20	248	1	2	..
....	......	Total............	....	3918	11841	11023	22864	10	5	15	4773	3091	456	8898	12	7	10

CLINTON COUNTY.

......82	....2e	Berlin............	....	248	272	199	471	....	....	....	90	69	12	177	..	..	1
......83	....3e	Bloomfield........	....	171	521	468	989	3	....	3	216	125	10	404	..	1	..
......83	....2e	Brookfield.........	Brookfield.............	152	454	369	823	....	....	....	164	118	21	325	..	..	..
...In 81	....6e	Camanche, city of....	Camanche..............	108	264	289	553	4	4	8	124	98	....	207	..	..	..
...80 81	....6e	Camanche, excl. city	....	88	255	234	489	....	1	1	108	75	9	203	..	..	..
82 pt 81	....5e	Center	Elvira [T. 82]	199	584	485	1069	....	....	....	173	208	250	359	..	..	..
...In 81	....7e	Clinton, city of......	Clinton	725	2271	2047	4318	12	6	18	1132	559	....	1360	..	..	..
......81	....6e	Clinton, excl. of city	....	166	462	446	908	1	....	1	169	89	14	321	..	..	..
......83	....5e	Deep Creek........	....	166	492	388	880	....	....	....	148	105	65	273	..	..	..
...In 81	....4e	De Witt, city of.....	De Witt...............	246	725	714	1439	6	4	10	313	230	24	517	..	..	..
80 81 82	..3 4e	De Witt, excl. of city	....	237	716	670	1386	2	....	2	274	181	38	606	..	..	..

CLINTON COUNTY—Continued.

No. of Township.	Range.	Names of Townships, Towns, and Cities.	Names of Post-Offices.	No. of Dwelling-Houses.	No. of White Males.	No. of White Females.	Total White Population.	No. of Colored Males.	No. of Colored Females.	Total Colored Population.	No. entitled to Vote.	No. of Militia.	No. of Foreigners not Naturalized.	No. between the ages of 5 and 21 years.	No. of Blind.	No. of Deaf and Dumb.	No. of Insane.
......81	....5e	Eden	Low Moor, Eden														
......81	....4e	"		140	418	367	785	...	....	....	153	144	36	334	..	..	..
......80	5 pt 4e	"															
......83	..6 7e	Elk River	Elk River (R. 6)	190	669	552	1221	1	1	2	217	126	63	457	3	1	..
......82	....6e	Hampshire	....	139	425	364	789				133	55	43	275	..	..	..
......82	....1e	Liberty	Toronto	122	372	363	735	....	....	....	127	96	23	298	..	..	..
...In 82	....7e	Lyons, City of	Lyons	501	1750	1708	3458	5	7	12	691	289	276	1241	1	1	..
......82	....7e	Lyons, excl. of city		69	188	176	364	3	3	6	61	64	14	138	..	..	..
.. .. 81	....2e	Olive	Calamus														
......81	....2e	"	Buena Vista	290	844	722	1566	....	....	....	242	122	469	588	..	..	..
.. ..80	....2e	"															
...pt 81	....3e	Orange	Grand Mound, Orange	92	258	250	508	1	....	1	99	66	38	210	..	..	..
......83	....1e	Sharon	Burgess	139	483	427	910	...	...	...	145	93	153	352	..	..	..
......81	....1e	Spring Rock	Wheatland	208	581	533	1114	4	...	4	214	156	23	426	1	..	..
...pt 82	....4e	Washington	....	124	393	354	747	....	....	....	136	....	15	256	..	..	..
......83	....4e	Waterford	Charlotte	167	486	455	941	...	....	...	173	113	30	357	..	..	..
...pt 82	....3e	Welton	Welton	123	383	319	702	1	....	1	124	79	26	291	..	..	..
		Total		4810	14266	12899	27165	43	26	69	5426	3260	1652	9975	5	3	1

CRAWFORD COUNTY.

No. of Township.	Range.	Names of Townships, Towns, and Cities.	Names of Post-Offices.	No. of Dwelling-Houses.	No. of White Males.	No. of White Females.	Total White Population.	No. of Colored Males.	No. of Colored Females.	Total Colored Population.	No. entitled to Vote.	No. of Militia.	No. of Foreigners not Naturalized.	No. between the ages of 5 and 21 years.	No. of Blind.	No. of Deaf and Dumb.	No. of Insane.
......82	41	Boyer		14	45	45	90	...	....	....	16	12	1	35	..	..	..
......83	39	Denison	Denison	46	180	158	338	...	....	....	80	55	6	99	..	..	1
...pt 85	.37-40			10	34	26	60	...	....	....	11	5	...	....	..	..	..

......84	38	Milford	Boyer River	56	157	141	298	....	....	....	68	56	....	138	..	..	..
.....82	40	Union		42	160	122	282	1	1	2	62	50	19	124	..	..	..
		Total		168	576	492	1068	1	1	2	237	178	26	396	..	..	1

DALLAS COUNTY.

......79	27	Adel, town of	Adel	70	280	255	535	4	4	8	82	47	....	186	..	..	..
pt 78–79	27	Adel, excl. of town															
...pt 79	28	"		292	1096	1041	2137	1	.	1	425	277	....	844	2	1	..
......78	28	"	Chattanooga														
......81	27	Beaver		20	56	65	121	1	1	2	32	25	....	40	..	..	..
......78	26	Boone	Boone	114	367	356	723	4	3	7	120	76	....	309	..	..	.
......81	29	Dallas	Linden	35	124	104	228	....	....	....	51	40	....	96	1	2	..
......81	26	Des Moines	Xenia														
......81	26	"	Snyder	118	356	330	686	....	....	....	135	98	5	296	..	..	..
...pt 80	26	"															
......79	29	Linn	Greenvale	100	314	291	605	....	....	....	122	78	....	252	..	..	..
......81	28	Spring Valley	Alton	63	229	173	402	....	....	....	81	58	....	161	..	..	..
......80	27	Sugar Grove	Pierce's Point	59	198	161	359	....	....	....	72	46	2	156	..	1	..
......78	29	Union	Redfield														
...pt 79	28	"		198	626	569	1195	....	....	....	262	202	2	489	..	..	1
...pt 79	29	"															
79 pt 80	26	Walnut		49	145	146	291	....	....	....	64	17	7	123	..	1	.
......80	28pt27	Washington		38	124	114	238	....	....	....	50	32	....	110	1	..	..
		Total		1156	3915	3605	7520	10	8	18	1296	996	16	3062	4	5	1

DAVIS COUNTY.

...In 69	... 14	Bloomfield, town of	Bloomfield	118	313	297	610	2	1	3	131	102	...	235	..	..	..
pt 68 69	13 14	" exc. of town		207	609	575	1184	3	6	9	244	165	...	553	..	..	..
...In 69	... 14	Drakeville, town of	Drakeville	33	123	124	247	....	....	....	49	39	1	121	..	..	..
...pt 69	14	" exc. of town		50	147	161	308	1	....	1	61	24	...	130	.	..	..
...67 68	15	Fabius	Monterey (T. 68)	191	558	522	1080	....	....	....	202	150	....	450	..	1	..
......69	15	Fox River	West Grove	164	530	517	1047	....	....	....	213	166	....	448	2	..	2
...67 68	13	Grove	Stiles (T. 67)	179	526	507	1033	2	....	2	205	140	9	435	..	..	..
......70	13	Lick Creek	Floris, Chequest	169	559	571	1130	....	....	....	225	173	1	475	3	1	1

DAVIS COUNTY—CONTINUED.

No. of Township.	Range.	Names of Townships, Towns, and Cities.	Names of Post-Offices.	No. of Dwelling-Houses.	No. of White Males.	No. of White Females	Total White Population.	No. of Colored Males.	No. of Colored Females.	Total Colored Population.	No. entitled to Vote.	No. of Militia.	No. of Foreigners not Naturalized.	No. between the ages of 5 and 21 years.	No. of Blind.	No. of Deaf and Dumb.	No. of Insane.
70	15	Marion	Oak Springs, Albany	138	418	398	816				175	135		347			
pt 69	13	Perry		133	366	373	739				156	120		285		1	3
pt 68	12	Prairie	Pulaski	86	292	269	561	4		4	113	82		223			1
67 pt 68	12	Roscoe		77	242	221	463	1		1	90	66	2	199			
70	12	Salt Creek		163	480	462	942	3	6	9	192	131		367	1		3
70	14	Soap Creek		148	433	401	834				173	127	1	379		2	2
69	12	Union	Troy	193	512	495	1007				228	162		435	2	1	
67 pt 68	14	Wycondah	Savannah (T. 67)	252	753	733	1486	1		1	279	228	5	666			
		Total		2301	6861	6626	13487	17	13	30	2736	2010	19	5748	8	6	12

DECATUR COUNTY.

No. of Township.	Range.	Names of Townships, Towns, and Cities.	Names of Post-Offices.	No. of Dwelling-Houses.	No. of White Males.	No. of White Females	Total White Population.	No. of Colored Males.	No. of Colored Females.	Total Colored Population.	No. entitled to Vote.	No. of Militia.	No. of Foreigners not Naturalized.	No. between the ages of 5 and 21 years.	No. of Blind.	No. of Deaf and Dumb.	No. of Insane.
68	27	Bloomington	Cross	23	83	73	156				33	23		61			
68	26	Burrell	Terrehaute	100	318	317	635	1		1	123	77		284			
69	25	Center	Leon	188	594	590	1184	5	2	7	246	143		510	2	1	
69	26	Decatur	Decatur [City]	124	357	472	829				123	95		312			
68	25	Eden		146	481	419	900				165	121	1	397		3	4
67	27	Fayette	Sedgwick	31	89	81	170				39	33		56			
70	25	Franklin		51	152	137	289				60	43		123		2	
70	24	Garden Grove	Garden Grove	86	318	283	601	1		1	139	96	1	241	1		
69	27	Grand River	Funk's Mills	29	110	109	219				47	16		106			
67	25	Hamilton	NineEagles, SpringValley	88	221	231	452		1	1	90	62		218			
69	24	High Point	High Point	113	303	326	629	8	10	18	127	88		250			
70	26	Long Creek		64	193	163	356	2	4	6	66	44		171			

......67	24	Morgan	....	97	274	282	556	....	....	....	100	73	2	259	..	..	1
......67	26	New Buda	New Buda	50	181	163	344	...	....	...	65	49	....	169	1	.	..
......70	... 27	Richland	Westerville	97	246	240	486	....	....	....	107	70	....	222	..	..	..
......68	24	Woodland	....	113	333	328	661	....	...	....	130	97	2	283	..		..
....	.....	Total	....	1400	4253	4214	8467	17	17	34	1660	1130	6	3662	4	6	5

DELAWARE COUNTY.

......87	6	Adams	Tower Hill	92	301	251	552	....	....	....	94	65	13	229	..	..	..
......89	3	Bremen	....	100	322	293	615	....	....	....	110	69	13	234	..	1	..
......89	6	Coffin's Grove	Masonville	122	324	330	654	2	....	2	130	75	9	249	2	1	..
......90	3	Colony	Colesburg	254	698	657	1355	....	....	....	265	182	30	548	..	..	..
......89	5	Delaware	Manchester	408	1098	1043	2141	1	....	1	513	384	11	679	..	..	..
......88	4	Delhi	Delhi	200	541	496	1037	1	....	1	229	171	13	416	1	..	..
......90	4	Elk	Greeley	154	440	408	848	....	....	....	175	124	16	363	..	..	..
......87	5	Hazel Green	Hazel Green	85	241	221	462	1	....	1	101	83	4	176	..	..	..
......90	5	Honey Creek	York	175	492	479	971	1	....	1	234	182	18	366	..	..	..
......88	5	Milo	....	129	398	341	739	....	....	....	164	127	5	331	..	..	..
......88	3	North Fork	....	128	356	352	708	....	....	....	128	110	29	309	..	..	.
......89	4	Oneida	Earlville, Delaware	193	526	478	1004	2	....	2	212	139	12	378	..	..	1
......88	6	Prairie	Barryville	45	128	135	263	1	....	1	50	34	10	104	..	..	..
......90	6	Richland	Forestville														
......90	6	"	Mount Hope	146	411	382	793	....	....	....	152	110	23	310	..	..	..
......90	6	"	Campton														
......87	3	South Fork	Hopkinton	309	776	769	1545	6	2	8	324	228	28	605	..	2	1
...pt 87	4	"	Sand Spring														
...pt 87	4	Union	Uniontown	130	380	379	759	....	....	....	148	87	12	265	.	..	..
....	.....	Total	....	2670	7432	7014	14446	15	2	17	3029	2170	246	5562	3	4	2

DES MOINES COUNTY.

.....69	4 pt 5	Augusta	Augusta (R. 4)	104	276	239	515	1	1	2	107	83		212	.	..	..
......71	...1 2	Benton	Kingston (R. 2)	226	618	573	1191	....	....	...	211	124	13	447	3	..	..
In 69 70	2	Burlington, city of	Burlington	1717	5383	5097	10480	76	60	136	2075	1476	257	3185	2	1	1
...pt 68	2	Burling'n, exc. of city	....														
......69	2	"	....	328	874	853	1727	8	5	13	344	206	14	543	1	1	..
......70	2	"	....														

DES MOINES COUNTY—Continued.

No. of Township.	Range.	Names of Townships, Towns, and Cities.	Names of Post-Offices.	No. of Dwelling-Houses.	No. of White Males.	No. of White Females.	Total White Population.	No. of Colored Males.	No. of Colored Females.	Total Colored Population.	No. entitled to Vote.	No. of Militia.	No. of Foreigners not Naturalized.	No. between the ages of 5 and 21 years.	No. of Blind.	No. of Deaf and Dumb.	No. of Insane.
70	4	Danville	Danville														
70	4	"	Parrish	278	836	783	1619	5	2	7	340	241	4	673	..	..	1
70	4	"	Middletown														
70	3	Flint River	......	176	494	497	991	5	3	8	175	114	4	342	..	..	..
71	3	Franklin	Dodgeville	243	688	660	1348	1	....	1	280	185	6	630	..	..	..
72	1 pt 2	Huron	Huron (R. 2)	112	324	299	623	....	....	....	135	32	2	287	..	..	..
71	4	Pleasant Grove	Pleas't Grove, South Flint	190	520	518	1038	10	8	18	209	140	10	441	6	..	1
69 pt 68	3	Union	......	194	624	582	1206	6	1	7	270	173	22	487	1	1	..
72	4	Washington	La Vega	127	446	408	854	1	....	1	146	135	7	331	1	..	..
pt 72	2	Yellow Springs	Kossuth														
pt 72	2	"	Northfield	318	885	774	1659	....	....	....	359	281	36	655	..	1	..
72	3	"	Linton														
......	......	Total	......	4013	11968	11283	23251	113	80	193	4651	3190	378	8233	14	4	3

DICKINSON COUNTY.

No. of Township.	Range.	Names of Townships, Towns, and Cities.	Names of Post-Offices.	No. of Dwelling-Houses.	No. of White Males.	No. of White Females.	Total White Population.	No. of Colored Males.	No. of Colored Females.	Total Colored Population.	No. entitled to Vote.	No. of Militia.	No. of Foreigners not Naturalized.	No. between the ages of 5 and 21 years.	No. of Blind.	No. of Deaf and Dumb.	No. of Insane.
pt 98 99	36 37	Okoboji	Okoboji (T. 99, R. 36)	32	91	87	178	....	....	....	44	25	....	....	..	..	..
pt 99 100	36	Spirit Lake	Spirit Lake (T. 99)	43	102	102	204	....	....	....	49	38	....	....	..	..	..
pt 99 100	36	Tusculum	......	22	81	46	127	....	....	....	31	18	....	....	..	..	..
......	......	Total	......	97	274	235	509	....	....	....	124	81	....	....	..	..	..

DUBUQUE COUNTY.

No. of Township.	Range.	Names of Townships, Towns, and Cities.	Names of Post-Offices.	No. of Dwelling-Houses.	No. of White Males.	No. of White Females.	Total White Population.	No. of Colored Males.	No. of Colored Females.	Total Colored Population.	No. entitled to Vote.	No. of Militia.	No. of Foreigners not Naturalized.	No. between the ages of 5 and 21 years.	No. of Blind.	No. of Deaf and Dumb.	No. of Insane.
87	2w	Cascade	Cascade	222	534	542	1076	....	....	....	179	132	23	337	..	..	..

......89	...1e	Center............	Lattner's...	216	585	531	1116	....	....	....	233	145	34	390	..	..	..
......90	...1w	Concord..........	Pin Oak, Cottage Hill...	157	474	472	946	....	...	...	165	92	20	436	..	..	..
......88	...2w	Dodge............	Farley, Worthington....	152	473	398	871	1	..	1	159	136	32	342	..	.	..
...In 89	....2e	Dubuque, city of....	Dubuque	3055	11056	10077	21133	42	47	89	3487	2608	350	5432	6	4	3
......89	...1w	Iowa.............	Tivoli, Bankston........	127	446	386	832	....	....	....	159	85	4	324	..	.	..
... ..90	....1e	Jefferson..........	Durango............														
......90	....1e	"	Sherrill's Mound......	214	597	561	1158	....	2	2	252	134	13	517	..	..	..
......90	....1e	"	Jefferson...........														
......89	...2e	Julien, ex. of Dubuque	....	221	695	670	1365	....	2	2	258	148	29	488	1	..	15
......90	...2w	Liberty	Allison..............	178	609	531	1140	...	.	...	219	140	21	496	1	1	..
......88	....3e	Mosalem..........	King....	126	404	374	778	....	....	...	128	82	13	386	..	..	..
......89	...2w	New Wine.........	Dyersville, New Vienna.	·315	839	755	1594	....	....	....	321	274	63	561	..	..	..
......90	...2e	Peru	....	167	512	409	921	..	....	....	184	121	16	362	..	..	..
......87	...1e	Prairie Creek.......	Ogden, Milleray........	152	488	427	915	....	....	....	169	102	13	425	..	1	..
......88	...2e	Table Mound.......	Ballyclough, Rockdale...	130	362	382	744	....	....	..	119	68	19	311	..	..	..
......88	...1w	Taylor...........	Epworth.............	209	599	589	1188	1	1	2	246	....	11	436	..	.	..
......88	...1e	Vernon	Peosta, Derrinane.......	177	604	512	1116	2	....	2	245	162	59	393	..	2	..
... ..87	....2e	Washington....	....	137	480	442	922	1	....	1	172	97	30	415	..	.	2
......87	...1w	White Water......	Fillmore............	175	478	468	946	....	....	....	175	92	31	405	..	.	..
......	......	Total...........	....	6130	20235	18526	38761	47	52	99	6870	4618	781	12456	8	8	20

EMMETT COUNTY.

98'9 p100	31	Armstrong Grove..	Armstrong's Grove......	15	44	33	77	....	....	....	17	13	....	39	..	..	..
.....100	32-34 p31	Emmett	Emmett (T. 100, R. 34)...	*25	*85	*75	*160	....	....	....	35	25	....	46	..	..	..
...98 99	...32-34	Estherville........	Estherville (T. 99, R. 34).	44	150	120	270	1	....	1	70	47	....	104	..	..	..
......98	32	Mud Lake.........	High Lake	*30	*125	*75	*200	....	....	....	*40	35	....	*50	..	..	..
....	.. ....	Total	....	114	404	303	707	1	....	1	162	120	...	239	..	..	..

NOTE.--Those marked thus (*) are estimated. No census returns have been made to this office from Mud Lake township, and only a partial report from Emmett township.—[CLERK DISTRICT COURT.

FAYETTE COUNTY.

......95	9	Auburn	Douglas...............	177	495	483	978	....	....	....	204	104	5	351	1	..	..
......93	10	Banks............	Wilson Grove	28	82	72	154	....	....	....	32	17	6	55	..	..	..
......93	9	Center...........	....	55	166	137	303	....	....	....	71	44	1	118	4	..	..
......95	7	Clermont	Clermont, Henderson's Pr	186	575	555	1130	....	....	....	231	137	66	416	1	..	1

FAYETTE COUNTY—Continued.

No. of Township.	Range.	Names of Townships, Towns, and Cities.	Names of Post-Offices.	No. of Dwelling Houses.	No. of White Males.	No. of White Females.	Total White Population.	No. of Colored Males.	No. of Colored Females.	Total Colored Population.	No. entitled to Vote.	No. of Militia.	No of Foreigners not Naturalized.	No. between the ages of 5 and 21 years.	No. of Blind.	No. of Deaf and Dumb	No. of Insane.
95	8	Dover	Eldorado	143	521	497	1018	1	...	1	163	108	36	409	.	..	2
95	10	Eden	Eden, Waucoma	145	462	425	887	...	...	...	191	117	7	319	..	..	..
92	7	Fairfield	Brush Cr'k, Taylorsville.	190	519	513	1032	...	...	...	216	140	8	410	..	..	..
93	10	Fremont	Mill	57	168	169	337	...	...	...	64	41	...	137	..	..	..
92	9	Harlan		28	102	96	198	...	...	...	47	32	...	76	..	..	..
93	7	Illyria	Leo														
93	7	"	Illyria	150	448	423	871	8	7	15	170	125	5	385	..	..	..
93	7	"	Waudena														
91	9	Jefferson	Otsego	83	248	237	485	...	...	...	97	71	30	195	..	..	..
91	10	Oran	Oran	93	289	286	575	...	...	...	113	86	4	247	..	..	..
94	7	Pleasant Valley	Elgin	155	549	492	1041	...	...	...	191	148	31	412	1	*1	..
91	7	Putnam	Putnam	110	318	274	592	...	...	...	124	88	8	251	1	..	..
94	10	Richland	Bethel	40	125	126	251	...	...	...	54	33	1	104	1	..	..
91	8	Scott	Scott Center	24	80	79	159	...	...	...	32	25	2	69	..	..	..
92	8	Smithfield	Seaton	93	284	255	539	...	...	...	119	71	4	214	..	..	..
93	8	Westfield	Fayette, Lima	281	838	790	1628	1	...	1	342	227	3	637	..	1	..
94	8	West Union	West Union	338	1064	1042	2106	3	3	6	480	316	10	839	1	..	3
94	9	Windsor	Windsor, Richfield	116	359	326	685	.	...	...	153	95	4	262	1	..	..
		Total		2492	7692	7277	14969	13	10	23	3094	2025	231	5906	11	2	6

* Idiotic.

FLOYD COUNTY.

No. of Township.	Range.	Names of Townships, Towns, and Cities.	Names of Post-Offices.	No. of Dwelling Houses.	No. of White Males.	No. of White Females.	Total White Population.	No. of Colored Males.	No. of Colored Females.	Total Colored Population.	No. entitled to Vote.	No. of Militia.	No of Foreigners not Naturalized.	No. between the ages of 5 and 21 years.	No. of Blind.	No. of Deaf and Dumb	No. of Insane.
97	15pt16	Cedar	Howardville (R. 16)	48	143	138	281	...	...	...	63	43	4	94	..	..	..

...pt 96	16	Floyd.............	Floyd........... ...														
pt 96 97	.. 17	"	....	186	579	543	1122	....	....	....	254	143	10	453	..	1	2
...pt 97	16	"	....														
......96	15	Niles..	....	64	159	156	315	....	....	....	82	69	....	117	..	..	..
......94	15	Riverton.........	....														
...pt 95	15	"	....	130	357	378	735	2	....	2	158	129	8	270	..	..	..
...pt 94	16	"	....														
pt 95 96	18	Rockford...........	Rockford (T. 95)........	103	285	275	560	....	....	....	143	101	21	200	..	..	..
...pt 96	17	Rock Grove.......	....														
...pt 97	17	"	....														
...pt 96	... 18	"	Rock Grove City	112	351	330	681	....	....	....	142	86	1	252	..	..	..
...pt 96	18	"	Nora Springs.........														
.. pt 97	18	"	....														
......95	16	St. Charles.........	Charles City														
...pt 95	15	"	....	347	989	904	1893	2	1	3	432	313	12	659	..	..	..
...pt 96	16	"	....														
94 pt 95	18	Scott..............	....	17	60	53	113	....	....	....	21	15	....	50	..	1	..
pt 95 96	17	Ulster..............	Ulster (T. 95)...........	42	122	90	212	....	....	....	51	35	2	72	..	..	..
......94	17	Union	Marble Rock..........														
...pt 94	16	"	....	140	420	393	813	1	....	1	179	147	....	292	..	1	..
......95	17	"	....														
....	......	Total............	....	1189	3465	3260	6725	5	1	6	1525	1081	58	2459	..	3	2

FRANKLIN COUNTY.

...pt 92	...20	Clinton............	....														
...92 93	21	"	Shobe's Grove (T. 93)..	51	150	139	289	....	....	....	64	51	....	116	..	..	..
......93	.20 22	"	Chapin (R. 20).........														
......91	19	Geneva....	Geneva ....(93)	41	115	117	232	....	....	....	50	42	....	86	..	..	..
...92 93	19	Ingham....	Ingham (92), Coldwater.	57	169	142	311	....	....	....	72	52	....	112	..	..	..
......90	... 22	Morgan....	Oakland Valley.......														
......91	22	"	Otisville.............	35	100	83	183	....	....	....	25	18	....	73	..	..	..
......92	...22	"	....														
......90	19pt20	Osceola...........	....	54	184	178	362	1	....	1	68	48	....	165	..	..	..
......90	21pt22	Reeve	....														
......91	20	"	Maysville............	112	306	274	580	....	....	....	123	103	....	246	..	..	..
......91	21	"	....														

FRANKLIN COUNTY—Continued.

No. of Township.	Range.	Names of Townships, Towns, and Cities.	Names of Post-Offices.	No. of Dwelling-Houses.	No. of White Males.	No. of White Females.	Total White Population.	No. of Colored Males.	No. of Colored Females.	Total Colored Population.	No. entitled to Vote.	No. of Militia.	No. of Foreigners not Naturalized.	No. between the ages of 5 and 21 years.	No. of Blind.	No. of Deaf and Dumb.	No. of Insane.
92	20	Washington	Hampton	57	187	175	362	1	...	1	95	82	....	144	..	..	..
		Total		407	1211	1108	2319	2	....	2	497	396	....	942	..	..	..

FREMONT COUNTY.

No. of Township.	Range.	Names of Townships, Towns, and Cities.	Names of Post-Offices.	No. of Dwelling-Houses.	No. of White Males.	No. of White Females.	Total White Population.	No. of Colored Males.	No. of Colored Females.	Total Colored Population.	No. entitled to Vote.	No. of Militia.	No. of Foreigners not Naturalized.	No. between the ages of 5 and 21 years.	No. of Blind.	No. of Deaf and Dumb.	No. of Insane.
68	44	Benton	Eastport														
pt 69	43	"		86	288	261	549	7	1	8	134	111	5	195	1	6	..
pt 69	44	"	Gaston														
67	40	Fisher															
68	40	"		38	127	96	223	....	....	....	50	31	14	78	1	..	..
pt 69	40	"	Manti														
67	43	Franklin															
pt 67	42	"	Hamburg	134	474	489	963	1	2	3	203	53	27	362	..	1	..
pt 68	42	"															
67	41	Madison															
68	41	"		109	354	275	629	....	1	1	136	88	....	269	2	3	..
pt 67	42	"															
pt 69	40 41	Monroe	Cora (R. 40)														
70	40	"		82	235	222	457	..	....	....	101	75	6	173	..		..
pt 70	41	"															
70	42pt41	Ross	Tabor (R. 42)	136	414	243	657	2	1	3	176	135	8	273	..	..	..
70	43	Scott	Plum Hollow														
70	43	"	Bartlett	260	635	657	1292	....	....	....	252	206	....	446	1	..	..
pt 69	43	"															

......69	42	Sidney	Sidney...............	304	1104	1121	2225	1	2	3	414	313	8	1008	..	2	1
...pt 69	41	"															
...pt 68	.42 43	"															
....	......	Total..........	....	1149	3631	3364	6995	11	7	18	1446	1012	68	2804	5	12	1

GREENE COUNTY.

......83	30	Jefferson	New Jefferson	198	570	518	1088	....	....	....	253	188	2	383	..	..	..
...84 85	30	"															
...w½ 82	30	"															
e⅔ 82 83	31	"															
e⅔ 84 85	31	"															
82 83 85	32	Kendrick		120	360	312	672	1	....	1	137	99	4	278	..	2	1
......84	32	"	Northville...........														
...w⅓ 82	31	"															
...w⅓ 83	31	"	Kendrick.............														
w⅓ 84 85	31	"															
......82	29	Washington	Rippey...............	106	298	294	592	....	....	....	112	86	2	244	..	..	..
83 84 85	29	"															
...e½ 82	30	"															
....	......	Total..........	....	424	1228	1124	2352	1	....	1	502	373	8	905	..	2	1

GRUNDY COUNTY.

......89	16	Reaver		25	65	65	130	....	....	....	26	24	....	49	..	1	..
..87 88	15	Black Hawk.........		22	62	60	122	....	....	....	30	17	3	47	..	..	..
......86	17	Clay	Wadaloup	24	60	56	116	....	....	....	24	19	2	48	..	..	..
......89	15	Fairfield..........		65	229	207	436	....	....	....	82	62	....	156	..	..	..
......86	18	Felix.............		46	145	142	287	....	....	....	52	39	....	127	..	..	..
......89	18	German............		54	160	137	297	....	....	....	44	15	....	105	..	..	..
......88	.16 18	Lincoln		10	25	31	56	....	....	....	13	8	11	16	..	..	..
......87	18	Melrose		33	118	94	212	....	....	....	47	38	5	82	..	..	..
......87	.16 18	Palermo	Grundy Center.........	50	136	136	272	....	....	....	70	53	....	79	..	..	..
......89	17	Pleasant Valley....		11	31	30	61	....	....	....	14	12	1	20	..	..	..
......88	18	Shiloh............		27	69	61	130	....	....	....	19	13	20	25	..	..	..
....	......	Total....	....	367	1100	1019	2119	....	....	....	421	300	42	754	..	1	..

GUTHRIE COUNTY.

No. of Township.	Range.	Names of Townships, Towns, and Cities.	Names of Post-Offices.	No. of Dwelling-Houses.	No. of White Males.	No. of White Females.	Total White Population.	No. of Colored Males.	No. of Colored Females.	Total Colored Population.	No. entitled to Vote.	No. of Militia.	No. of Foreigners not naturalized.	No. between the ages of 5 and 21 years.	No. of Blind.	No. Deaf and Dumb.	No. of Insane.
78 pt 79	... .31	Beaver		18	48	54	102				26	18		44			
.....79	33 w½32	Bear Grove	Bear Grove (R. 33)	35	138	104	242				55	42		103			
..80 81	... .30	Cass	Panora (T. 80)														
..pt 79	..30 31	"		204	605	559	1164	1	2	3	287	223		469			
..pt 80	31	"															
pt 79 80	..31 32	Center	Guthrie Center (80, 32)	98	286	276	562				116	80	2	230	1		
81 pt 80	31	Dodge	Moffitt's Grove (T. 80)	26	66	75	141				33	28		43			
.....81	32	Highland	Dodge	21	54	51	105				27	21		37			
pt 78 79	30	Jackson	Dale City (T. 78)	119	388	361	749				160	109	6	272			
.....81	33	Orange		16	60	59	119				25	17		48			
.....78	30	Penn	Macksville	65	173	178	351				75	56		130	1		
....78	..32 33	Thompson	Dalmanutha (R. 33)	39	152	125	277				51	42		124	1		
.....80	33 e½ 32	Union		13	48	43	91				18	14		37			
		Total		654	2018	1885	3903	1	2	3	873	650	11	1537	3		

HAMILTON COUNTY.

No. of Township.	Range.	Names of Townships, Towns, and Cities.	Names of Post-Offices.	No. of Dwelling-Houses.	No. of White Males.	No. of White Females.	Total White Population.	No. of Colored Males.	No. of Colored Females.	Total Colored Population.	No. entitled to Vote.	No. of Militia.	No. of Foreigners not naturalized.	No. between the ages of 5 and 21 years.	No. of Blind.	No. Deaf and Dumb.	No. of Insane.
.pt 88	...24-26	Boone	Webster City (R. 26)	135	417	392	809		1	1	201	148	1	296			
....89	23'4 pt25	Cass	Blairsburg (R. 24)	36	131	129	260				54	44	2	119	3		
....86	24	Ellsworth		21	61	52	113				19	8	7	35			
....89	...25 26	Fremont		28	79	70	149	1		1	36	26		22		1	
....87	25pt24 26	Hamilton		78	150	175	325				75	55		150			
....87	23 pt 24	Lyon	Lakin's Grove (R. 24)	18	59	45	104				24	14		41			
....86	25	Marion															
....86	26	"	Hook's Point	77	267	241	508	1		1	90	75	4	226			
.pt 87	26	"															

......88	23pt24	Rose Grove.........	Rose Grove (R. 23)......	22	69	58	127	....	....	....	36	28	5	44	..	..	..
......86	23	Scott	Randall	24	68	60	128	....	....	....	20	9	39	54	..	..	..
pt 87 88	26	Webster...........	Homer (T. 87).........	107	325	303	628	....	....	....	129	73	1	269	..	..	.
....	......	Total..........	....	546	1626	1525	3151	2	1	3	684	480	59	1256	3	1	..

HANCOCK COUNTY.

.....94	.24-26	Amsterdam	....														
.w ¼ 94	...23	"	Upper Grove..........	16	52	52	104	....	....	....	26	14	....	40	..	..	..
.w ¾ 95	...26	"	....														
.....95	.23-25	Avery	....														
..e ¾ 94	23	"	....	11	30	27	57	....	....	....	16	13	....	21	..	..	..
..e ¼ 95	...26	"	....														
.....96	.23-25	Ellington	....														
..e ⅙ 96	26	"	....	22	70	61	131	....	....	....	27	18	....	52	1	1	..
.e 5-6 97	23	"	Ellington														
.....97	24-26	Madison	....														
w 5-6 96	.. 26	"	....	14	34	31	65	....	....	....	15	14	....	30	..	..	..
w 1-6 97	. . 23	"	....														
....	......	Total..........	....	63	186	171	357	....	....	....	84	59	....	143	1	1	..

HARDIN COUNTY.

....89	22 w ½ 21	Alden...............	Alden (R. 21)...........	87	209	205	414	....	1	1	91	72	2	151	..	..	..
....88	19	Clay................	Lithopolis..............	150	465	445	910	....	....	.. .	199	132	9	376	..	..	..
....87	19	Eldora	Eldora, Delanti.........	210	657	574	1231	....	....	....	272	211	2	456	2	..	..
....88	...21 22	Ellis	Cottage (R. 21)..........	75	215	195	410	....	....	....	99	60	....	159	..	..	..
....89	 19	Ætna...............	Ackley	192	563	487	1050	....	....	....	242	151	22	354	..	..	1
....89	20 e ½ 21	Hardin	Iowa Falls (R. 20).......	379	972	896	1868	5	6	11	452	343	29	667	1	..	1
....88	 20	Jackson.............	Berlin, Hardin City......	111	315	308	623	....	....	....	122	93	9	252	..	..	..
....87	20	Pleasant...........	Point Pleasant.........	110	295	278	573	1	....	1	119	76	7	218	..	..	..
... 86	20 21 22	Providence	New Providence (R. 20).	173	483	458	941	....	....	....	208	172	4	386	..	2	1
... 87	...21 22	Tipton.............	Tipton Grove...........	72	216	196	412	....	....	....	91	47	8	167	..	..	..
....86	19	Union..............	Union..................	162	447	452	899	1	....	1	187	151	....	291	..	..	..
......	......	Total..........	....	1721	4837	4494	9331	7	7	14	2082	1508	92	3477	3	2	3

HARRISON COUNTY.

No. of Township.	Range.	Names of Townships, Towns, and Cities.	Names of Post-Offices.	No. of Dwelling Houses.	No. of White Males.	No. of White Females.	Total White Population.	No. of Colored Males.	No. of Colored Females.	Total Colored Population.	No. entitled to Vote.	No. of Militia.	No. of Foreigners not Naturalized.	No. between the ages of 5 and 21 years.	No. of Blind.	No. of Deaf and Dumb.	No. of Insane.
80	41	Boyer															
80	42	"	Woodbine, Bigler's Grv.	81	365	276	641	....	....	....	150	101	....	252	..	..	..
81	42	"															
79	43	Calhoun	Calhoun	49	183	166	349	....	....	....	67	51	5	136	..	..	..
79	41	Cass	Jeddo City	22	87	75	162	....	....	....	36	25	1	108	..	..	..
78	45	Cincinnati	Yazoo	59	243	176	419	....	....	....	105	71	19	157	..	..	..
79	45	Clay	Modail	82	226	276	502	....	....	....	101	73	....	144	4	..	..
81	41	Harrison	Harrison	26	83	70	153	....	....	....	38	41	7	49	1	..	..
81	44	Jackson		27	77	67	144	....	....	....	38	26	....	47	..	..	..
79	42	Jefferson	Logan														
79	42	"	Whitesboro	78	289	225	514	....	....	....	131	91	9	216	..	..	..
79	42	"	Reeder's Mills														
78	43pt42	Lagrange	Harris Grove [R. 42]	43	146	125	271	....	....	....	64	56	....	147	..	..	..
81	45	Little Sioux	Little Sioux	106	*	*	472	....	....	....	160	118	....	167	1	..	..
80 81	43	Magnolia	Magnolia [T. 81]	105	315	280	595	1	....	1	140	110	5	234	..	..	..
80	44 45	Raglan		72	266	227	493	....	....	....	98	80	2	184	..	..	..
78	44	St. John	St. John, Missouri Valley	202	407	340	747	....	....	....	160	121	....	726	1	..	..
79	44	Taylor		39	146	114	260	....	....	....	51	41	....	102	..	..	..
78	41pt42	Union		18	60	53	113	..	....	....	24	19	....	46	1	..	..
		Total		1009	*2893	*2470	5835	1	....	1	1363	1024	48	2715	8	..	..

* No return is made of the population of Little Sioux township by sexes. The total enumeration is, however, given.

HENRY COUNTY.

70	5	Baltimore	Lowell	166	466	467	933	....		....	189	127	1	381	1	2	....
72	5	Canaan		81	248	221	469	6	4	10	98	64	..	182		.	...
71	6	Center, exc. of Mt. Pl't.		291	995	923	1918	33	30	63	379	306	18	604	2	3	*331
70	6	Jackson		190	575	506	1081	16	11	27	228	159	2	422	..	..	....
73	7	Jefferson	Marshall	260	749	697	1446	....		....	276	198	10	615	1	2	2
72	6	Marion		197	656	665	1321	9	11	20	280	174	4	558	..	..	..
In 71	6	Mt. Pleasant, city of	Mt. Pleasant	725	1998	2112	4110	126	101	227	947	719	16	1616	2	3	2
71	5	New London, ex. of city		217	602	593	1195	7	4	11	285	241	..	446	..	1	2
In 71	5	New London, city of	New London	84	230	266	496	2	1	3	101	64	.	190	..	..	....
70	7	Salem, excl. of city		229	718	651	1369	1		1	300	194	.	560	1	..	....
In 70	7	Salem, city of	Salem	99	258	253	511	2	2	4	124	90	..	192	..	..	....
73	5	Scott	Winfield	144	448	412	860	2		2	194	141	3	342	..	..	....
71	7	Tippecanoe		280	793	753	1546	16	12	28	314	244	17	625	..	5	1
72	7	Trenton	Trenton	240	780	722	1502	2	1	3	309	183	26	651	..	2	1
73	6	Wayne		171	510	442	952	1	1	2	206	159	..	381	..	..	...
		Total		3374	10026	9683	19709	223	178	401	4230	3063	97	7765	7	18	*339

* Inclusive of the inmates of the State Hospital for the Insane.

HOWARD COUNTY.

97 98	14	Afton	Busti	85	255	224	479	....	....	....	109	67	....	169	..	..	1
100	11	Albion	Osborne	90	256	212	468	....	....	....	113	83	3	154	..	..	..
100	13	Chester	Eatonville	46	130	105	235	....	....	....	52	39	....	94	2	..	..
100	12	Forest City	Foreston, Lime Springs	60	207	168	375	....	....	....	88	77	1	142	2	..	..
97 98	13	Howard	Howard	23	72	58	130	....	....	....	25	19	2	54	.	..	..
99	12	Howard Center	Howard Center	32	76	84	160	..	....	....	37	25	....	59	..	2	..
99	14	Jamestown		45	116	111	227	....	....	....	46	35	3	98	..	..	2
97 98	11	New Oregon	New Oregon	166	533	483	1016	....	....	....	220	153	19	380	..	..	..
100	14	Oakdale		16	55	41	96	....	....	....	23	12	....	40	..	..	..
97 98	12	Paris		54	153	125	278	....	....	....	55	35	17	64	..	..	..
99	13	Saratoga	Saratoga	10	24	17	41	....	....	....	11	7	....	10	..	..	..
99	11	Vernon Springs	Vernon Springs, Cresco	149	474	418	892	4	....	4	231	149	9	352	..	1	..
		Total		776	2351	2046	4397	4	....	4	1010	701	54	1616	4	3	3

HUMBOLDT COUNTY.

No. of Township.	Range.	Names of Townships, Towns, and Cities.	Names of Post-Offices.	No. of Dwelling-Houses.	No. of White Males.	No. of White Females.	Total White Population.	No. of Colored Males.	No. of Colored Females.	Total Colored Population.	No. entitled to Vote.	No. of Militia.	No. of Foreigners not Naturalized.	No. between the ages of 5 and 21 years.	No. of Blind.	No. of Deaf and Dumb.	No. of Insane.
.....91	28	Dakota	Dakota (§ 6)														
.....91	28	"	Sylvan Retreat (§ 29) ..														
.....91	27 29 30	"	....	126	382	298	680	....	....	....	158	128	9	216	..	1	..
.....92	30	"	Humboldt														
.....92	..28 29	"	.. ..														
.....93	.28 29	Humboldt	Lott's Creek (R. 29)......	55	176	146	322	....	....	....	76	59	3	125	..	..	..
..92 93	27	Vernon........	....	49	146	122	268	....	....	....	58	40	....	103	..	..	..
.....93	30	Wacousta...........	Wacousta (§ 32).........	7	18	19	37	....	....	....	9	7	1	8	..	..	.
... ...	....	Total...........	....	237	722	585	1307	....	....	....	301	234	13	452	..	1	.

IDA COUNTY.

No. of Township.	Range.	Names of Townships, Towns, and Cities.	Names of Post-Offices.	No. of Dwelling-Houses.	No. of White Males.	No. of White Females.	Total White Population.	No. of Colored Males.	No. of Colored Females.	Total Colored Population.	No. entitled to Vote.	No. of Militia.	No. of Foreigners not Naturalized.	No. between the ages of 5 and 21 years.	No. of Blind.	No. of Deaf and Dumb.	No. of Insane.
86 87 88 89	39 40 41	Corwin...........	Ida (T. 87, R. 40)........	18	51	39	90	....	....	....	25	19	....	32	..	..	..

IOWA COUNTY.

No. of Township.	Range.	Names of Townships, Towns, and Cities.	Names of Post-Offices.	No. of Dwelling-Houses.	No. of White Males.	No. of White Females.	Total White Population.	No. of Colored Males.	No. of Colored Females.	Total Colored Population.	No. entitled to Vote.	No. of Militia.	No. of Foreigners not Naturalized.	No. between the ages of 5 and 21 years.	No. of Blind.	No. of Deaf and Dumb.	No. of Insane.
pt 80 81	..9 10	Amana.............	....	141	606	583	1189	....	....	....	299	142	103	182	..	1	2
...pt 81	11 12	Cono	Cono (R. 12)...........	40	120	110	230	....	....	....	52	31	....	91	..	..	..
......78	12	Dayton............	....	119	363	318	681	1	....	1	153	116	2	258	..	..	2
......78	...11	English....	Millersburg............	244	734	714	1448	...	....	....	289	246	3	627	..	..	1
......78	10	Fillmore...........	Lyle City.............	162	461	427	888	...	....	...	170	94	5	375	..	.	..
......78	9	Greene	Jone, Foote....	137	419	359	778	. ..	....	....	149	107	3	329	..	..	..
......80	...12	Hartford	Victor, Ladora..........	103	301	309	610	1	....	1	145	110	6	219	..	..	2

...pt 80	10	Hilton........	....	50	153	120	273	....	....	....	54	42	9	91	..	..	..
...pt 81	11 12	Honey Creek........	Koszta (R. 12)........	177	463	449	912	1	2	3	197	153	1	383	3	..	1
...pt 80	9	Iowa........	Homestead........	136	363	351	714	..	..	..	147	79	20	234	..	..	..
......81	9	Lenox........	....	67	213	182	395	....	....	....	84	57	4	168	..	..	..
......79	12	Lincoln........	....	37	119	110	229	....	....	....	47	35	4	86	..	1	..
...80 81	10 11	Marengo, exc. of city	....	120	421	378	799	....	....	....	152	109	8	287	..	3	..
...In 81	11	Marengo, city of	Marengo........	187	524	523	1047	1	3	4	271	210	5	355	1	1	1
......79	11	Pilot........	....	59	201	164	365	....	....	....	68	51	2	171	..	2	1
......80	11	Sumner........	Genoa Bluffs........	71	186	205	391	....	....	....	90	70	1	152	..	..	..
......79	...10	Troy........	Stellapolis........	117	370	309	679	....	....	....	139	98	14	297	..	..	..
...pt 81	10 11	Washington........	....	68	223	209	432	....	....	....	79	56	7	187	..	..	..
......79	9	York........	....	55	159	162	321	....	....	....	69	47	3	129	..	..	..
....	....	Total........	....	2090	6399	5982	12381	4	5	9	2654	1853	200	4618	4	8	10

JACKSON COUNTY.

..In 85	....3e	Andrew, town of....	Andrew........	46	155	144	299	....	....	....	74	48	3	109	..	..	..
...In 86	...5e	Bellevue........	Bellevue........	217	560	614	1174	5	3	8	248	170	11	424	1	..	..
......86	..4 5e	Bellevue, exc. of town	....	139	440	429	869	1		1	149	81	15	367	..	2	..
......85	....1e	Brandon........	Canton, Ozark........	212	607	514	1121	1	....	1	220	142	....	470	1	..	..
......86	...1e	Butler........	Garry Owen........	135	403	397	800	....	....	....	154	74	11	319	..	..	..
......84	....4e	Fairfield........	Rolly........	142	400	341	741	2	....	2	149	115	14	313	..	..	..
......85	....2e	Farmers' Creek........	Farmers' Creek........														
......85	....2e	"	Fulton........	268	770	724	1494	....	....	....	328	195	8	613	3	..	2
......85	....2e	"	Iron Hill........														
pt 84 85	...6e	Iowa........	Sterling (T. 84)........	206	606	515	1121	....	....	....	256	127	71	405	..	..	..
......85	....4e	Jackson........	Spring Brook........	140	397	407	804	1	....	1	153	115	15	309	..	..	..
...In 84	..2 3e	Maquoketa, city of...	Maquoketa........	274	669	717	1386	....	....	....	329	209	12	500	..	..	..
......84	...3e	Maquoketa, ex. of city	....	134	373	315	688	....	....	....	147	57	....	291	1	..	..
......84	....1e	Monmouth........	Monmouth, Mill Rock..	159	561	541	1102	....	....	....	221	166	10	450	..	..	..
......86	....2e	Otter Creek........	Otter Creek........	157	433	451	884	1	....	1	168	109	11	394	..	1	..
......85	....3e	Perry, exc. of Andrew	....	141	422	402	824	....	....	....	184	92	3	318	1	..	1
......87	....3e	Prairie Springs........	....	200	604	545	1149	....	....	....	207	115	43	438	..	..	..
......86	....3e	Richland........	Cottonville, Lamotte........	180	523	484	1007	....	....	....	204	115	24	384	..	2	..
...In 84	....7e	Sabula, town of........	Sabula........	144	319	310	629	....	....	....	137	89	1	264	1	..	..
......84	....2e	South Fork, excl. of Maquoketa........	Waterford........	150	427	431	858	....	...	....	184	113	2	338	..	..	..
......87	..4 5e	Tete des Morts........	St. Donatus (R. 4)........	165	509	417	926	....	....	....	150	90	66	364	..	1	..

JACKSON COUNTY—Continued.

No. of Township.	Range.	Names of Townships, Towns, and Cities.	Names of Post-Offices.	No. of Dwelling-Houses.	No. of White Males.	No. of White Females.	Total White Population.	No of Colored Males.	No. of Colored Females.	Total Colored Population.	No. entitled to Vote.	No. of Militia.	No. of Foreigners not Naturalized.	No. between the ages of 5 and 21 years.	No. of Blind.	No. of Deaf and Dumb.	No. of Insane.
.....84	7 pt 6e	Union, exc. of Sabula	....	25	109	100	209	....	....	....	45	32	6	72	..	1	..
..pt 84	....5e	Van Buren	Van Buren, Spragueville	171	504	466	970	....	....	....	201	138	22	348	..	1	..
......85	....5e	Washington.........	Wickliffe .... }														
...pt 85	....6e	"	.... }	170	454	447	901	....	....	....	162	113	15	336	..	..	..
.... .84	....5e	"	.... }														
....	......	Total..........	....	3575	10245	9711	19956	11	3	14	4070	2505	363	7826	8	8	4

JASPER COUNTY.

No. of Township.	Range.	Names of Townships, Towns, and Cities.	Names of Post-Offices.	No. of Dwelling-Houses.	No. of White Males.	No. of White Females.	Total White Population.	No of Colored Males.	No. of Colored Females.	Total Colored Population.	No. entitled to Vote.	No. of Militia.	No. of Foreigners not Naturalized.	No. between the ages of 5 and 21 years.	No. of Blind.	No. of Deaf and Dumb.	No. of Insane.
......79	...18	Buena Vista........	....	243	756	664	1420	1	...	1	293	228	13	521	2	..	3
..... 81	...21	Clear Creek.........	Clyde..................	141	474	459	933	....	....	....	183	126	3	392	..	.	..
......78	21	Des Moines	Vandalia, Prairie City...	292	943	869	1812	1	....	1	373	231	12	767	..	2	..
... ..78	18	Elk Creek	Galesburg	130	477	458	935	....	....	....	208	160	6	374	..	..	..
......78	.19 20	Fairview....	Monroe..............	249	787	746	1533	1	....	1	317	85	..	674	1	1	1
......81	...17	Hickory Grove......	....	19	74	62	136	....	....	...	28	20	...	47	..	..	..
......81	20	Independence	....	129	415	387	802	....	....	....	170	144	1	326	..	..	2
......78	17	Lynn Grove.........	Lynnville..............	175	533	461	994	....	....	....	233	196	4	373	..	..	2
......81	19	Malaka..............	....	97	356	300	656	3	1	4	136	92	2	262	..	1	..
...80 81	18	Mariposa....	Kimball...............	114	280	260	540	2	5	7	105	89	10	181	..	..	..
......79	. 20	Mound Prairie	Colfax.................	105	311	276	587	....	....	...	126	108	2	231	..	..	..
.... .80	19 20	Newton	Newton...............	464	1599	1438	3037	24	19	43	699	561	22	1081	1	..	..
......79	19	Palo Alto...........	....	141	336	261	597	....	...	....	125	90	13	210	..	..	..
......80	21	Poweshiek..........	Greencastle............	192	681	597	1278	1	....	1	261	193	4	449	2	1	1

......79	17	Richland	....	58	208	177	385	....	1	1	96	76	....	128	..	..	..
......80	17	Rock Creek........	....	54	173	147	320	....	....	....	59	32	....	130	..	1	..
......79	21	Washington........	Woodville............	36	105	110	215	....	....	....	68	48	2	81	..	..	..
....	......	Total........	....	2639	5508	7672	16180	33	26	59	3480	2479	94	6227	6	6	9

JEFFERSON COUNTY.

......73	10	Black Hawk	Baker................	121	382	348	730	...	....	...	149	120	...	289	..	..	..
......72	9	Buchanan........	Salina...............	240	688	658	1346	1	....	1	280	194	18	559	..	..	..
......71	9	Cedar...........	Wooster..............	146	410	373	783	3	6	9	157	98	11	327	..	..	..
......71	11	Des Moines	....	181	570	605	1175	....	1	1	242	154	2	539	1	..	..
...In 72	10	Fairfield, city of.....	Fairfield............	320	958	1060	2018	6	9	15	389	266	17	675	..	..	..
......72	10	" exc of city.	....	263	765	693	1458	....	....	...	305	213	7	577	..	..	..
......71	10	Liberty...........	Libertyville..........	162	520	504	1024	....	....	....	239	184	3	510	1	..	2
......72	8	Lockridge.........	Lockridge............	286	806	778	1584	11	6	17	284	160	54	695	3	..	..
......72	11	Locust Grove	Batavia, Brookville	233	707	670	1377	1	...	1	294	227	5	582	1	..	..
......73	9	Penn.............	Pleasant Plain........	230	748	708	1456	...	1	1	320	221	....	602	..	..	..
......73	11	Polk.............	Abingdon.............	211	620	597	1217	....	....	....	248	197	1	558	..	..	..
......71	8	Round Prairie......	Glasgow..............	191	528	521	1049	....	....	....	215	165	1	453	1	..	1
......73	8	Walnut.	Germanville, Merrimac..	229	585	573	1158	....	....	....	226	150	2	564	..	..	..
....	......	Total.......	....	2811	8287	8088	16375	22	23	45	3348	2349	121	7030	7	..	3

JOHNSON COUNTY.

...pt 81	6	Big Grove	Solon................	192	604	569	1173	4	2	6	235	143	11	491	..	..	..
......81	5	Cedar...........	....	148	409	406	815	....	....	....	134	101	24	313	..	..	..
pt 79 80	7	Clear Creek.........	Copi (T. 80).........	104	303	297	600	....	....	....	111	81	10	233	..	..	..
......77	5	Fremont..........	Palestine............	120	370	327	697	....	....	....	164	94	1	262	1	..	..
...pt 80	5	Graham...........	Oasis................	109	309	318	627	....	....	....	116	84	3	264	..	..	2
......79	8	Hardin	Windham..............	71	200	205	405	....	....	....	86	56	2	151	..	..	..
...In 79	6	Iowa City, city of...	Iowa City............	1025	3221	3163	6384	12	22	34	1200	802	37	1721	..	2	..
......79	6	" exc. of city	....	352	1040	1006	2046	16	18	34	360	245	43	899	1	1	1
......81	7	Jefferson...........	Shueyville...........	135	392	352	744	....	....	....	....	....	....	....	1	2	2
......78	6	Liberty...........	Bon Accord, Seventy eight	120	357	301	658	....	....	....	133	75	5	269	..	..	..
pt 80 81	7	Madison..........	....	103	315	294	609	....	....	....	117	92	12	249	1	..	1
pt 80 81	8	Monroe..........	Danforth	136	398	392	790	....	....	....	123	66	27	325	..	..	..
...pt 80	...5 6	New Port.........	New Port Center (R. 6)...	103	328	314	642	1	1	2	110	66	9	248	..	..	..
pt 80 81	8	Oxford...........	Nemora...............	134	387	362	749	....	....	....	150	109	14	311	..	..	1

JOHNSON COUNTY—Continued.

No. of Township.	Range.	Names of Townships, Towns, and Cities.	Names of Post-Offices.	No. of Dwelling-Houses.	No. of White Males.	No. of White Females	Total White Population.	No. of Colored Males.	No. of Colored Females.	Total Colored Population.	No. entitled to Vote.	No. of Militia.	No. of Foreigners not Naturalized.	No. between the ages of 5 and 21 years.	No. of Blind.	No. of Deaf and Dumb.	No. of Insane.
...pt 80	6	Penn	....														
...pt 80	7	"	....	109	311	308	619	....	....	....	118	51	....	274	..	..	..
...pt 81	6	"	North Liberty														
.....78	5 pt 6	Pleasant Valley	....	142	426	389	815	2	....	2	162	132	12	319	..	..	..
......79	5	Scott	....	130	391	376	767	....	....	....	167	121	9	303	..	..	..
......78	7	Sharon	....	165	513	505	1018	....	....	..	203	142	14	401	..	1	..
......79	7	Union	....	90	287	243	530	....	....	...	95	78	21	208	..	1	..
......78	8	Washington	Frank Pierce, Amish	146	467	407	874	1	....	1	181	135	4	376	..	1	..
....	......	Total..........	....	3634	11028	10534	21562	36	43	79	3965	2673	258	7617	4	8	7

JONES COUNTY.

No. of Township.	Range.	Names of Townships, Towns, and Cities.	Names of Post-Offices.	No. of Dwelling-Houses.	No. of White Males.	No. of White Females	Total White Population.	No. of Colored Males.	No. of Colored Females.	Total Colored Population.	No. entitled to Vote.	No. of Militia.	No. of Foreigners not Naturalized.	No. between the ages of 5 and 21 years.	No. of Blind.	No. of Deaf and Dumb.	No. of Insane.
...In 84	4	Anamosa, town of...	Anamosa..............	316	870	881	1751	8	4	12	388	320	21	594	..	6	6
......85	4	Cass	....	110	360	294	654	....	....	....	142	100	....	233	2	1	..
......86	4	Castle Grove.......	Castle Grove, Grove Creek	131	426	368	794	....	....	....	169	105	18	310	..	..	..
......85	1	Clay	Clayford....	149	465	458	923	....	....	....	178	107	3	399	..	..	..
......84	4	Fairview, excl. of Anamosa	Fairview, Highland Grove	150	498	498	996	....	....	....	208	154	2	463	..	1	1
......83	4	Greenfield..........	....	164	480	457	937	....	....	....	198	150	4	378	..	2	..
......83	2	Hale............	....	122	388	362	750	....	....	....	143	127	8	179	1	..	..
......84	3	Jackson.............	....	104	324	284	608	....	....	....	127	90	5	242	..	..	..
......84	2	Madison............	Madison	158	373	336	709	....	....	....	167	36	....	252	..	..	.
......86	3	Monticello..........	Monticello	303	863	853	1716	4	2	6	409	266	21	543	1	..	1
......83	1	Oxford	Oxford Mills............	124	392	308	700	....	....	....	152	90	33	296	..	..	..

86	2	Richland	Bowen's Prairie, Zurich	150	419	343	762	....	1	1	166	81	15	310	..	..	..
83	3	Rome	Walnut Fork	160	515	501	1016	6	3	9	209	140	....	425	..	..	..
85	2	Scotch Grove	Johnson														
85	2	"	Fuller's Mills	130	422	383	805	....	....	....	166	124	7	346	..	..	..
85	2	"	Scotch Grove														
86	1	Washington	....	145	455	406	861	....	....	....	165	79	21	397	..	..	5
85	3	Wayne	Langworthy, Edinburg	150	477	460	937	....	....	....	189	140	25	367	1	..	..
84	1	Wyoming	Wyoming	226	653	628	1281	....	....	....	270	202	12	512	..	1	2
....	......	Total	....	2792	8380	7820	16200	18	10	28	3446	2311	195	6246	5	11	15

KEOKUK COUNTY.

77	12	Adams	Aurora	97	335	272	607	....	....	....	132	94	3	253	1	1	..
74	13	Benton	Butler	158	487	474	961	....	....	....	189	145	....	429	..	..	..
75	10	Clear Creek	Talleyrand	147	365	470	835	....	....	....	170	89	4	315	..	..	..
77	11	English River	White Pigeon														
77	11	"	Webster	192	575	579	1154	....	....	....	233	190	4	485	..	..	..
77	11	"	South English														
76	11	German	Baden														
pt 75	11	"	Garibaldi	206	670	580	1250	....	....	....	229	148	17	525	2	..	1
74	11	Jackson	Ioka	234	692	635	1327	....	....	....	267	217	1	586	1	2	1
76	10	Lafayette	....	110	308	302	610	....	....	....	132	100	5	220	..	..	..
pt 74 75	11 12	Lancaster	Lancaster (T. 75, R. 11)	182	648	640	1288	....	....	....	260	185	1	543	1	8	5
77	10	Liberty	Chandler	134	437	420	857	....	....	....	171	116	....	351	..	1	1
77	13	Prairie	Coal Creek	67	210	181	391	....	....	....	82	65	3	146	..	..	..
74	10	Richland	Richland	262	795	764	1559	....	....	....	319	245	....	650	1	1	..
In 75	12	Sigourney, town of	Sigourney	151	433	471	904	1	....	1	215	157	3	337	..	..	..
pt 75 76	12	Sigourney, excl. town	....	66	241	219	460	2	....	2	91	60	....	213	..	..	..
74	12	Steady Run	Martinsburg	149	461	441	902	....	....	....	173	140	....	415	..	1	..
76	12	Van Buren	....	143	437	435	872	....	....	....	164	129	17	377	..	..	2
75	13	Warren	....	89	286	293	579	....	....	....	114	78	....	267	1	..	2
76	13	Washington	Springfield, What Cheer	224	457	412	869	1	....	1	179	94	....	389	..	..	1
....	......	Total	....	2611	7837	7588	15425	4	....	4	3120	2252	58	6501	7	14	13

KOSSUTH COUNTY.

No. of Township.	Range.	Names of Townships, Towns, and Cities.	Names of Post-Offices.	No. of Dwelling-Houses.	No. of White Males.	No. of White Females.	Total White Population.	No of Colored Males.	No. of Colored Females.	Total Colored Population.	No. entitled to Vote.	No. of Militia.	No. of Foreigners not Naturalized.	No. between the ages of 5 and 21 years.	No. of Blind.	No. of Deaf and Dumb.	No. of Insane.
96	27–30	Algona	Kossuth Center (R. 28).														
97	27–30	"	Buffalo Fork (R. 28)														
98	27–30	"	Greenwood (R. 28)	169	586	515	1101	....	..	....	269	196	....	439	..	..	..
98 99 100	27–30	"	Seneca (T. 98, R. 30)														
pt 95	27–30	"	Algona (R. 29)														
pt 94 95	29 30	Cresco		44	109	97	206	....	....	....	56	33	....	77	..	..	..
pt 94 95	27 28	Irvington	Irvington (R. 28)	46	137	128	265	1	....	1	55	46	....	109	..	..	..
		Total		259	832	740	1572	1	....	1	380	275	....	625	..	..	..

LEE COUNTY.

No. of Township.	Range.	Names of Townships, Towns, and Cities.	Names of Post-Offices.	No. of Dwelling-Houses.	No. of White Males.	No. of White Females.	Total White Population.	No of Colored Males.	No. of Colored Females.	Total Colored Population.	No. entitled to Vote.	No. of Militia.	No. of Foreigners not Naturalized.	No. between the ages of 5 and 21 years.	No. of Blind.	No. of Deaf and Dumb.	No. of Insane.
69	7	Cedar	Big Mound	199	546	525	1071	11	6	17	225	172	5	446	1	..	1
67	6	Charleston	Charleston	202	593	499	1092	....	....	....	228	133	3	483	..	..	..
69	4	Denmark	Denmark [(R. 7)	162	408	434	842	13	8	21	193	132	4	326	..	..	1
66	6 7	Des Moines.	Vincennes (R. 6), Belfast	198	502	475	977	39	45	84	212	151	9	365	..	1	..
68	6	Franklin	Franklin Center, Dover	302	879	882	1761	....	....	....	325	263	37	757	2	1	..
68	2	Green Bay															
68	3	"	Jollyville	121	360	314	674	....	....	....	166	126	9	256	..	1	..
69	3	"															
68	7	Harrison	Primrose	174	481	462	943	19	12	31	215	155	7	377	..	..	..
65	5	Jackson, exc. Keokuk		188	468	444	912	74	57	131	165	101	24	379	2	..	..
67	5	Jefferson	Jeffersonville	165	510	456	966	8	8	16	212	171	6	372	..	..	3
In 65	5	Keokuk, city of	Keokuk	1739	4719	4852	9571	437	481	918	2079	1499	115	3433	2	1	4
67	4	Madison.	Fort Madison	629	1864	1769	3633	31	23	54	651	384	29	1237	..	..	..

... ..69	6	Marion	St. Paul..............	220	694	609	1303	3	....	3	283	220	5	488	..	1	..
......69	6	"	Pilot Grove														
......69	6	"	Clay's Grove..........														
......66	5	Montrose, exc. of city	Sandusky, Summitville..	183	443	456	899	21	24	45	182	133	5	369	..	.	..
...In 66	5	" city of....	Montrose	85	305	332	637	1	....	1	130	97	....	226	..	.	..
......69	5	Pleasant Ridge......	....	156	444	431	875	7	9	16	188	119	1	365	..	.	..
......67	7	Van Buren..........	Croton, Warren.........	120	554	506	1060	1	....	1	225	149	16	448	1	.	..
......68	4	Washington	....	191	553	503	1056	12	7	19	233	152	13	427	..	.	1
......68	5	West Point,exc.of city	....	170	505	442	947	4	4	8	199	120	13	387	2	2	1
...In 68	5	" city of ...	West Point.............	144	411	422	833	....	....	...	164	107	7	318	..	1	..
....	......	Total..............	....	5388	15239	14813	30052	681	684	1365	6275	4384	308	11459	10	8	11

LINN COUNTY.

.pt 82 '3	6	Bertram	Bertram (T. 83).........	175	532	450	982	....	....	....	220	166	....	390	1	..	..
......86	5	Boulder...........	Prairieburg.............	94	311	288	599	....	....	....	117	64	4	268	..	..	..
......84	5	Brown	Springville, Viola......	208	677	616	1293	....	....	....	279	208	....	515	..	..	..
...pt 85	5	Buffalo	Necot...................	64	192	188	380	....	....	....	60	26	1	130	..	..	..
...In 83	7	Cedar Rapids, city of	Cedar Rapids...........	482	1451	1445	2896	15	14	29	615	470	95	952	..	..	2
......83	8	Clinton...........	Sisley's Grove..........	174	502	489	991	....	....	...	212	159	16	371	..	..	..
......82	7	College...........	Western College........	183	464	454	918	2	....	2	183	143	22	475	2	..	..
......82	8	Fairfax...........	Fairfax.................	121	339	312	651	....	....	....	136	74	19	256	.	..	1
.pt 84 '5	8	Fayette...........	Palo (T. 84)............	129	437	422	859	1	....	1	178	132	....	351	1	..	..
......82	5	Franklin..........	Mt. Vernon, Lisbon.....	439	1314	1319	2633	6	1	7	567	319	14	1122	2	..	..
......86	6	Jackson	Valley Farm............	146	395	398	793	1	....	1	170	111	1	257	..	..	..
......86	6	"	Nugent's Grove.........														
......86	6	"	Paris...................														
......83	5	Linn..............	Prospect Hill...........	187	494	469	963	....	....	....	195	135	...	363	..	..	..
......85	6	Maine.............	Central City...........	148	481	472	953	....	....	....	230	169	3	376	..	..	..
......85	6	"	Wapsa..................														
...pt 85	7	"	Waubeck................														
.pt 83 '4	...6 7	Marion, city of......	Marion	313	935	927	1862	5	1	6	449	328	14	682	1	1	2
... ..84	6	Marion, exc. of city..	....	293	884	798	1682	1	....	1	380	278	5	716	1	1	..
...pt 84	7	" ..	....														
...pt 83	7	" ..	....														
...pt 84	...7 8	Monroe	Dry Creek (R. 7)........	148	437	417	854	...	....	....	174	127	....	350	..	..	..

LINN COUNTY—Continued.

No. of Township.	Range.	Names of Townships, Towns, and Cities.	Names of Post-Offices.	No. of Dwelling-Houses.	No. of White Males.	No. of White Females.	Total White Population.	No. of Colored Males.	No. of Colored Females.	Total Colored Population.	No. entitled to Vote.	No. of Militia.	No. of Foreigners not Naturalized.	No. between the ages of 5 and 21 years.	No. of Blind.	No. of Deaf and Dumb.	No. of Insane.
......85	7	Otter Creek.........	Lafayette..............														
......85	7	"	Flemingville...........	228	697	624	1321	....	....	....	240	187	9	593	2	1	..
...pt 85	8	"	....														
......82	6	Putnam	....	108	350	305	655	1	1	2	116	84	21	260	..	..	..
......83	7	Rapids, exc. of city..	....	298	915	893	1808	....	....	....	324	73	63	541	..	..	..
......86	7	Spring Grove.........	Spring Grove........														
......86	7	"	Troy Mills*...........	61	226	194	420	....	....	....	74	59	1	133	..	1	..
......86	7	"	West Prairie*.........														
86 pt 85	8	Washington.........	Center Point............	149	515	472	987	...	....	....	199	157	....	445	..	..	..
....	......	Total..........	....	4148	12548	11952	24500	32	17	49	5118	3469	288	9546	10	4	5

*These offices may be in Jackson Township, as they are reported in both.

LOUISA COUNTY.

No. of Township.	Range.	Names of Townships, Towns, and Cities.	Names of Post-Offices.	No. of Dwelling-Houses.	No. of White Males.	No. of White Females.	Total White Population.	No. of Colored Males.	No. of Colored Females.	Total Colored Population.	No. entitled to Vote.	No. of Militia.	No. of Foreigners not Naturalized.	No. between the ages of 5 and 21 years.	No. of Blind.	No. of Deaf and Dumb.	No. of Insane.
...pt 74	...4 5	Columbus City......	....														
...pt 75	4	"	....	457	933	891	1824	8	4	12	406	327	11	704	1	..	1
...pt 75	5	"	Columbus City, Clifton.														
pt 74 75	4	Concord....... ...	Fredonia (R. 75).........	144	417	390	807	....	....	...	159	121	12	323	1	..	1
...pt 73	...1 2	Eliot....	Palo Alto (R. 2).........	47	202	161	363	....	....	....	80	63	10	124	..	..	..
...pt 74	...4 5	Elm Grove.........	....	196	358	314	672	1	1	2	132	104	4	264	..	..	..
...pt 74	3	Grandview....	Grandview	253	751	721	1472	8	9	17	332	238	11	578	1	..	1
...pt 75	3	"	Letis..................														
pt 73 74	.1 2 3	Jefferson............	Toolsboro (T. 73, R. 2)..	120	307	286	593	9	3	12	131	100	...	244	4	..	..

pt 73 74	4	Marshall........ ..	Cairo (T. 74)............	157	500	434	934	....	....	....	199	141	16	383	..	..	..
...pt 73	4	Morning Sun.... ...	Virginia Grove	195	530	502	1032	....	....	....	216	166	....	397	..	1	..
...pt 73	4	"	Morning Sun..........														
...pt 73	3	"	....														
pt 75 76	5	Oakland...........	Port Allen (T. 76)	71	260	238	498	....	....	....	113	87	1	180	..	..	..
...pt 74	2	Port Louisa.........	Port Louisa	253	737	704	1441	....	....	....	301	225	2	557	..	..	..
...pt 74	3	"	....														
pt 74 75	...2 3	"	....														
pt 75 76	5	Union..............	....	93	265	251	516	....	....	....	116	90	1	222	..	..	..
pt 73 74	.2 3 4	Wapello, exc. of city.	....	162	465	443	908	....	....	....	196	143	3	376	1	..	1
...In 74	3	Wapello, city of.....	Wapello...............	127	400	380	780	2	....	2	187	130	2	273	1	..	..
....	......	Total...........	....	2275	6125	5715	11840	28	17	45	2568	1935	73	4625	9	1	4

LUCAS COUNTY.

......71	20	Benton............	....	88	473	454	927	....	....	....	105	70	....	237	..	..	..
......72	20	Cedar..............	Lagrange, Ola..........	121	342	325	667	2	3	5	129	100	1	290	..	..	..
......72	21	Chariton, exc. of town	....	82	282	272	554	....	....	....	102	47	2	170	..	..	..
...In 72	21	Chariton, town of....	Chariton...............	138	544	440	984	6	2	8	287	244	....	360	..	1	..
......73	... 21	English............	....	124	399	357	756	....	....	....	130	99	....	354	..	..	..
......72	23	Jackson.....	Tallahoma..............	61	181	183	364	....	....	....	72	57	1	144	..	..	..
......73	22	Liberty...........	....	71	250	209	459	....	....	....	83	68	....	198	..	..	..
......73	23	Otter Creek.........	....	94	274	253	527	....	....	....	100	84	....	235	..	..	..
......73	20	Pleasant...........	Belinda................	63	199	191	390	....	....	....	69	52	....	189	..	..	1
......71	23	Union.............	Argo, Last Chance......	114	302	305	607	....	....	....	115	94	....	255	1	..	..
......71	22	Warren............	Freedom................	96	302	306	608	6	3	9	125	94	....	280	..	..	..
......71	20	Washington........	Russell................	78	213	187	400	....	....	....	91	73	....	164	1	..	..
..... 72	22	Whitebreast........	....	83	248	233	481	....	....	....	92	73	....	216	..	..	..
....	......	Total..........	....	1213	4009	3715	7724	14	8	22	1500	1155	4	3092	2	1	1

LYON COUNTY—Not Organized.

MADISON COUNTY.

..76, &c	28, &c.	Center, exc. of Wint'st	....	16	30	30	60	....	....	....	13	10	....	20	..	..	..
......76	26	Crawford	Ellsworth..............	104	316	283	599	1	1	2	120	87	6	259	..	3	..

MADISON COUNTY—Continued.

No. of Township.	Range.	Names of Townships, Towns, and Cities.	Names of Post-Offices.	No. of Dwelling-Houses.	No. of White Males.	No. of White Females.	Total White Population.	No. of Colored Males.	No. of Colored Females.	Total Colored Population.	No. entitled to Vote.	No. of Militia.	No. of Foreigners not Naturalized.	No. between the ages of 5 and 21 years.	No. of Blind.	No. of Deaf and Dumb.	No. of Insane.
76	28	Douglas		88	347	340	687				154	117		266			
74	29	Grand River	Venus	64	176	179	355				65	59		49		1	
76	29	Jackson		49	179	156	335				78	59		91		2	
77	27	Jefferson		71	222	195	417				93	71	3	134	1		
77	26	Lee		36	121	105	226				37	25	1	103			
75	28	Lincoln		86	317	274	591				125	107	1	248			
77	28	Madison	North	92	299	277	576				127	92	2	219			
74	28	Monroe	Kasson, Clanton	60	171	154	325				74	55		130	2		
74	26	Ohio	Ohio	92	254	258	512				99	87		229			
77	29	Penn		42	117	108	225				50	48		60			
75	27	Scott		148	471	462	933				182	146		414			
75	26	South	St. Charles	162	482	444	926	2		2	204	147		397			
76	27	Union		97	360	306	666				116	81	2	289			
74	27	Walnut	Peru	99	356	331	687				124	86	1	297			
75	29	Webster	Middle River	52	151	129	280	1		1	61	40	2	108			
In 76	28	Winterset, City of	Winterset	204	683	674	1357	1	1	2	308	214	4	521			
		Total		1562	5052	4705	9757	5	2	7	2025	1531	22	3832	3	6	

MAHASKA COUNTY.

No. of Township.	Range.	Names of Townships, Towns, and Cities.	Names of Post-Offices.	No. of Dwelling-Houses.	No. of White Males.	No. of White Females.	Total White Population.	No. of Colored Males.	No. of Colored Females.	Total Colored Population.	No. entitled to Vote.	No. of Militia.	No. of Foreigners not Naturalized.	No. between the ages of 5 and 21 years.	No. of Blind.	No. of Deaf and Dumb.	No. of Insane.
76	15	Adams	Buck Horn	119	357	314	671				137	95		306			
76	17	Black Oak		124	376	347	723	1		1	150	90	16	279		1	
74	14	Cedar	Fremont	134	429	511	940	3	3	6	187	151	1	366			
74	16	Des Moines	Given	141	413	398	811				155	131		344			

......74	15	Harrison..........	....	191	558	518	1076	5	2	7	237	184	10	434	..	..	..
......74	17	Jefferson..........	Eveland Grove..........	166	504	448	952	....	....	....	191	155	2	406	1	..	1
......76	16	Madison..........	Farmersville..........	113	364	325	689	....	....	....	168	118	10	261	..	..	..
......76	14	Monroe	Indianapolis, Hopewell..	201	561	541	1102	....	....	....	238	188	1	407	2	..	..
......75	.15 16	Oskaloosa, exc. of city	Beacon (R. 15)........	487	1588	1488	3076	20	7	27	636	445	20	1236	2	1	1
...In 75	16	Oskaloosa, city of....	Oskaloosa..........	438	1276	1391	2667	25	29	54	580	432	6	941	..	..	..
......77	14	Pleasant Grove......	Agricola..........	131	389	365	754	....	....	....	143	86	8	349	..	..	..
......77	16	Prairie..........	New Sharon, Flint......	178	527	474	1001	2	6	8	213	181	11	390	..	..	..
......77	17	Richland..........	Peoria, Granville......	231	719	659	1378	....	....	....	288	191	4	549	2	..	..
......75	17	Scott	Auburn..........														
......75	17	"	Belle Fontaine........	162	485	448	933	....	....	....	192	147	2	387	1	1	..
......75	17	"	Leighton Station......														
......77	15	Union..........	Union Mills..........	153	448	452	900	5	4	9	174	127	6	382	..	..	..
......75	14	White Oak..........	White Oak..........	159	440	468	908	....	....	....	162	119	....	389	1	..	..
....	......	Total..........	....	3128	9434	9147	18581	61	51	112	3851	2840	97	7426	9	3	2

MARION COUNTY.

.....pt 75	18	Clay..........	Iola..........														
.....pt 75	18	"	English Settlement..	218	650	628	1278	..	....	....	246	185	....	598	..	..	..
.....pt 76	18	"	....														
........74	21	Dallas..........	Dallas..........	144	459	441	900	....	....	....	173	119	6	389	..	..	..
........75	...21	Franklin..........	Caloma, Starr........	70	246	212	458	....	....	....	93	77	....	192	..	..	..
........74	19	Indiana..........	Attica..........	184	536	544	1080	....	....	....	198	160	....	439	1	1	..
........75	... 19	Knoxville, exc. of city	....														
........75	20	" " "	....	384	1216	1142	2358	1	....	1	473	326	1	1020	2	..	1
.....pt 76	19 20	" " "	....														
..In § 7 75	19	Knoxville, city of...	Knoxville..........	164	543	557	1100	3	3	6	248	201	1	345	..	1	..
77 pt 75 76	18	LakePrairie, exc. Pella	....	478	1415	1272	2687	2	....	2	528	450	88	1050	2	..	3
........74	18	Liberty..........	Ely, Hamilton........	238	624	665	1289	....	....	....	280	215	16	584	..	1	.
In(§3,10)76	18	Pella, city of	Pella..........	375	923	910	1833	....	....	....	353	209	62	688	3	..	..
...n pt 77	...21	Perry..........	Bennington..........	68	193	196	389	....	....	....	77	52	4	168	..	..	..
.....pt 76	...21	Pleasant Grove......	Pleasantville........	205	573	547	1120	....	....	....	207	149	....	492	3	..	..
.....n ⅔ 76	...19	Polk..........	....	147	455	399	854	....	....	....	152	123	9	334	1	..	2
...n pt 77	20	Red Rock..........	Red Rock, Mennon...	214	627	591	1218	....	....	....	226	150	....	551	..	..	2
...n pt 77	19	Summit..........	Newark..........	196	560	522	1082	....	....	....	219	173	....	396	..	..	2
..pt 76 77	...21	Swan..........	Wheeling (T. 76)......	178	494	450	944	...	....	....	203	136	....	377	..	..	..

MARION COUNTY—CONTINUED.

No. of Township.	Range.	Names of Townships, Towns, and Cities.	Names of Post-Offices.	No. of Dwelling-Houses.	No. of White Males.	No. of White Females.	Total White Population.	No. of Colored Males.	No. of Colored Females.	Total Colored Population.	No. entitled to Vote.	No. of Militia.	No. of Foreigners not Naturalized.	No. between the ages of 5 and 21 years.	No. of Blind.	No. of Deaf and Dumb.	No. of Insane.
pt 76 77	20	Union		97	272	279	551	....	..	....	119	94	....	211	1	2	..
74	20	Washington	Gosport, Columbia	196	528	503	1031	....	....	....	219	172	....	412	1	1	..
		Total		3556	10314	9858	20172	6	3	9	4014	2991	187	8246	14	6	10

MARSHALL COUNTY.

No. of Township.	Range.	Names of Townships, Towns, and Cities.	Names of Post-Offices.	No. of Dwelling-Houses.	No. of White Males.	No. of White Females.	Total White Population.	No. of Colored Males.	No. of Colored Females.	Total Colored Population.	No. entitled to Vote.	No. of Militia.	No. of Foreigners not Naturalized.	No. between the ages of 5 and 21 years.	No. of Blind.	No. of Deaf and Dumb.	No. of Insane.
85	19	Bangor	Bangor	118	333	265	598	5	6	11	118	99	....	273	..	..	2
82	20	Eden	Edenville	78	233	208	441	....	....	....	100	....	....	169	..	..	..
82	17	Green Castle		65	197	188	385	1	....	1	81	66	5	162	1	..	..
85	18	Iowa	Albion, Norris	268	681	653	1334	....	...	...	302	225	....	529	..	..	1
82	18	Jefferson		57	175	155	330	....	...	...	65	39	4	135	..	..	..
83	17	Legrand	Legrand	172	538	376	914	....	....	....	215	169	22	362	..	..	..
85	20	Liberty	Illinois Grove	85	271	238	509	....	....	....	101	88	....	207	..	1	..
84	19	Marietta	Marietta	125	448	395	843	3	5	8	164	112	3	340	1	..	..
84	17	Marion		130	404	355	759	....	....	....	165	123	2	310	..	..	..
84	18	Marshall, exc. of city		117	321	327	648	7	10	17	140	107	3	308	..	..	..
In 84	18	Marshalltown, city of	Marshalltown	500	1154	1103	2257	15	7	22	562	....	25	683	..	..	..
84	20	Minerva	Minerva	82	268	237	505	2	3	5	98	81	....	200	..	..	..
83	20	State Center	State Center	61	227	186	413	1	....	1	97	77	....	164	..	..	..
85	17	Vienna	Vienna	76	246	222	468	....	....	....	102	72	2	176	1	..	..
83	18	Timber Creek	Timber Creek	115	378	333	711	....	....	....	135	108	6	308	..	..	1
82 83	19	Washington		53	164	169	333	....	....	....	67	56	131	128	..	1	..
		Total		2102	6038	5410	11448	34	31	65	2512	1422	203	4454	3	2	4

MILLS COUNTY.

....73	.....40 e½ 41	Anderson........	Benton (R. 41)........	57	180	169	349	....	....	...	72	56	2	146	1	..	..
....72	..w½ 42 e½ 43	Glenwood, exc. city	....	84	350	308	658	....	....	....	128	91	2	227	1	1	..
.In 72	43	Glenwood, city of..	Glenwood...........	126	448	437	885	5	5	10	193	136	3	324	1	..	..
....72	.....40 e½ 41	Indian Creek.....	....	58	187	169	356	...	....	....	71	55	....	146	..	..	..
....73	..w½ 41 e½ 42	Ingraham........	Ward (R. 42).........	32	108	96	204	....	....	..	37	24	....	82	..	..	..
....71	43	Lyons...........	Egypt..............	194	710	639	1349	....	....	....	270	280	9	519	..	4	.
....73	w½ 42 e 5-6 43	Oak..............	....	96	275	225	500	1	....	1	99	71	31	194	..	..	..
....72	....44 w½ 43	Platteville........	....	104	400	380	780	....	....	....	125	65	..	222	1	..	..
....71	42	Rawles...........	Wahaghbonsy.......	89	297	250	547	2	....	2	107	82	....	112	..	..	..
....73	....44 w⅙ 43	St. Mary.........	....	46	189	144	333	3	5	8	95	79	8	106	..	..	..
....72	..w½ 41 e½ 42	Silver Creek......	....	296	300	292	592	...	..	...	133	105	1	207	..	..	..
....71	.......40 41	White Cloud......	White Cloud (R. 41)...	67	225	195	420	....	..	....	98	96	1	178	..	..	..
......	....	Total.........	....	1249	3669	3304	6973	11	10	21	1428	1140	57	2463	4	5	..

MITCHELL COUNTY.

...pt 98	16	Burr Oak..........	Cardiff, Brownsville.														
...pt 98	17	"	....	64	181	144	325	....	....	....	73	42	7	132	..	..	..
...pt 99	...16 17	"	....														
pt 97 98	...17 18	Cedar..........	....	107	326	285	611	....	....	....	133	89	17	232	..	..	..
......98	15	Douglas..........	Nelson.............	35	101	90	191	....	....	....	44	36	1	65	..	..	..
......99	15	Jenkins..........	Doran, Riceville.....	82	229	222	451	....	....	...	94	62	....	161	..	..	..
...pt 97	...15 16	Lincoln..........	....	42	124	123	247	....	....	....	48	35	....	104	..	..	..
.. pt 98	17	Mitchell..........	Mitchell............														
...pt 98	17	"	West Mitchell.......	149	551	510	1061	....	....	...	248	164	9	381	1	4	..
...pt 99	...17 18	"	....														
...pt 99	18	Newburg..........	Newburg............	49	186	182	368	....	....	....	63	49	7	105	..	..	..
...pt 97	...16 17	Osage..........	....														
...pt 98	16	"	....	239	752	696	1448	1	....	1	354	233	10	564	..	..	..
...pt 98	17	"	Osage..............														
.....100	.18 pt 17	Otranto..........	Otranto (R. 18)......	56	177	172	349	....	....	....	66	36	9	114	..	..	1
...pt 99	...17 18	St. Ansgar..........	St. Ansgar (R. 18)....	67	206	177	383	....	....	....	83	34	1	134	..	..	..
...pt 99	..16 17	Stacyville..........	....														
.....100	16	"	Stacyville..........	83	226	220	446	1	....	1	*90	50	....	163	..	..	..
..pt 100	17	"	....														

* Number of voters not returned—estimated at 90.—[CLERK OF THE DISTRICT COURT.

MITCHELL COUNTY—CONTINUED.

No. of Township.	Range.	Names of Townships, Towns, and Cities.	Names of Post-Offices.	No. of Dwelling Houses.	No. of White Males.	No. of White Females.	Total White Population.	No. of Colored Males.	No. of Colored Females.	Total Colored Population.	No. entitled to Vote.	No. of Militia.	No. of Foreigners not Naturalized.	No. between the ages of 5 and 21 years.	No. of Blind.	No. of Deaf and Dumb.	No. of Insane.
100	15	Wayne	Wentworth	52	139	129	268				58	35		105			
		Total		1025	3198	2950	6148	2		2	1354	865	61	2260	1	4	1
		MONONA COUNTY.															
84	45	Ashton		10	23	23	46				12	7		17			
		Belvidere	Belvidere (T. 83, R. 44)	10	50	38	88	10	13	23	16	8	1	52			
		Center	Castana (T. 84, R. 44)	19	48	45	93				17	11		43			
		*Franklin		53	149	127	276				67	50		90	1	1	
		Grant		14	53	42	95				24	14		42			
		Kennebec	Arcola (T. 84, R. 44)	42	148	129	277				66	44	2	117			
		Lake		23	75	55	130				24	19		58			
		Lincoln		34	84	86	170				43	34	2	41			
		Maple	Mapleton (T. 85, R. 43)	30	79	79	158				29	20		53			
In 83	45	*Onawa City, town of	Onawa City									40					
		St. Clair	St. Clair (T. 83, R. 42)	13	39	39	78				14	16		21			
		Sherman	Bottom (T. 82, R. 45)	29	100	69	169				39			70			
		Spring Valley		4	33	24	57			†4	9			28			
		‡West Fork	West Fork (T. 85, R. 46)								8	6					
		Total		281	881	756	1637	10	13	†27	368	169	5	632	1	1	

* No report of the town of Onawa City is returned from the county, except of the number of militia. The figures for the other items are probably included in the statistics of Franklin township, in which Onawa City is located.

† Number of each sex not reported in Spring Valley township.

‡ No returns from this township of the several items except as indicated.

MONROE COUNTY.

In 72	17	Albia, city of	Albia	173	468	469	937	19	8	27	233	131	2	302	..	..	..
73	17	Bluff Creek	Half Way Prairie	145	439	392	831	...	...	...	163	114	...	393	..	2	..
73	19	Cedar	Coalton														
73	19	"	Thompsonville	105	329	310	639	...	...	...	119	88	...	256	..	2	..
73	19	"	Weller														
71	18	Franklin	Tyrone	91	267	245	512	...	...	...	98	67	...	224	..	..	..
72	18	Guilford	Georgetown	147	419	351	770	...	...	...	153	71	4	349	2	..	..
71	19	Jackson	East Melrose, Osprey	93	344	324	668	...	...	...	125	99	7	293	..	..	..
72	16	Mantua	Frederick	152	454	448	902	...	...	...	163	108	3	402	..	..	..
71	17	Monroe	...	85	266	234	500	...	1	1	105	67	...	210	..	2	..
73	16	Pleasant	...	175	525	536	1061	...	...	...	191	137	8	379	..	2	..
72	17	Troy, exc. of Albia	...	163	433	450	883	12	12	24	184	130	...	381	1	3	..
73	18	Union	Lovilla	195	581	586	1167	...	...	...	230	157	...	497	..	..	..
71	16	Urbana	...	123	339	353	692	...	...	...	131	86	3	262	1	1	..
72	19	Wayne	...	88	290	304	594	...	...	...	113	90	13	252	..	..	..
...	...	Total	...	1735	5154	5002	10156	31	21	52	1998	1345	40	4190	4	12	..

MONTGOMERY COUNTY.

73	36pt37	Douglas	Grant [R. 36]	57	147	148	295	...	...	...	62	51	2	124	..	1	..
73	.38 39	Frankfort	...														
pt 73	37	"	...														
pt 72	37	"	Frankfort	80	258	227	485	...	...	...	102	96	...	145	..	..	..
n ½ 72	38	"	...														
n ½ 72	39	"	...														
pt 71	.36 37	Jackson	Valiska [R. 36]	50	173	141	314	...	...	...	69	57	...	96	..	..	..
71	.. 38	Red Oak	...														
pt 71	37	"	...														
pt 71	39	"	...	95	302	273	575	...	...	...	130	109	...	202	2	..	..
pt 72	.37 39	"	...														
pt 72	38	"	Red Oak Junction														
72	36	Washington	Sciola														
pt 71	.36 37	"	...	44	153	136	289	...	...	...	56	35	...	101	..	..	..
pt 72	37	"	...														
pt 71 72	39	West	Carr's Point [T. 71]	18	65	49	114	...	...	...	24	19	...	46	..	..	..
...	...	Total	...	344	1098	974	2072	...	...	...	443	367	2	714	2	1	..

MUSCATINE COUNTY.

No. of Township.	Range.	Names of Townships, Towns, and Cities.	Names of Post-Offices.	No. of Dwelling-Houses.	No. of White Males.	No. of White Females.	Total White Population.	No. of Colored Males.	No. of Colored Females.	Total Colored Population.	No. entitled to Vote.	No. of Militia.	No. of Foreigners not Naturalized.	No. between the ages of 5 and 21 years.	No. of Blind.	No. of Deaf and Dumb.	No. of Insane.
76 pt 77	...2w	Bloomington, exc. of Muscatine	....	2426	647	617	1264	10	12	22	306	198	17	576	2	1	..
...pt 76	....4w	Cedar	....	63	225	233	458	....	....	....	95	70	3	177	..	..	..
......78	....1e	Fulton	Prairie Mills, Pleas't Pr'e.	200	574	504	1078	....	....	....	186	150	31	414	..	..	..
......78	.. 3w	Goshen	Atalissa	231	648	623	1271	3	3	6	277	210	11	505	1	1	1
...pt 77	2,3,4 w	Lake	....	112	408	357	765	5	4	9	153	114	11	337	..	..	..
......77	... 1e	Montpelier	....	124	374	328	702	1	....	1	150	101	13	267	..	..	..
...pt 78	...2w	Moscow	Moscow	156	384	391	775	1	....	1	168	90	5	250	..	2	..
...In 77	...2w	Muscatine, city of	Muscatine	2042	3760	3800	7560	52	53	105	1493	1219	180	2395	3	2	2
...pt 76	...4w	Orono	Orono	42	149	134	283	....	....	....	63	48	....	125	..	..	..
...pt 77	...3w	Pike	....														
...pt 77	...4w	“	Pike, Lacey	89	270	232	502	....	....	....	107	77	9	193	..	..	..
......76	...3w	Seventy-Six	....	159	468	460	928	1	....	1	202	143	8	356	1	1	..
......77	...1w	Sweetland	Fairport														
......77	...1w	“	Sweetland Center	263	758	729	1487	....	....	....	301	135	22	135	1	1	1
...pt 78	...1w	“	Milpine														
......78	...4w	Wapsinonoc	West Liberty	261	773	702	1475	9	4	13	341	257	38	531	.	1	..
......78	1pt2w	Wilton, exc. of town	....	168	543	456	999	4	3	7	219	149	29	363	..	..	..
...In 78	...1w	Wilton, town of	Wilton	139	504	481	985	1	1	2	184	173	22	356	..	..	..
... .	......	Total	....	6475	10485	10047	20532	87	80	167	4245	3134	399	6980	8	9	4

O'BRIEN COUNTY.

No. of Township.	Range.	Names of Townships, Towns, and Cities.	Names of Post-Offices.	No. of Dwelling-Houses.	No. of White Males.	No. of White Females.	Total White Population.	No. of Colored Males.	No. of Colored Females.	Total Colored Population.	No. entitled to Vote.	No. of Militia.	No. of Foreigners not Naturalized.	No. between the ages of 5 and 21 years.	No. of Blind.	No. of Deaf and Dumb.	No. of Insane.
... ..94	...39	Watterman	....	7	12	8	20	...	....	....	11	10	....	9	..	..	..

OSCEOLA COUNTY—Not Organized.

PAGE COUNTY.

......67	37	Amity.......	College Springs..............	75	302	245	547	15	23	38	116	93	1	233	1	..	..
......67	36	Buchanan....	Centre.......	88	313	306	619	....	....	....	109	87	....	295	..	..	3
......70	... 37	Douglas......	....	35	123	97	220	1	....	1	40	30	....	96	..	..	..
......68	... 36	East River....	....	120	410	405	815	....	1	1	147	113	4	388	..	..	..
......70	38	Fremont.....	....	24	68	64	132	....	....	....	24	17	....	60	..	..	..
......68	37	Harlan	....	84	249	209	458	10	12	23	99	78	10	171	..	..	..
......68	38 39	Lincoln	....	49	142	131	273	2	..	2	60	49	1	141	..	..	..
......69	pt 36	Nebraska.....	Hawleyville...........	88	257	273	530	9	11	20	122	94	....	221	..	..	..
......69	37pt36	Nodaway.....	Clarinda (R. 36).............	231	647	603	1250	24	40	64	273	179	2	547	1	..	1
......70	39	Pierce	Franklin Grove..............	18	58	61	119	....	....	....	27	19	....	47	..	..	..
......69	38 39	Tarkio........	Tarkio (R. 38)...............	31	122	100	222	....	....	....	54	23	....	97	1	..	..
......70	36	Valley	....	68	219	202	421	....	....	....	87	58	....	167	..	..	..
......67	38 39	Washington ..	Union Grove (R.39)..........	45	140	130	270	1	....	1	43	30	....	156	..	..	..
....	.....	Total......	....	956	3050	2826	5876	62	87	149	1201	870	18	2619	3	..	4

PALO ALTO COUNTY.

...*..	..*.	Emmettsburg.	Emmettsburg (T. 96, R. 33)...	21	70	56	126	....	....	....	27	18	2	43	..	..	..
......	....	Nevada.......	Soda Bar (95, 32), Great Oak (96, 33)	25	79	64	143	....	....	....	31	29	..	55	..	..	..
......	....	West Bend...	West Bend (94, 31), Fern Valley (95, 31)	25	81	63	144	....	....	....	35	31	..	51	..	..	..
......	....	* Total.....	....	71	230	183	413	....	....	....	93	78	2	149	..	..	..

* No report.

PLYMOUTH COUNTY.

......90	48pt46	Lincoln.......	....	....	50	42	92	....	....	....	24	17	1	31	..	..	..
......91	46	Plymouth	.... }	....													
......92	45	"	.... }	....	64	58	122	....	....	....	29	9	....	36	..	..	..
......90	..pt 46	"	.... }	....													
....	.....	Total.......	....	....	114	100	214	....	....	....	53	26	1	67	..	..	..

POCAHONTAS COUNTY.

No. of Township.	Range.	Names of Townships, Towns, and Cities.	Names of Post-Offices.	No. of Dwelling Houses.	No. of White Males.	No. of White Females.	Total White Population.	No. of Colored Males.	No. of Colored Females.	Total Colored Population.	No. entitled to Vote.	No. of Militia.	No. of Foreigners not Naturalized.	No. between the ages of 5 and 21 years.	No. of Blind.	No. of Deaf and Dumb.	No. of Insane.
92	31	Clinton		11	33	27	60	....	...	....	14	7	1	13	..	..	..
93	31	Des Moines	Rolfe	25	68	58	126	....	...	....	30	21	....	46	..	..	..
90	31	Lizard		37	107	101	208	....	...	....	40	28	9	92	..	..	..
93	32	Powhattan		14	31	28	59	....	...	....	13	13	4	10	..	..	..
		Total		87	239	214	453	....	....	...	97	69	14	161	..	..	..

POLK COUNTY.

No. of Township.	Range.	Names of Townships, Towns, and Cities.	Names of Post-Offices.	No. of Dwelling Houses.	No. of White Males.	No. of White Females.	Total White Population.	No. of Colored Males.	No. of Colored Females.	Total Colored Population.	No. entitled to Vote.	No. of Militia.	No. of Foreigners not Naturalized.	No. between the ages of 5 and 21 years.	No. of Blind.	No. of Deaf and Dumb.	No. of Insane.
78	22 23	Allen	Avon (R. 23)	107	288	256	544	....	....	....	105	91	....	..	..	..	1
n pt 79	22	Beaver	Mitchell, Apple Grove	100	342	273	615	....	....	....	154	106	25	242	1	..	..
s pt 78	24 25	Bloomfield		130	393	375	768	4	4	8	161	107	8	309	..	..	..
77 78	pt 22	Camp	Adelphi (T. 73)	198	665	674	1339	....	....	....	266	202	1	585	..	..	2
79	23	Delaware		95	337	307	644	2	3	5	134	99	1	278	1	..	..
In 78	24*	Des Moines, tp. & pt. city	Des Moines	1136	3629	3509	7138	27	41	68	1198	948	29	1917	5	3	6
In 78	24*	Des Moines (E., Lee tp)		415	1672	1486	3158	78	69	147	658	515	63	943	.	2	..
80	23	Douglass	Greenwood	59	182	148	330	....	....	....	68	54	1	133	..	.	..
81	24	Elkhart	Elkhart	83	244	237	481	....	....	....	108	83	3	174	..	..	..
pt 78	22 23	Four Mile	Rising Sun (R. 23)	85	268	263	531	....	....	....	115	97	1	226	..	..	..
80	22	Franklin		60	211	189	400	2	4	6	83	60	....	166	..	..	..
pt 80	24	Jefferson															
pt 80	25	"	Ridgedale, Lincoln	114	333	334	667	3	3	6	135	107	...	257	..	..	..
pt 81	25	"															

...pt 78	23	Lee, exc. of D. M. city	....														
...pt 78	24	.." .. " ...."	....	129	447	411	858	5	4	9	183	157	12	319	..	..	..
...pt 79	24	." ...." ...."	....														
.....81	25	Madison	....														
...pt 80	.24 25	"	Polk City (R. 25)......	342	1138	1038	2176	1	....	1	400	287	20	872	2	2	3
...pt 81	24	"	....														
pt 79 80	24	Saylor..............	Saylorville (T. 79)........	145	548	494	1042	1	....	1	222	130	....	438	2	..	3
...pt 79	24	Valley.........	....	60	239	219	458	1	....	1	115	71	4	182	..	..	..
......79	25	Walnut...........	....														
...pt 78	24	"	....	118	404	356	760	5	5	10	160	138	....	316	..	..	..
...pt 78	25	"	....														
......81	22	Washington........	Peoria City............	60	239	219	458	1	...	1	115	71	3	101	..	..	..
....	......	Total............	....	3436	11579	10788	22367	130	133	263	4380	3286	171	7458	11	7	15

* That part of the city of Des Moines lying west of the Des Moines river constitutes the township of Des Moines. The remainder of the city is in Lee township.

NOTE.—The townships of Allen, Bloomfield, Des Moines, Jefferson, Valley, and Walnut lie south and west of the Des Moines river; of these, Allen, Bloomfield, and a portion of Des Moines lie south of the Raccoon Fork.

POTTAWATTAMIE COUNTY.

......77	.42 43	Boomer.........	....	49	189	165	345	....	....	....	61	40	14	142	..	..	..
......75	39	Center	....														
....$\frac{1}{6}$ 75	49	"	Big Grove..........	57	178	149	327	....	....	....	67	53	....	115	..	1	..
....$\frac{1}{3}$ 75	39 $\frac{1}{8}$ 40	"	....														
...In 75	.43 44	Council Bluffs, city of	Council Bluffs (R. 43)....	698	2700	2102	4802	19	11	30	1214	754	138	1472	1	1	.
......76	43	Crescent.........	....														
......76	44	"	Crescent City.........	130	410	411	821	....	....	....	142	85	27	316	..	..	..
..w $\frac{1}{2}$ 76	42	"	....														
......74	39	Grove..........	Wheeler's Grove........	34	122	116	238	2	....	2	41	29	8	118	..	..	..
......75	41	James.........	....														
...5-6 11	40	"	....	28	99	80	179	...	....	....	38	19	....	75	..	..	..
....$\frac{7}{8}$ 76	40	"	....														
......74	.43 44	Kane, exclusive of	....														
......75	.42–44	Council Bluffs...	....	125	378	327	705	1	....	1	138	89	14	288	..	..	2
...76 77	38	Knox...........	....														
......77	.39 40	"	Nishna (R. 39).........	51	152	150	302	....	....	....	57	41	1	130	..	..	..
....$\frac{2}{3}$ 76	39	"	....														
......74	40	Macedonia.........	Macedonia............	28	90	89	179	....	....	....	35	29	....	85	..	..	..

POTTAWATTAMIE COUNTY—Continued.

No. of Township.	Range.	Names of Townships, Towns, and Cities.	Names of Post-Offices.	No. of Dwelling-Houses.	No. of White Males.	No. of White Females.	Total White Population.	No. of Colored Males.	No. of Colored Females.	Total Colored Population.	No. entitled to Vote.	No. of Militia.	No. of Foreigners not Naturalized.	No. between the ages of 5 and 21 years.	No. of Blind.	No. of Deaf and Dumb.	No. of Insane.
77	44	Rockford	Loveland Mills	67	193	176	369	....	....	....	78	44	....	151	..	..	..
74	41 42	Silver Creek		253	66	52	118	....	....	....	24	18	....	66	..	..	..
74 75	38	Walnut Creek		30	91	95	186	....	....	....	39	19	....	78	..	..	..
76	41	York															
77	41	"		21	64	65	129	....	....	....	19	13	9	54	..	..	..
e½76	42	"															
		Total		1571	4723	3977	8700	22	11	33	1953	1233	211	3090	1	4	2

POWESHEIK COUNTY.

No. of Township.	Range.	Names of Townships, Towns, and Cities.	Names of Post-Offices.	No. of Dwelling-Houses.	No. of White Males.	No. of White Females.	Total White Population.	No. of Colored Males.	No. of Colored Females.	Total Colored Population.	No. entitled to Vote.	No. of Militia.	No. of Foreigners not Naturalized.	No. between the ages of 5 and 21 years.	No. of Blind.	No. of Deaf and Dumb.	No. of Insane.
80	14	Bear Creek	Brooklyn	191	533	494	1027	2	....	2	233	168	3	365	1	..	..
81	16	Chester		27	97	99	196	4	....	4	48	45	1	66	..	..	..
78	13	Deep River	Deep River	111	365	320	685	1	....	1	136	105	8	285	..	..	1
80	16	Grinnell, ex. of town		79	233	199	432	2	....	2	93	68	....	176	..	..	..
In 80	16	Grinnell, town of	Grinnell	165	495	474	969	10	14	24	199	200	1	417	..	..	..
78	14pt15	Jackson	Montezuma (R.14), Sherman	250	800	753	1553	1	....	1	318	250		600	..	..	..
81	13	Jefferson	Prairie Creek (R.15)	86	296	236	532	....	....	....	90	70	4	255	1	4	..
79	13	Lincoln		75	235	193	428	....	....	....	91	71	12	148	..	..	..
81	14	Madison		67	216	187	403	....	....	....	90	81	3	167	..	..	1
80	15	Malcom	Malcom	57	178	141	319	1	....	1	83	67	7	99	..	..	..
79	15	Pleasant		64	215	195	410	6	1	7	85	78	....	190	..	3	..
79	14	Scott		39	139	123	262	....	....	....	42	35	2	106	..	1	..
81	15	Sheridan		16	60	47	107	....	....	....	28	22	....	40	..	..	..
78	16	Sugar Creek	Mill Grove	121	358	301	659	1	....	1	125	100	4	284	..	..	..

...pt 78	15	Union	Forest Home	119	389	357	746	1	...	1	143	89	5	231	2	1
......80	13	Warren		107	369	327	696	....	....	....	139	104	5	288	..	..
......79	16	Washington	Tyro	79	213	207	420	....	....	....	84	51	5	163	..	..
		Total		1653	5191	4653	9844	29	15	44	2027	1604	60	3980	4	9

Last column of the above rows: .., .., 3, 5.

RINGGOLD COUNTY.

...67 68	28	Athens	Cross (T. 68)	46	150	130	280	....	....	....	59	45	1	117	..	2	..
.....69	28pt29	East Fork		53	143	157	300	2	2	4	57	50	....	130	..	..	..
......67	29	Lott's Creek															
......68	29	"	Caledonia	69	243	217	460	....	....	....	94	71	3	211	..	..	..
.....68	29	"	Ringgold														
67 pt 68	30	Middle Fork	Ingart Grove (T. 67)	35	139	141	280	....	....	....	51	38	2	126	..	..	..
...pt 68	29	Mount Ayr	Mount Ayr														
...pt 68	30	"	Estella	116	340	349	689	....	....	....	135	114	6	254	..	..	..
...pt 69	.29 30	"															
...69 70	31	Platt	[gene (R. 29)	61	189	172	361	....	....	....	61	45	....	148	.	..	..
......70	28pt29	Sand Creek	Union Hill (R. 28), Eu-	46	144	144	288	...	....	....	56	40	....	116	..	..	..
......70	... 30	Washington															
...pt 70	... 29	"		112	402	373	775	1	1	2	134	91	9	353	1	1	1
...pt 69	.29 30	"															
...67 68	31	West Fork	Redding (R. 67)	72	229	219	448	1	....	1	88	65	1	197	2	1	..
		Total		610	1979	1902	3881	4	3	7	735	559	22	1652	3	4	1

SAC COUNTY.

.. ...89	.35-38	Douglas		19	37	44	81	....	....	....	27	14	....	32	..	.	..
.. ...88	.35-38	Jackson	Sac City (R. 36)	41	158	153	311	....	....	....	70	39	3	106	..	.	..
...86 87	.35-38	Sac	Grant City (T. 86, R. 35)	43	102	101	203	....	....	....	42	26	....	90	..	..	..
		Total		103	297	298	595	....	....	....	139	79	3	228	..	..	..

SCOTT COUNTY.

......80	....2e	Allen's Grove	Allen's Grove	103	343	290	633	1	....	1	109	119	36	245	..	..	..
......78	....2e	Blue Grass	Blue Grass, Walcott	158	630	571	1201	1	....	1	216	153	82	402	2	1	..
......77	....2e	Buffalo	Buffalo	198	574	519	1093	4	2	6	246	140	14	414	1	..	..
......80	....4e	Butler	Walnut Grove	132	349	308	657	1	3	4	134	89	41	260	..	..	1

SCOTT COUNTY—CONTINUED.

No. of Township.	Range.	Names of Townships, Towns, and Cities.	Names of Post-Offices.	No. of Dwelling-Houses.	No. of White Males.	No. of White Females.	Total White Population.	No. of Colored Males.	No. of Colored Females.	Total Colored Population.	No. entitled to Vote.	No. of Militia.	No. of Foreigners not Naturalized.	No. between the ages of 5 and 21 years.	No. of Blind.	No. of Deaf and Dumb.	No. of Insane.
79	1e	Cleona	New Liberty	118	371	299	670	....	...	....	92	152	91	212	..	..	..
78	3 pt 4e	Davenport, exc. of city	Gilbert	470	1564	1515	3079	15	8	23	536	539	30	1435	4	1	7
In 78	3e	" city of.	Davenport	2778	8987	8316	17303	118	129	247	2838	1709	973	5533	4	1	5
79	2e	Hickory Grove	Amity	205	661	569	1230	1	1	2	195	248	142	415	1	..	..
pt 78 79	5e	LeClaire, exc. of town		162	443	398	841	3	....	3	187	129	14	307	2	..	..
In 78 79	5e	" town of.	Le Claire	254	675	636	1311	1	1	2	298	215	29	496	..	1	1
80	1e	Liberty	Dixon														
80	1e	"	Big Rock	149	453	369	822	....	....	....	183	174	44	309	..	..	..
80	1e	"	Round Grove														
79	4e	Lincoln		161	512	432	944	....	....	....	193	127	25	315	..	..	..
pt 78	4 5e	Pleasant Valley	Valley City	130	377	344	721	4	1	5	171	108	16	270	..	..	1
79 pt 80	5e	Princeton, exc. of city		116	327	319	646	....	....	....	141	93	8	265	..	..	..
In 79	5e	" city of.	Princeton	112	289	289	578	....	....	....	145	97	3	206	..	1	..
77	3e	Rockingham		48	144	140	284	2	...	2	49	33	16	107	..	..	..
79	3e	Sheridan	Mount Joy	193	592	526	1118	1	....	1	177	201	94	391	1	..	..
80	3e	Winfield		151	497	436	933	1	....	1	167	102	58	322	..	..	..
		Total		5638	17788	16276	34064	153	145	298	6078	4428	1716	11904	15	5	15

SHELBY COUNTY.

No. of Township.	Range.	Names of Townships, Towns, and Cities.	Names of Post-Offices.	No. of Dwelling-Houses.	No. of White Males.	No. of White Females.	Total White Population.	No. of Colored Males.	No. of Colored Females.	Total Colored Population.	No. entitled to Vote.	No. of Militia.	No. of Foreigners not Naturalized.	No. between the ages of 5 and 21 years.	No. of Blind.	No. of Deaf and Dumb.	No. of Insane.
78	37 38 39	Fairview		37	129	99	228	....	....	...	49	36	....	101	..	..	..
81	38 39	Galland's Grove															
81	40	" "	Manteno	81	260	219	479	....	....	...	96	68	....	191	..	..	..
n ½ 80	39 40	" "															

19	39 40	Harlan															
w ½ 79 80	38	"	Harlan (T. 79)	35	101	93	194	....	....	....	38	24	3	75	..	..	..
s ½ 80	39 40	"															
79	37	Jackson	Botany														
80 81	37	"		51	165	147	312	....	....	....	58	51	....	142	..	..	..
e ½ 79 80	38	"															
		Total		204	655	558	1213	....	....	....	241	179	3	509	..	..	..

SIOUX COUNTY.

95		Buncombe	Calliope	4	11	7	18	..	....	...	8	7	...	9	..	..	..

STORY COUNTY.

82	21	Collins		54	170	180	350	....	....	....	61	40	2	170	..	..	1
84	24	Franklin		85	306	295	601	2	....	2	116	90	....	247	..	..	..
83	23	Grant*		....	....	....	....	....	....	....	....	....	....	....	..	..	..
85	23 w ½ 22	Howard	Sheffield (R. 23)	92	288	287	575	....	....	....	83	48	38	183	..	5	..
82	22	Indian Creek	Iowa Center	134	444	460	904	....	....	....	183	131	1	375	..	..	..
85	24	La Fayette	Story City	37	102	90	192	....	....	....	26	17	22	74	..	..	..
85	21 c ½ 22	Lincoln		14	40	45	85	....	....	....	17	13	2	33	..	..	..
84	23	Milford		52	179	155	334	....	....	....	66	61	3	135	..	..	..
83	pt 22	Nevada	Nevada														
83	e ½ 23	"		284	754	766	1520	....	1	1	341	234	5	634	..	1	..
84	21 22	"															
83	21 pt 22	New Albany	Colo	74	244	229	473	....	....	....	76	58	3	169	..	..	1
82	24	Palestine	Pt. Palestine	71	277	236	513	1	....	1	67	47	16	215	1		
84	21 e ½ 22	Sherman†		....	....	....	....	....	....	....	....	....	....	....	..	..	..
82	23	Union	Cambridge	71	251	248	499	....	....	....	96	84	6	179	..	..	..
83	24	Washington	Ames														
83	24	"	New Philadelphia	143	432	405	837	....	1	1	170	148	39	339	1	..	..
83	w ½ 23	"															
		Total		1111	3487	3396	6883	3	2	5	1302	971	137	2753	2	6	2

* Not organized; included in Nevada and Washington.
† " " " " Nevada.

TAMA COUNTY.

No. of Township.	Range.	Names of Townships, Towns, and Cities.	Names of Post-Offices.	No. of Dwelling-Houses.	No. of White Males.	No. of White Females.	Total White Population.	No. of Colored Males.	No. of Colored Females.	Total Colored Population.	No. entitled to Vote.	No. of Militia.	No. of Foreigners not Naturalized.	No. between the ages of 5 and 21 years.	No. of Blind.	No. of Deaf and Dumb.	No. of Insane.
86	14 15	Buckingham	Buckingham (R. 14)	69	227	208	435	1		1	72	56	18	161			
84	16	Carlton		120	359	348	707				148	83	5	263			
84	14	Carroll		63	112	103	215				43	29	2	95			
85	13	Clark		19	49	50	99				24	17	5	32			
82	15	Columbia		76	226	210	436	1		1	100	77	1	155			
85	15	Crystal	Crystal	46	141	132	273				53	44	10	118			
86	13	Geneseo		58	180	147	327				59	48	10	132			
82	16	Highland		30	103	90	193				43	37		78			
84	15	Howard		157	451	385	836				179	149	3	347			
83	16	Indian Village	Orford, Butlerville	197	686	643	1329	1		1	281	205	97	499			
86	16	Lincoln		7	20	18	38				10			16			
84	13	Oneida		36	152	120	272				56	39		110			
83	14	Otter Creek		114	378	363	741				116	87	17	325			
85	14	Perry	Wolf Creek	77	246	205	451				83	66	13	179			
82	14	Richland	Helena	125	395	377	772		1	1	164	129	4	302			2
82	13	Salt Creek	Chelsea, West Irving	151	482	445	927				182	163	16	370			
85	16	Spring Creek	Badger Hill, Spring Creek	37	121	118	239				65	29		93			
83	15	Toledo, exc. of village	Tama City	278	715	658	1373	1		1	317	240	3	503		3	
In 83	15	" village of	Toledo	123	380	379	759	22	24	46	181	139		299			
83	13	York	Waltham	108	371	321	692				107	93	41	291			
		Total		1891	5794	5320	11114	26	25	51	2283	1730	245	4368		3	2

TAYLOR COUNTY.

68	34	Benton	Bedford	117	307	300	603	15	13	28	135	81	1	258			
68	33	Clayton		57	162	170	332	1	1	2	64	46		132			
69	35	Dallas	Memory	59	197	195	392	3	1	4	79	70		155			
70	34	Holt	Holt	27	75	73	148	6	6	12	27	24	1	86			
67	33	Jackson		40	153	145	298	3	4	7	56	43		122			
67 68	32	Jefferson	Platteville (T. 68)	79	237	230	467	3	4	7	85	67		299			
69 70	33	Marshall		33	93	97	190	7	11	18	38	29	3	82			1
68	35	Mason		72	224	184	408				82	67	1	164			
70	35	Nodaway		51	130	112	242	13	12	25	46			108			
69 70	32	Platte		14	47	42	89				20	14		25			
67	35	Polk	Siam	70	338	295	633	1		1	85	63		157			
67	34	Ross		56	215	195	410				60	62		188			
69	34	Washington	Gravity	31	127	103	230				51	43		83			
			Jenks														
		Total		706	2301	2141	4442	52	52	104	828	609	6	1859			1

UNION COUNTY.

73	29	Dodge		27	77	67	144				29	17		56			
72 73	31	Douglas		10	25	31	56				14	9		18			
71 pt 72	30	Highland		22	67	69	136				22	14		65			
72	28	Jones		81	226	223	449				97	70		183		2	
73 pt 72	30	Lincoln		38	124	110	234				45	31		117			
73	28	New Hope		33	109	104	213				45	40		96			
71	31	Platt	Union City	49	151	128	279	1		1	47	45	1	129			
71	28	Pleasant		198	230	222	452				89	59		182			
71	29	Sand Creek		23	55	60	115				23	19		46			
72	29	Union	Afton	174	492	439	931				186	150	1	343			
		Total		655	1556	1453	3009	1		1	597	454	2	1235		2	

VAN BUREN COUNTY.

In 69	9	Bentonsport, city of	Bentonsport	90	246	268	514		1	1	109	82	2	214	1		
In 70	9	Birmingham, city of	Birmingham, city of	99	269	272	541	4	4	8	128	89		224	1		
pt 68	8	Bonaparte	Bonaparte	178	582	573	1155	5		5	233	176	16	492	1	1	1

VAN BUREN COUNTY—CONTINUED.

No. of Township.	Range.	Names of Townships, Towns, and Cities.	Names of Post-Offices.	No. of Dwelling-Houses.	No. of White Males.	No. of White Females	Total White Population.	No. of Colored Males.	No. of Colored Females.	Total Colored Population.	No. entitled to Vote.	No. of Militia.	No. of Foreigners not Naturalized.	No. between the ages of 5 and 21 years.	No. of Blind.	No. of Deaf and Dumb.	No. of Insane.
70	8	Cedar		198	590	559	1149	....	....	....	237	177	3	449	..	1	1
69	11	Chequest	Lebanon	142	449	423	872	....	....	....	180	141	....	357	..	1	..
67	10	Des Moines	Upton														
67	10	"		172	486	441	927	9	11	20	219	128	....	337	..	..	..
68	10	"	Home														
67 pt 68	8	Farmington, excl. city		150	393	410	803	8	12	20	159	99	9	334	3	1	2
In 68	8	Farmington, city of	Farmington	115	363	349	712				153	81	....	251	..	..	..
69	8	Harrisburg		179	437	513	950	1		1	243	120	1	369	..	..	..
67	11	Jackson															
68	11	"	Milton	220	625	605	1230	1	....	1	285	184	3	431	..	1	..
In 69	10	Keosauqua, city of	Keosauqua	99	319	327	646	27	15	42	139	81	1	241	..	..	..
70	10	Lick Creek		185	497	504	1001	8	12	20	200	127	...	441	..	..	2
70	9	Union, excl. of Birmingham	Winchester	187	554	474	1028	9	10	19	249	164	1	....	..	..	..
69	10	Van Buren, excl. of Keosauqua	Kilbourne, Pittsburg	254	726	687	1413	12	10	22	276	200	2	628	..	1	..
67 68	9	Vernon	Vernon(68), MtSterling(67)	263	718	657	1375	2	2	4	309	242	4	559	1	..	..
70	11	Village	Iowaville														
70	11	"		157	617	571	1188	....	....	....	242	172	1	508	..	..	..
70	11	"	Doud's Station														
69	9	Washington, excl. of Bentonsport	Mt. Zion														
69	9	Washington, do	Pierceville, Utica	92	314	311	625	....	....	....	130	95	5	247	2	..	..
		Total		2780	8185	7944	16129	86	77	163	3491	2359	48	6082	9	6	6

WAPELLO COUNTY.

.....71	... 15	Adams.	Blakesburg, Cooperville.	237	708	639	1347	....	....	....	259	166	1	563	2	3	..
...pt 71	13	Agency	....														
...pt 72	12	Agency	....	97	345	304	649	....	....	...	137	112	2	281	1	..	..
...pt 72	13	Agency, excl. of city	....														
...In 72	13	Agency City	Agency City	90	290	298	588	....	...	....	124	64	3	230	..	1	1
...pt 72	.14, 15	Cass	....														
...pt 73	14	Cass	....	106	322	319	641	....	....	....	117	90	2	271	..	..	..
...pt 73	15	Cass	Chillicothe														
...pt 72	.13, 14	Center, exc. Ottumwa	Port Richmond (R. 14)	395	1106	1041	2147	6	5	11	459	292	13	834	1	2	2
...pt 73	15	Columbia, exclusive of Eddyville	....	133	447	373	820	5	6	11	171	137	1	344	..	..	..
......73	12	Competine	Competne	127	434	407	841	....	...	....	162	106	....	378	..	..	..
...pt 72	...13	Dahlonega	Dahlcnega	101	290	285	575	....	....	....	119	81	....	237	..	..	2
...In 73	15	Eddyville, city of	Eddyville	226	672	672	1344	3	8	11	295	206	10	508	1	2	..
......71	14	Green	Point Isabel	193	602	547	1149	....	...	....	217	100	1	499	2	..	..
......73	13	Highland	....	122	406	373	779	....	....	....	171	100	....	299	..	1	..
...pt 71	...13	Keokuk	....	99	270	258	528	5	2	7	102	78	2	237	..	..	..
...In 72	... 14	Ottumwa, city of	Ottumwa	556	1470	1442	2912	21	21	42	676	566	14	970	..	2	1
...pt 72	12	Pleasant	....	187	531	548	1079	....	....	....	226	54	....	456	1	..	..
...pt 72	15	Polk	Christiansburg.... [tion	163	480	452	932	....	....	....	164	116	28	368	1	..	1
...pt 73	14	Richland	Kirkville, Comstock's Sta-	224	636	592	1228	2	....	2	261	189	1	480	..	2	1
......71	12	Washington	Ashland	157	674	613	1287	....	....	....	278	198	3	565	..	1	..
....	......	Total	....	3213	9683	9163	18846	42	42	84	3938	2655	81	7520	9	14	8

WARREN COUNTY.

...pt 77	23	Allen	Carlisle, Summerset	105	347	292	639	..	....	....	126	96	3	224	..	..	..
......75	22	Belmont	Rose Mount	103	343	298	641	...	....	....	133	114	....	280	..	..	..
......77	...24	Greenfield	Fort Plain	195	592	583	1175	5	5	10	229	190	3	498	..	..	..
...In 76	24	Indianola, city of	Indianola	193	512	511	1023	9	10	19	238	196	3	394	..	..	..
......75	...25	Jackson	....	53	172	181	352	...	....	....	59	41	....	155	..	..	..
......76	...25	Jefferson	Linn, Oswego....[Center	142	406	381	787	....	1	1	163	135	3	345	1	..	..
......74	23	Liberty	Lawrenceburg, Liberty	88	315	290	605	...	....	....	120	84	....	270	..	..	..
......77	25	Lynn	Norwalk	109	329	325	654	...	....	....	136	88	1	275	1	..	..
......75	23	Otter	Hammondsburg	90	344	317	651	7	3	10	132	105	....	293	..	1	..

WARREN COUNTY—CONTINUED.

No. of Township.	Range.	Names of Townships, Towns, and Cities.	Names of Post-Offices.	No. of Dwelling-Houses.	No. of White Males.	No. of White Females.	Total White Population.	No. of Colored Males.	No. of Colored Females.	Total Colored Population.	No. entitled to Vote.	No. of Militia.	No. of Foreigners not Naturalized.	No. between the ages of 5 and 21 years.	No. of Blind.	No. of Deaf and Dumb.	No. of Insane.
pt 76 77	.22 23	Palmyra...........	Palmyra (T. 77, R. 22)...	176	558	563	1121	1	....	1	219	167	....	491	..	..	1
...pt 77	22	Richland	Hartford...............	241	674	697	1371	....	....	....	277	195	....	588	..	..	..
......74	24	Squaw	Sharon................	69	238	233	471	....	....	....	86	59	....	211	1	2	..
......76	22	Union.............	Sandyville	129	455	425	880	....	....	....	168	126	....	402	..	1	..
......74	25	Virginia..........	New Virginia..........	41	107	113	220	1	....	1	46	34	...	83	..	1	..
......76	24pt23	Washington, excl. of Indianola........	....	220	708	623	1331	2	1	3	263	208	...	568	1	1	2
......74	22	White Breast	Lacona................	137	372	390	762	....	....	....	149	112	....	278	2	..	..
......75	24	White Oak.........	....	63	212	221	433	....	....	....	90	81	....	170	..	..	..
....	.....	Total............	....	2154	6674	6443	13117	25	20	45	2634	2031	13	5525	6	6	3

WASHINGTON COUNTY.

No. of Township.	Range.	Names of Townships, Towns, and Cities.	Names of Post-Offices.	No. of Dwelling-Houses.	No. of White Males.	No. of White Females.	Total White Population.	No. of Colored Males.	No. of Colored Females.	Total Colored Population.	No. entitled to Vote.	No. of Militia.	No. of Foreigners not Naturalized.	No. between the ages of 5 and 21 years.	No. of Blind.	No. of Deaf and Dumb.	No. of Insane.
...pt 74	8	Brighton	Brighton..............	218	555	545	1100	4	5	9	246	194	....	446	1	1	..
...pt 76	8	Cedar.............	Cedarville	155	452	394	846	....	....	....	177	132	1	355	..	..	..
...pt 74	9	Clay..............	Clay..................	127	434	380	814	....	....	....	169	138	....	345	..	..	..
......74	6	Crawford..........	Crawfordsville.........	216	645	566	1211	....	....	....	278	189	3	478	1	..	1
... ..75	9	Dutch Creek	Dutch Creek.......... }														
......75	9	"	Valley .... }	212	655	585	1240	....	....	....	262	160	7	515	..	..	1
.n pt 74	9	"	.... }														
......77	8 pt 7	English River.......	Richmond (R. 7)........	250	748	710	1458	6	3	9	266	138	24	629	1	7	..
pt 74 75	8	Franklin...........	....	123	375	362	737	7	2	9	168	110	5	296	..	..	..
......76	6	Highland..........	Dairy.................	85	259	224	483	....	....	....	99	68	3	192	..	..	..

......77	6	Iowa...............	Yatton (R. 6).........														
......77	6	"	Davis Creek (R. 6). ...	180	566	530	1096	...	....	....	209	127	28	409	1	2	1
......77	.e pt 7	"	....														
......76	7	Jackson...........	....	149	459	452	911	3	....	3	177	140	12	392	..	4	..
......77	9 pt 8	Lime Creek.........	Wassonville (R. 9)......	240	706	675	1381	2	....	2	287	234	20	543	4	1	..
......74	8 pt 7	Marion............	....	167	526	476	1002	....	....	....	186	150	60	413	..	..	..
......75	6	Oregon.............	Ainsworth..............	194	561	566	1127	....		...	246	199	5	404	1	..	..
......76	9	Seventy-Six.... ..	....	77	256	245	501	1	....	1	106	69	....	199	1	..	..
...pt 74	7	Washington.........	....														
......75	7	" exc. city.	....	210	630	588	1218	3	....	3	305	216	9	638	..	..	..
...pt 75	8	"	....														
...In 75	7	" city of...	Washington...........	402	1207	1253	2460	26	28	54	511	315	8	780	..	2	..
....	......	Total..........	....	3005	9034	8551	17585	52	38	90	3692	2579	185	7034	10	17	3

WAYNE COUNTY.

......69	22	Benton........ ...	....	115	334	319	653	....	....	....	129	100	2	270	..	..	*1
......69	22	Clay..............	Lewisburgh............	42	145	136	281	....	....	....	52	41	....	121	..	..	..
......67	22	Clinton...........	....	83	241	237	478	....	....	....	92	70	....	203	1	2	2
......69	21	Corydon...........	Corydon.	174	331	334	665	2	....	2	146	113	..	313	..	..	..
......67	23	Grand River........	Grand River, Clio.......	70	273	277	550	....	....	...	95	61	...	219	..	..	..
......67	21	Howard...........	Warsaw...............	69	214	195	409	....	....	....	85	70	....	166	1	1	2
......68	21	Jackson....... ...	....	30	90	76	166	....	....	....	35	28	....	69	..	..	..
......68	23	Jefferson	....	78	243	228	471	....	....	....	92	56	....	203	..	1	..
......67	...20	Monroe	Genoa.................	74	228	263	491	....	....	....	75	53	....	237	1	..	1
......70	23	Richman.........	Selma, Lucerne.........	40	140	112	252	....	....	....	57	34	....	112	..	..	1
......69	20	South Fork........	Promise City..	91	300	295	595	....	....	....	118	91	....	252	1	1	..
......70	21	Union.............	Bethlehem, New York..	128	390	326	716	1	...	1	148	112	....	295	..	..	..
......68	20	Walnut...........	Kniffin....	75	217	232	449	....	....	....	89	56	....	207	..	..	..
......68	22	Warren...........	....	36	120	91	211	....	....	....	35	25	1	109	..	..	..
......70	22	Washington..	Cambria.......	99	286	292	578	....	....	....	113	85	1	256	..	..	..
......70	20	Wright............	Confidence.............	113	356	333	689	....	....	....	142	114	....	413	..	..	..
....	......	Total..........	... ...	1317	3908	3746	7654	3	....	3	1503	1109	4	3445	4	5	*7

* 1 Idiot.

WEBSTER COUNTY.

......90	.27 28	Badger......... ...	....	23	77	74	151	....	....	....	36	21	.. .	57	..	..	..

WEBSTER COUNTY—CONTINUED.

No. of Township.	Range.	Names of Townships, Towns, and Cities.	Names of Post-Offices.	No. of Dwelling-Houses.	No. of White Males.	No. of White Females.	Total White Population.	No of Colored Males.	No. of Colored Females.	Total Colored Population.	No. entitled to Vote.	No. of Militia.	No. of Foreigners not Naturalized.	No. between the ages of 5 and 21 years.	No. of Blind.	No. of Deaf and Dumb.	No. of Insane.
......86	28pt27	Dayton............	West Dayton (R. 28).....	112	336	306	642	....	....	....	113	89	19	239	..	..	..
......90	29	Deer Creek.........	....	23	73	64	137	....	....	....	34	22	....	51	..	..	..
......89	. ..29	Douglas........	....	45	123	123	246	....	....	....	63	46	....	93	..	..	..
...e½ 88	30	"	....														
......86	29e½27	Hardin........	....	54	193	146	339	....	....	....	43	57	48	126	..	..	2
......90	... 30	Jackson.	....	40	123	101	224	....	....	....	43	28	1	94	..	..	..
89 w½ 88	30	Johnson.......	....	35	122	109	231	....	....	....	46	35	2	96	..	1	..
......88	29pt28	Otho...........	Otho (R. 28)............	56	143	166	309	....	....	....	71	52	4	80	..	..	..
......87	.28 29	Sumner	Hesperian............	65	135	120	255	....	....	....	72	59	....	130	..	..	..
... ..89	27	Wahkonsa.........	....														
......89	28	"	Fort Dodge...........	384	921	893	1814	5	1	6	406	....	14	605	..	..	..
...pt 88	28	"	....														
......88	27pt28	Washington........	Border Plains (R. 27)	68	250	204	454	....	....	....	108	60	..	199	1	1	1
......87	30ep27	Webster.........	....	69	210	207	417	....	....	....	80	52	3	171	..	..	..
......86	30	Yell.	....	65	206	200	406	....	....	....	94	60	1	70	..	.	..
...pt 87	27	"	....														
....	.....	Total.........	....	1039	2912	2713	5625	5	1	6	1209	581	92	2011	1	2	3

WINNEBAGO COUNTY.

No. of Township.	Range.	Names of Townships, Towns, and Cities.	Names of Post-Offices.	No. of Dwelling-Houses.	No. of White Males.	No. of White Females.	Total White Population.	No of Colored Males.	No. of Colored Females.	Total Colored Population.	No. entitled to Vote.	No. of Militia.	No. of Foreigners not Naturalized.	No. between the ages of 5 and 21 years.	No. of Blind.	No. of Deaf and Dumb.	No. of Insane.
......98	 23	Center...........	....														
.pt 98,99	24	"	Benson Grove (T.99,§36)	65	210	190	400	....	....	....	64	47	27	167	1	..	..
...pt 99	23 25 26	"	....														
......98	25'6pt24	Forest....	Forest City (R. 24, § 35).	24	72	62	134	...	....	....	26	19	....	54	..	..	..

..pt 100	23, 24,25,26	Norway..........	....	14	52	53	105	....	....	....	17	8	....	41	..	..	..
pt 99,100	23, 24,25,26	Pleasant..........	Lake Mills (§11, 99, 23)	25	79	67	146	....	....	....	29	23	....	49	..	..	..
....	....	Total..........	....	128	413	372	785	....	....	....	136	97	27	311	1	..	..

WINNESHIEK COUNTY.

......96	7	Bloomfield........	Castalia........	179	549	534	1083	....	....	....	235	152	7	431	..	..	..
......99	9	Bluffton..........	Bluffton....	91	314	250	564	....	....	....	104	61	49	341	..	..	..
.....100	9	Burr Oak.........	Burr Oak.............	129	457	385	842	....	....	....	176	116	23	359	1	1	..
......97	9	Calmer....	Calmer............														
......97	9	"	Spillville...........	269	791	589	1380	5	1	6	243	192	46	439	1	..	..
......97	9	"	Conover...........														
......99	 8	Canoe............	Springwater	146	432	380	812	....	....	....	164	139	26	309	2	..	..
......98	 8	Decorah,exc. of city	Freeport....	222	759	618	1377	1	....	1	247	169	42	485	..	..	..
......98	8	Decorah, city of...	Decorah....	245	850	805	1655	11	9	20	371	265	37	522	1	..	..
... ..97	7	Frankville	Frankville...	166	533	494	1047	....	....	....	207	169	12	370	..	..	..
.....100	10	Fremont......... .	Plymouth Rock.......	101	290	282	572	....	....	....	120	79	5	209	1	.	..
......98	7	Glenwood.........	Woodville...........	186	557	529	1086	....	....	....	151	97	69	401	..	..	..
.....100	8	Hesper...........	Hesper....	166	503	506	1009	1	....	1	162	144	26	381	..	..	4
.....100	12	Highland.........	....	119	429	413	842	....	....	....	100	66	103	316	2	2	1
......96	10	Jackson.........	....	72	196	204	400	....	....	....	68	50	15	152	..	..	..
......98	10	Lincoln..........	....	84	296	293	589	....	....	....	64	38	30	250	..	1	..
......98	9	Madison..........	Burr Oak Springs.....	99	413	320	733	....	....	....	90	87	55	301	..	1	2
......96	8	Military.....	Ossian...............	208	626	574	1200	....	....	....	198	153	76	438	1	..	2
... ..99	10	Orleans...........	....	104	268	261	529	....	....	....	122	90	....	185	..	..	..
......99	7	Pleasant....	Locust Lane..........	139	507	435	942	....	....	....	165	81	209	304	..	..	..
......97	8	Springfield.......	....	173	520	479	999	....	....	....	146	95	102	440	..	2	..
......97	10	Sumner..........	....	394	351	308	659	....	....	....	99	84	82	236	..	..	..
......96	9	Washington	Fort Atkinson......														
......96	9	"	Festina.............	146	512	441	953	1	....	1	181	96	46	336	..	..	..
... ..96	9	"	Old Mission........														
....	....	Total.........	....	3438	10173	9100	19273	19	10	29	3413	2423	1060	7205	9	7	9

WOODBURY COUNTY.

.....89	... .42	Correctionville....	Correctionville.... ...	27	91	90	181	....	....	....	36	24	....	51	..	..	..

WOODBURY COUNTY—Continued.

No. of Township.	Range.	Names of Townships, Towns, and Cities.	Names of Post-Offices.	No. of Dwelling-Houses.	No. of White Males.	No. of White Females.	Total White Population.	No. of Colored Males.	No. of Colored Females.	Total Colored Population.	No. entitled to Vote.	No. of Militia.	No. of Foreigners not Naturalized.	No. between the ages of 5 and 21 years.	No. of Blind.	No. of Deaf and Dumb.	No. of Insane.
86	46	Lakeport	Hamlin *														
86	44	Little Sioux	Smithland, Oto	87	252	218	470				117	53	1	166			
89	47	Sioux City tp., ex. city		8	31	17	48				17	10		18			
In 89	47	Sioux City, city of	Sioux City	187	549	481	1030				274	225	6	323			
88	48	Woodbury	Woodbury	37	134	106	240	1		1	66	39	25	85			
		Total		346	1057	912	1969	1		1	510	351	32	643			

* Reported by Postmaster at Sioux City—probably new township, created since census was taken.

WORTH COUNTY.

No. of Township.	Range.	Names of Townships, Towns, and Cities.	Names of Post-Offices.	No. of Dwelling-Houses.	No. of White Males.	No. of White Females.	Total White Population.	No. of Colored Males.	No. of Colored Females.	Total Colored Population.	No. entitled to Vote.	No. of Militia.	No. of Foreigners not Naturalized.	No. between the ages of 5 and 21 years.	No. of Blind.	No. of Deaf and Dumb.	No. of Insane.
pt 99	21 22	Bristol	Bristol (R. 22)	50	143	126	269				44	26		105			
pt 98 99	20 21	Brookfield		18	58	54	112				16	12	6	54			
98	22	Fertile															
pt 98	21	"		8	18	27	45				8	5	1	18			
pt 99	22	"															
100 pt 99	21	Hartland	Hartland (T. 100)	76	234	212	446				52	31	17	156			
pt 99	19 20	Northwood															
100	19	"		62	191	176	367				72	62		122			
100	20	"	Northwood														
100	22	Silver Lake		39	97	93	190				24	22	12	67			
98	19	Union															
pt 98	20	"		16	53	61	114				17	12		50			
pt 99	19 20	"															
		Total		269	794	749	1543				233	170	36	572			

WRIGHT COUNTY.

93 pt 92	24	Belmond........	Belmond (T. 93)........	31	99	91	190	2	....	2	42	31	2	62	..	..	..
......93	.25 26	Boone.............	Luni (R. 26)...........	22	48	46	94	....	1	1	22	16	....	41	..	..	..
......91	.25 26	Eagle Grove..	Eagle Grove (R. 26).....	21	62	42	104	....	....	....	23	22	18	38	..	..	..
...pt 91	.23 24	Iowa...............	....														
...pt 92	23	"	Freyburg..............	28	98	75	172	....	....	....	42	23	2	69	..	..	..
...pt 92	24	"	....														
......92	.25 26	Liberty.....	Goldfield (R. 26)........	35	102	90	192	....	....	....	40	26	4	79	..	..	..
93 pt 92	23	Pleasant...........	....	42	120	106	226	....	....	....	41	21	9	93	1	..	..
......90	.25 26	Troy..	Bach Grove (R. 26)......	29	98	90	188	....	....	....	37	24	4	80	..	..	..
90 pt 91	23	Vernon............	....	8	40	50	90	....	....	....	14	10	....	38	..	..	..
90 pt 91	24	Wall Lake..........	....	15	41	31	72	....	....	....	19	12	....	19	..	..	..
....	......	Total............	....	231	708	621	1329	2	1	3	280	185	39	519	1	..	..

TABLE I.

SHOWING THE POPULATION FOR **1867** BY COUNTIES, ALPHABETICALLY ARRANGED, GIVING THE VARIOUS CLASSIFICATIONS THEREOF.

COUNTIES.	No. of Dwelling-Houses.	No. of White Males.	No. of White Females.	Total White Population.	No. of Colored Males.	No. of Colored Females.	Total Colored Population.	No. entitled to Vote.	No. of Militia.	No. of Foreigners not Naturalized.	No. between the ages of 5 and 21 years.	No. of Blind.	No. of Deaf and Dumb.	No. of Insane.	No. Students attending College.
Adair	262	839	755	1594	....	....	....	339	264	14	638	....	....	1	....
Adams	390	1215	1093	2308	2	7	9	483	369	9	979	....	....	1	...
Allamakee	2762	8268	7709	15977	15	11	26	3081	1998	493	6083	9	8	8	5
Appanoose	2072	6703	6321	13024	22	18	40	2592	1891	12	5649	8	16	5	....
Audubon	139	400	390	790	....	....	....	177	127	....	288	....	....	..	....
Benton	2464	7750	7015	14765	4	3	7	3064	2282	191	5774	*45	1	3	13
Black Hawk	2742	8220	7804	†16024	9	3	12	3350	2276	266	5891	2		2	53
Boone	1482	5169	4689	9858	3	....	3	2118	1655	183	3624	3	11	....	2
Bremer	1586	4927	4400	9327	5	5	10	1947	1330	129	3405	1	1	2	42
Buchanan	2090	6309	5915	12224	6	1	7	2589	1734	114	4174	1	2	1	6
Buena Vista	29	87	64	151	....	....	....	38	28	6	49	....	8	1	....
Butler	1144	3364	3175	6539	1	2	3	1448	989	53	2783	2	....	1	12
Calhoun	114	298	248	546	....	....	....	135	99	13	192	1	2	....	....
Carroll	132	350	338	688	....	....	....	138	112	....	307	....	....	....	....
Cass	388	1299	1178	12477	2	....	2	519	431	19	1025	3	....	1	....
Cedar	2747	8299	7736	6035	24	17	41	3415	2302	269	2072	20	....	14	44
Cerro Gordo	326	1000	988	1988	....	....	....	444	292	8	782	2	7	1	....
Cherokee	40	113	96	209	....	....	....	53	24	....	82	....	....	....	....
Chickasaw	1048	3233	2983	6216	4	....	4	127	770	97	2420	1	....	3	2
Clarke	1025	3121	3087	6208	19	17	36	1266	918	3	2753	2	2	4	3

Clay	58	204	165	369	....	....	....	98	60	....	128	....	1	....	3
Clayton	3918	11841	11023	22864	10	5	15	4773	3091	456	8898	12	7	10	30
Clinton	4810	14266	12899	27165	43	26	69	5426	3260	1652	9975	5	3	1	13
Crawford	168	576	492	1068	1	1	2	237	178	26	396	....	....	1	....
Dallas	1156	3915	3605	7520	10	8	18	1296	996	16	3062	4	5	1	2
Davis	2301	6861	6626	13487	17	13	30	2736	2010	19	5748	8	6	12	126
Decatur	1400	4253	4214	8467	17	17	34	1660	1130	6	3662	4	6	5	23
Delaware	2670	7432	7014	14446	15	2	17	3029	2170	246	5562	3	4	2	46
Des Moines	4013	11968	11283	23251	113	80	193	4651	3190	378	8233	14	4	3	29
Dickinson	97	274	235	509	....	....	...	124	81	....	....	....	....	....	....
Dubuque	6130	20235	18526	38761	47	52	99	6870	4618	781	12456	8	8	20	226
Emmett‡	114	404	303	707	1	....	1	162	120	....	239	....	....	....	....
Fayette	2492	7692	7277	14969	13	10	23	3094	2025	231	5906	11	2	6	173
Floyd	1189	3465	3260	6725	5	1	6	1525	1081	58	2459	....	3	2	2
Franklin	407	1211	1108	2319	2	....	2	497	396	....	942	....	....	....	....
Fremont	1149	3631	3364	6995	11	7	18	1446	1012	68	2804	5	12	1	163
Greene	424	1228	1124	2352	1	....	1	502	373	8	905	....	2	1	....
Grundy	367	1100	1019	2119	....	....	....	421	300	42	754	....	1	....	....
Guthrie	654	2018	1885	3903	1	2	3	873	650	11	1537	3	....	....	....
Hamilton	546	1626	1525	3151	2	1	3	684	480	59	1256	3	1	....	1
Hancock	63	186	171	357	....	....	....	84	59	....	145	1	1	....	....
Hardin	1721	4837	4494	9331	7	7	14	2082	1508	92	3477	3	2	3	3
Harrison	1009	2893	2470	§5835	1	....	1	1363	1024	48	2715	8	....	....	5
Henry	3374	10026	9683	19709	223	178	401	4230	3063	97	7765	7	18	‖339	716
Howard	776	2351	2046	4397	4	....	4	1010	701	54	1616	4	3	3	....
Humboldt	237	722	585	1307	....	....	....	301	234	13	452	...	1	....	....
Ida	18	51	39	90	...	....	...	25	19	....	32	....	....	....	....
Iowa	2090	6399	5982	12381	4	5	9	2654	1853	200	4618	4	8	10	15
Jackson	3575	10245	9711	19956	11	3	14	4070	2505	363	7826	8	8	4	16

9

* Inclusive of inmates of State Asylum for the Blind.
§ There are 472 persons returned from this county, sex not given.
† Inclusive of 300 children at the State Orphans' Home.
‖ Includes inmates of Iowa Insane Hospital.
‡ Partly estimated.

TABLE I.—CONTINUED.

COUNTIES.	No. of Dwelling-Houses.	No. of White Males.	No. of White Females.	Total White Population.	No. of Colored Males.	No. of Colored Females.	Total Colored Population.	No. entitled to Vote.	No. of Militia.	No. of Foreigners not Naturalized.	No. between the ages of 5 and 21 years.	No. of Blind.	No. of Deaf and Dumb.	No. of Insane.	No. of Students attending College.
Jasper	2639	8508	7672	16180	33	26	59	3480	2479	94	6227	6	6	9	33
Jefferson	2811	8287	8088	16375	22	23	45	3348	2349	121	7030	7	....	3	78
Johnson	3634	11028	10534	21562	36	43	79	3965	2673	258	7617	4	8	7	112
Jones	2792	8380	7820	16200	18	10	28	3446	2311	195	6246	5	11	15	18
Keokuk	2611	7837	7588	15425	4	....	4	3120	2	58	6501	7	14	13	10
Kossuth	259	832	740	1572	1	....	1	380	275	....	625	....	....	....	....
Lee	5388	15239	14813	30052	681	684	1365	6275	4384	308	11459	10	8	11	100
Linn	4148	12548	11952	24500	32	17	49	5118	3469	288	9546	10	4	5	534
Louisa	2275	6125	5715	11840	28	17	45	2568	1935	73	4625	9	1	4	20
Lucas	1213	4009	3715	7724	14	8	22	1500	1155	4	3092	2	1	1	....
Lyon (not organized)	....	....	....	....	..	....	....	....	... .	....	....	....	....	....	....
Madison	1562	5052	4705	9757	5	2	7	2025	1531	22	3832	3	6	....	4
Mahaska	3128	9434	9147	18581	61	51	112	3851	2840	97	7426	9	3	2	89
Marion	3556	10314	9858	20172	6	3	9	4014	2991	187	8246	14	6	10	189
Marshall	2102	6038	5410	11448	34	31	65	2512	1422	203	4454	3	2	4	173
Mills	1249	3669	3304	6973	11	10	21	1428	1140	57	2463	4	5	....	3
Mitchell	1025	3198	2950	6148	2	...	2	1354	865	61	2260	1	4	1	2
Monona	281	881	756	1637	10	13	*27	368	169	5	632	1	1	....	....
Monroe	1735	5154	5002	10156	31	21	52	1998	1345	40	4190	4	12	....	1
Montgomery	344	1098	974	2072	....	....	....	443	367	2	714	2	1	....	23
Muscatine	6475	10485	10047	20532	87	80	167	4245	3134	399	6980	8	9	4	95

O'Brien	7	12	8	20	....	....	....	11	10	....	9	....	....	....	....
Osceola (not organized)	....	....	....	....	....	....	....	....	....	....	....	....	....	....	....
Page	956	3050	2826	5876	62	87	149	1201	870	18	2619	3	....	4	....
Palo Alto	71	230	183	413	....	....	....	93	78	2	149	....	....	....	....
Plymouth	....	114	100	214	....	....	....	53	26	1	67	....	....	....	....
Pocahontas	87	239	214	453	....	....	....	97	69	14	161	....	....	....	....
Polk	3436	11579	10788	22367	130	133	263	4380	3286	171	7458	11	7	15	46
Pottawattamie	1571	4723	3977	8700	22	11	33	1953	1233	211	3090	1	4	2	2
Poweshiek	1653	5191	4653	9844	29	15	44	2027	1604	60	3980	4	9	5	144
Ringgold	610	1979	1902	3881	4	3	7	735	559	22	1652	3	4	1	....
Sac	103	297	298	595	....	....	....	139	79	3	228	....	....	....	....
Scott	5638	17788	16276	34064	153	145	298	6078	4428	1716	11904	15	5	15	154
Shelby	204	655	558	1213	....	....	....	241	179	3	509	....	....	....	....
Sioux	4	11	7	18	....	....	....	8	7	....	9	....	....	....	....
Story	1111	3487	3396	6883	3	2	5	1302	971	137	2753	2	6	2	2
Tama	1891	5794	5320	11114	26	25	51	2283	1730	245	4368	....	3	2	28
Taylor	706	2301	2141	4442	52	52	104	828	609	6	1859	....	....	1	....
Union	655	1556	1453	3009	1	....	1	597	454	2	1235	....	2	....	....
Van Buren	2780	8185	7944	16129	86	77	163	3491	2359	48	6082	9	6	6	118
Wapello	3213	9683	9163	18846	42	42	84	3938	2655	81	7520	9	14	8	5
Warren	2154	6674	6443	13117	25	20	45	2634	2031	13	5525	6	6	3	7
Washington	3005	9034	8551	17585	52	38	90	3692	2579	185	7034	10	17	3	88
Wayne	1317	3908	3746	7654	3	....	3	1503	1109	4	3445	4	5	7	2
Webster	1039	2912	2713	5625	5	1	6	1209	581	92	2011	1	2	3	....
Winnebago	128	413	372	785	....	....	....	136	97	27	311	1	....	....	....
Winneshiek	3438	10173	9100	19273	19	10	29	3413	2423	1060	7205	9	7	9	88
Woodbury	346	1057	912	1969	1	....	1	510	351	32	643	....	....	....	3
Worth	269	794	749	1543	....	....	....	233	170	36	572	....	....	....	....
Wright	231	708	621	1329	2	1	3	280	185	39	519	1	....	....	1
Total	155,758	463,537	433,316	†897,325	2508	2203	4715	181,749	125,646	13,503	339,618	412	368	644	3951

* 4 colored persons, sex not reported. † 472 sex not reported.

TABLE II.

SHOWING THE EXTENT OF RAILROAD FINISHED, THE NUMBER OF COLLEGES, &C., THE AMOUNT OF LANDS INCLOSED AND OF HEDGING, AND THE VALUE OF AGRICULTURAL IMPLEMENTS, &C., IN THE STATE; AS WELL AS THE VALUE OF MANUFACTURES, AND THE AMOUNT OF COAL AND THE VALUE OF OTHER MINERALS RAISED, DURING THE YEAR 1866, IN IOWA; BY COUNTIES, ALPHABETICALLY ARRANGED.

COUNTIES.	No. miles railroad finished.	No. colleges, academies, and universities.	Value of manufactures.	No. bushels coal raised, 80 lbs. per bushel.	Value minerals raised, not including coal.	Value agricultural implements, machinery, and wagons.	No. rods hedging.	No. acres land inclosed.
Adair	......	....	$ 2169	......	$ ..	$ 22307	344	6134
Adams	......	....	16645	1755	....	27330	998	12388
Allamakee	5	....	11772	....	....	162797	234	117620
Appanoose	......	....	103957	109988	....	154395	8375	95920
Audubon	......	....	....	....	....	5972	480	3429
Benton	25	....	26216	....	....	154814	9251	118236
Black Hawk	34¼	1	583873	....	....	151047	2258	98693
Boone	27½	....	15783	3670	30	81074	2064	341471½
Bremer	6½	1	17429	....	....	116477	3340	70964
Buchanan	24½	....	44782	....	90	130899	5738	96629
Buena Vista	......	....	....	....	....	....	......	344
Butler	25	....	8700	....	....	106812	5429	57167
Calhoun	......	....	....	....	....	8998	40	1619
Carroll	......	....	....	....	....	5634	105	2371
Cass	......	....	2060	....	....	39614	1308	13209
Cedar	......	1	13713	....	....	244904	19601	177749
Cerro Gordo	......	....	....	....	....	19983	615	13337

Cherokee						2027		208
Chickasaw			24704			77455	206	47399
Clarke			34490			81543	2961	45634
Clay						2870		751
Clayton	25	1	217083		110300	293877	1566	172416
Clinton	38¼		1038512		22000	370899	28442	228390
Crawford	31¾		4295			10403	85	5347
Dallas			47479	1765		99980	5320	48926¾
Davis	½	1	105063	29727		179013	15073	117096
Decatur			59360			89858	1646	58141
Delaware	32½	2	89847		85	170406	5164	156644
Des Moines	17¼	4	2671015			538150	24622	126321
Dickinson						915		1435
Dubuque	37¾	6	3300774	400	134760	444391	409	169433
Emmett						5415	25	1423
Fayette		2	83846		400	180972	7531	128431
Floyd			25973			103944	2770	45460
Franklin	1					39196	443	12520
Fremont	18	1	40011			70551	5679	42376
Greene	24½		2077	1200		22623	550	10548
Grundy			1024			37785	2662	20306
Guthrie			85452	12675		61399	3966	24115
Hamilton			5652			31363	861	15781
Hancock			3			4819	738	1919
Hardin	11¼		85323	30000	900	130456	9558	64476
Harrison	26¾		5241			77133	504	24811
Henry	19½	5	162141	10035		257378	37658	132534
Howard	22		7884			57207	1731	35821
Humboldt			3017			10576	1499	4842
Ida						1940		115
Iowa	25		173351			165784	7112	97789

TABLE II.—CONTINUED.

COUNTIES.	No. miles railroad finished.	No. colleges, academies, and universities.	Value of manufactures.	No. bushels coal raised, 80 lbs. per bushel.	Value minerals raised, not including coal.	Value agricultural implements, machinery, and wagons.	No. rods hedging.	No. acres land inclosed.
Jackson	....	....	$ 134980	....	$.....	$ 236909	3469	168152
Jasper	51	....	41903	89215	....	210053	4585	107596
Jefferson	25¾	1	218501	358675	15700	229955	18898	121471
Johnson	27	2	242737	70	177	224126	9835	160821
Jones	19¾	1	27265	....	15	225991	6339	158527
Keokuk	....	....	77483	59000	....	205747	12411	124119
Kossuth	....	....	....	....	....	10570	63	4007
Lee	55	3	1337331	5040	200	215256	70952	164223
Linn	49	2	855522	....	....	241517	12414	175220
Louisa	19	2	31225	....	....	163145	13629	108619
Lucas	12	....	82577	23155	....	73529	12628	45128
Lyon (not organized)	....	....	....	....	....	....	....	....
Madison	....	....	49680	1854	....	127907	10385	64333
Mahaska	20	1	119149	638381	....	229841	9178	134232
Marion	16	1	102680	181206	4177	178775	4236	120276
Marshall	26	3	11416	....	....	159529	8808	79230
Mills	18	....	35852	....	....	87539	4123	35950
Mitchell	....	1	39881	....	....	97693	3646	38947
Monona	....	....	18000	....	....	21085	35	6937
Monroe	27	....	74600	38684	3834	110043	6480	70218

Montgomery	......	....	5204	....	....	20747	....	9363
Muscatine	45¼	4	384164	49462	425	200425	32639	150718
O'Brien	......	....	....	....	....	1600	....	123
Osceola (not organized)	......	....	....	....	....	....	....	....
Page	......	....	24763	10500	100	99392	5885	34191
Palo Alto	......	....	....	....	....	....	....	951
Plymouth	......	....	....	....	....	2390	....	1695
Pocahontas	......	....	....	....	....	5105	400	1424
Polk	32	4	601733	332769	....	773380	4744	78802
Pottawattamie	25	....	95967	....	....	82183	1083	22580
Poweshiek	25½	1	19221	100	21	116426	3420	69417
Ringgold	......	....	23315	....	....	33773	5620	23130
Sac	......	....	....	....	....	5430	260	2592
Scott	13½	3	1126614	99200	145	328384	39681	193591
Shelby	......	....	1293	....	....	16855	730	4616
Sioux	......	....	....	....	....	175	....	40
Story	24½	1	17417	....	....	77555	17909	42373
Tama	25½	....	61339	....	4	139972	4529	77354
Taylor	......	....	10181	2700	65	41683	4163	26941
Union	......	....	8317	....	....	37346	3043	18271
Van Buren	30	1	263236	71170	27312	196280	32840	123684
Wapello	56¾	1	320675	164381	80	162399	18928	113821
Warren	......	1	43042	93840	....	168117	9633	83076
Washington	11	2	102387	4000	....	246405	26167	155347
Wayne	......	....	49286	18800	....	79485	3297	57874
Webster	......	....	24307	39593	....	71000	4765	27117
Winnebago	......	....	3425	....	....	5271	....	1429
Winneshiek	30	1	146162	....	....	284773	991	179265
Woodbury	......	....	1250	....	....	22416	....	3413
Worth	......	....	2337	....	....	21260	752	7593
Wright	......	....	466	....	....	19580	509	6932
Total	1152¼	61	15957599	2483010	320820	11362402	663063	8263174

TABLE III.

EXHIBITING THE STATISTICS, BY COUNTIES, OF THE GRAIN CROPS OF THE STATE OF IOWA FOR THE YEAR 1866.

COUNTIES.	No. acres spring wheat.	No. bushels harvested.	No. acres winter wheat.	No. bushels harvested.	No. acres oats.	No. bushels harvested.	No. acres corn.	No. bushels harvested.	No. acres rye.	No. bushels harvested.	No. acres barley.	No. bushels harvested.
Adair	1073	16235	15	225	324	10490	3999	97132	2	25	....	....
Adams	1473	20477	9	134	535	14715	6264	110558	61	654	¾	15
Allamakee	30817	423232	896	11775	8424	228405	21731	529653	174	2435	266	6193
Appanoose	1752	18393	2191	26486	9117	296042	41467	815281	470	5790	15	349
Audubon	699	11344	....	....	333	6107	1773	22868	....	....	½	11
Benton	29417½	458309	33	384	8936	326757	31060	901480	140	1796	702	18355
Black Hawk	31892	500081	7	70	7639	318833	19468	484949	447	6712	271	6182
Boone	4301	55406	22	274	2181	72521	16384	463556	49½	977	16½	460
Bremer	17611	239772	5	90	6993	212187	12296½	300662	164½	2460	191	5177
Buchanan	25312	351264	21	130	9075	246545	20096	426611	100½	1546	329	7027
Buena Vista	21	378	....	....	20	460	142	3430	....	....	....	....
Butler	15584	216590	21½	315	4435	130390	12165	274037	126	1762	67	1888
Calhoun	308	6191	....	....	178	7172	654	19310	....	....	1	40
Carroll	497	8663	....	....	77	2771	1007	30123	....	....	4	100
Cass	3134	54307	1	26	975	33961	9103	186070	....	....	39	768
Cedar	30798	421655	1614	12490	15147	487830	50295	1529540	1142	18192	3576	85709
Cerro Gordo	2139	26011	....	....	1974	57786	2635	55669	....	4	74	1261
Cherokee	10	150	....	....	8	240	300	3511	....	....	....	....
Chickasaw	8898	117087	....	....	4246	112484	7046	126438	16	321	122	2426
Clarke	2048	27576	116	1305	4497	129263	22819	451166	120	1528	....	....

Clay	92	1680	......	......	77	2071	205	2675	......	......	......	......
Clayton	51208	780517	937	7986	15868	423337	32440	921185	390	6122	857	22456
Clinton	55291	795742	80	897	19773	628357	52594	1408933	392	6535	4220	108179
Crawford	808	17943	......	......	360	12864	1823	47315	4	110	¼	15
Dallas	8469	117551	55	497	3442	118700	25537½	856234	100	1364	36½	911
Davis	2490	18106	4276	47966	11439	311599	44171	800143	1018	11370	¼	18
Decatur	1030	11266	630	6860	3668	104382	25069	299820	282	3686	28	271
Delaware	28831	418364	15	90	14095	444275	29212	661934	229	3784	1162	29103
Des Moines	10916	116760	4789	43235	8349	249752	47028	1547549	1144	14554	720	15534
Dickinson	92	1456	......	......	42	1345	248	3685	......	......	2	60
Dubuque	25244	364567	466	2229	20853	661993	42594	1224272	818	15229	1350	34315
Emmett	200	3309	......	......	1	20	442	10585	......	......	......	......
Fayette	24403	327850	56	751	12322	339093	23676	575156	22	210	508	10699
Floyd	11612	140696	10	80	4568	120534	8535	192599	21	295	85	1473
Franklin	4365	60583	......	......	1691	45448	4294	100199	......	......	34	250
Fremont	4637	85266	27	261	1998	64970	52162	749597	45	830	200	3469
Greene	1837	29281	......	......	684	25353	6180	169074	13	105	6	90
Grundy	7110	106380	......	......	2375	88287	4975	128554	32	328	74	1621
Guthrie	4738	73653	121	1879	1428	55528	12711	439134	37	444	⅛	20
Hamilton	2353	31047	13	167	1399	47283	4996	115726	2	24	27	620
Hancock	416	4349	......	......	328	11949	595	10655	......	......	7	265
Hardin	13791	209566	......	......	4615	174568	18482	509022	52	622	100	1942
Harrison	6218	126868	19	273	1888	77291	11918	344676	32	575	756	2558
Henry	10940	102980	4258	44802	8478	263768	45029	1622322	1987	20946	261	4920
Howard	10348	108447	......	.....	5879	111153	4664	81741	15	195	323	5785
Humboldt	654	12159	......	.....	419	15758	1063	33790	......	......	9	253
Ida	45	930	......	......	74	3230	95	1585	......	....	4	130
Iowa	19697	292512	237	1782	6392	228610	28438	950207	345	5616	630	17744
Jackson	19596	273735	2067	20052	22352	678297	45645	1324190	1319	19302	669	15231
Jasper	18912	353515	67	568	6978	252296	48908	1956396	111	1719	85	2695
Jefferson	5251	49593	7079	68887	10199	293846	47849	1630553	2430	31159	76	1415

TABLE III.—CONTINUED.

COUNTIES.	No. acres spring wheat.	No. bushels harvested.	No. acres winter wheat.	No. bushels harvested.	No. acres oats.	No. bushels harvested.	No. acres corn.	No. bushels harvested.	No. acres rye.	No. bushels harvested.	No. acres barley.	No. bushels harvested.
Johnson	16700	253908	2237	20935	14639	512399	50146	1629207	1930	31622	424	9776
Jones	19583	282909	194	1931	15995	444853	45161	1185238	592	10629	462	11106
Keokuk	11340	125391	4369	41233	7879	306636	48313	1616568	1422	20055	142	3863
Kossuth	502	7200	.....	......	501	12904	1089	17335	.....	......	5	83
Lee	10747	101346	3331	25234	9884	266524	52891	1544206	4110	52738	955	18604
Linn	27549	364558	79	867	15435	506088	50651	1415373	724	11301	545	12044
Louisa	11319	127552	3010	32665	6833	211737	41779	1530637	1501	19826	18	359
Lucas	2198	21568	289	2934	4962	154334	23930	548024	385	5434	89	1452
Lyon (not organized)	....	....	.....	......	....	......	......	....	.....	......	.....	......
Madison	6420	99259	312	3627	4737	148480	32498	998176	265	3553	2	84
Mahaska	13474	174877	2550	28777	8564	291911	55354	2163056	510	7339	232	4583
Marion	13088	168703	2519	25059	9597	303431	58685	2182452	638	9027	62	1268
Marshall	25662	368935	16	251	5808	280892	23939	727015	75	855	145	3770
Mills	8082	133058	3	15	1772	67329	17449	552236	16	294	308	8562
Mitchell	10380	142346	.....	......	5261	162531	4717	98659	8	75	529	12104
Monona	1390	32960	.....	......	354	15808	2597	65402	2	31	1	59
Monroe	3329	32351	2847	34287	5766	161617	29053	705810	770	10991	7	114
Montgomery	1656	23084	12	176	445	15097	5545	146616	19	184	2	40
Muscatine	20685	264365	2366	18005	11563	405923	41023	1338990	2230	32990	3118	83519
O'Brien*	30	600	.....	......	70	2100	60	2100	.....	......	.....	......
Osceola (not organized)	....	....	.....	......	....	......	......	....	.....	......	.....	......

Page	5355	56486	88	1313	2449	70969	18367	329959	42	530	22	294
Palo Alto	155	3203	......	......	77	2131	577	7755	......	......	......	......
Plymouth	453	10141	......	......	120	4109	270	7555	......	......	24	739
Pocahontas	245	3846	......	......	75	2121	483	9750	......	......	......	......
Polk	9184	136513	177	2414	5164	193864	39405	1481567	196	2886	333	7161
Pottawattamie	4168	67779	......	......	1100	35333	8930	232757	15	478	99	2274
Poweshiek	16167	247787	25	315	3994	140530	25721	931720	120	2089	205	3946
Ringgold	775	8672	51	406	1930	52093	13653	157800	52	548	5	90
Sac	373	8485	......	......	302	10151	865	18645	......	......	......	......
Scott	48717	713619	147	1480	13993	407638	43693	1436464	310	5105	20299	555572
Shelby	1150	20914	......	......	313	10227	2459	54006	......	......	......	......
Sioux	......	......	......	......	10	40	10	200	......	......	......	......
Story	5555	71520	1	15	3006	104312	15200	410760	39	478	10	168
Tama	22802	423015	5	43	4310	158351	21864	705072	57	952	116	3362
Taylor	2820	34036	33	166	2043	55512	14104	234129	32	484	......	......
Union	1240	14093	104	1151	1553	46361	8019	136290	150	1995	1½	15
Van Buren	6224	50069	7734	69052	8469	248627	36864	999460	1860	22599	44	759
Wapello	5595	56461	4912	53726	7740	210203	47060	1289370	1256	16995	127	655
Warren	8618	129381	648	8763	6482	214564	41311	1417940	549	6898	138	1013
Washington	17216	202869	4676	39410	11076	388726	52115	1807035	1586	21622	80	2035
Wayne	1275	8401	529	5756	4950	155350	25707	432793	219	2846	½	10
Webster	3439	58887	......	......	1603	51112	12821	201707	6	49	8	192
Winnebago	318	4595	......	......	197	5713	270	6370	......	......	33	307
Winneshiek	55159	792507	2	30	14580	417594	20732	489955	61	989	1256	29195
Woodbury	625	15985	6	150	243	10342	1676	40370	......	8	248	380
Worth	1250	17139	......	......	693	21392	1144	23162	......	......	5	74
Wright	1523	21203	......	......	676	22619	1943	48697	5	20	9	155
Total	983906	13912368	73425	723152	504362	15861494	1992326	56928938	35604	492841	48013	1197729

* Estimated.

TABLE IV.

EXHIBITING THE STATISTICS, BY COUNTIES, OF THE SORGHUM AND GRASS CROPS OF THE STATE OF IOWA FOR THE YEAR 1866.

COUNTIES.	No. acres sorghum.	No. gallons syrup from sorghum.	No. pounds sugar from sorghum.	No. acres Hungarian grass.	No. tons hay from Hungarian grass.	No. acres tame grasses.	No. tons hay from tame grasses.	No. tons hay from wild grass.	No. bushels grass-seed.
Adair	73	5614	......	5	11	109	168	3765	35
Adams	110	6961	......	161	296	203	320	4291	59
Allamakee	185	11915	206	282	480	8787	9568	5689	233
Appanoose	471	34403	207	5019	2223	8478	11203	2154	2193
Audubon	24	1981	......	44	104	31	10	3104	22
Benton	394	31070	......	23	72	4590	6013	18124	1550
Black Hawk	394	24563	......	269	444	2840	2801	17466	197
Boone	255	19731	30	198	497	653	1054	11695	69
Bremer	338	21100	402	431	914	1866	2126	13836	306
Buchanan	381	30402	400	48	97	4223	5190	15498	622
Buena Vista	2½	117	......	......	......	......	......	782	......
Butler	224	14205	23	321	856	718	854	12608	238
Calhoun	16	1382	......	6	11	4	3	1775	......
Carroll	27	2737	......	......	......	6	10	1652	......
Cass	102	8692	15	170	428	67	104	6913	34
Cedar	473	45550	60	166	355	23137	19391	10110	7292
Cerro Gordo	55	3034	......	137	343	91	126	6778	......
Cherokee	13	682	......	......	......	......	......	1113	......
Chickasaw	156	10034	*6780	70	161	1816	1913	15744	1700
Clarke	301	18812	15	1638	2177	1951	2248	4793	297

Clay	16	816	......	......	......	....	....	1643	....
Clayton	293	32593	60	139	266	12159	12346	11432	1525
Clinton	398	43466	20	809	1723	17729	17791	17867	2200
Crawford	24	1423	......	48	125	18	5	3878	......
Dallas	769	33403	200	369	926	618	772	10158	22
Davis	563	37603	197	4777	5889	11008	12304	307	1151
Decatur	356	15653	109	2229	2335	4056	5647	6258	530
Delaware	426	31740	78	276	716	9503	11735	20382	1213
Des Moines	418	37729	16	26	350	19377	19121	1954	887
Dickinson	28	938	......	......	......	....	....	1962	....
Dubuque	485	33862	......	150	320	18584	20392	12098	830
Emmett	32	1235	200	......	......	3	5	4178	....
Fayette	296	20593	120	51	106	8543	8816	20133	2233
Floyd	136	7736	......	474	900	687	983	13008	193
Franklin	50	2479	......	103	300	107	62	6920	....
Fremont	291	29301	40	241	627	103	92	14410	23
Greene	98	9563	......	30	66	59	60	4393	17
Grundy	61	3401	......	46	71	344	325	6324	30
Guthrie	153	16709	2	292	626	182	305	6886	55
Hamilton	111	6687	......	12	31	79	47	9507	....
Hancock	8	237	......	......	......	4	8	1458	11
Hardin	324	21129	100	131	303	1042	1089	17251	101
Harrison	201	14755	......	530	755	6	18	16179	98
Henry	687	66687	340	104	149	23300	22260	1539	6014
Howard	45	2303	......	99	249	568	636	12099	164
Humboldt	48	2577	......	7	16	25	11	5881	....
Ida	2	180	......	......	......	....	....	610	....
Iowa	389	36580	......	59	136	5624	6930	20794	1224
Jackson	672	60299	1	292	476	20816	24018	6140	1405

* Maple sugar.

TABLE IV.—CONTINUED.

COUNTIES.	No. acres sorghum.	No. gallons syrup from sorghum.	No. pounds sugar from sorghum.	No. acres Hungarian grass.	No. tons hay from Hungarian grass.	No. acres tame grass.	No. tons hay from tame grasses.	No. tons hay from wild grass.	No. bushels grass seed.
Jasper	539	50477	......	259	610	2025	2512	21806	162
Jefferson	796	81619	106	78	302	24544	25796	296	13510
Johnson	579	52410	1161	472	960	15000	17304	17141	5494
Jones	581	52135	1005	499	1087	13492	16775	14580	636
Keokuk	705	63151	10	151	286	13042	15590	6210	2044
Kossuth	26	734	......	.....	......	13	15	5853	....
Lee	628	60763	174	193	327	30930	25687	518	19957
Linn	880	72855	......	127	160	18428	20187	22869	1205
Louisa	504	50345	109	178	342	13862	13408	7037	1370
Lucas	280	19728	173	2019	3269	2363	3337	5237	583
Lyon (not organized)	.....	....	.....	.....	......	....	....	....	....
Madison	432	35946	50	401	693	2636	3777	9186	235
Mahaska	599	65640	1005	326	599	13459	17366	9130	685
Marion	676	64354	2	779	1504	7475	9774	7009	739
Marshall	332	23852	24	318	642	1749	1720	16170	172
Mills	102	8060	6	290	616	63	115	12341	2
Mitchell	83	4892	......	710	1884	547	818	12501	128
Monona	84	4709	......	......	......	....	....	7787	....
Monroe	451	26983	135	2226	3575	7967	9520	2429	919
Montgomery	63	4862	......	12	25	170	225	4007	16
Muscatine	525	53072	52	167	257	15550	14144	8274	2916

O'Brien	4	......	......	......	......	......	......	200	......
Osceola (not organized)	......	......	......	......	......	......	......	......	......
Page	167	9042	......	430	745	304	977	9564	117
Palo Alto	7	498	......	......	......	......	......	3444	......
Plymouth	3	210	......	......	......	......	......	1176	......
Pocahontas	17	731	......	......	......	......	......	2304	......
Polk	621	39855	101	715	1552	1334	1788	17690	160
Pottawattamie	103	8653	85	272	494	24	266	11696	43
Powesheik	313	27616	32	129	434	2623	7468	16671	419
Ringgold	170	7139	......	345	475	863	1533	6751	175
Sac	22	1290	......	6	15	......	......	1581	......
Scott	234	27329	......	292	603	12033	13002	13365	573
Shelby	43	3529	100	122	306	6	8	3146	......
Sioux	......	......	......	......	......	......	......	50	......
Story	308	21103	330	84	209	397	349	17827	86
Tama	285	25455	......	161	440	2140	2566	18886	671
Taylor	164	6581	......	456	535	720	1132	6675	202
Union	127	7262	......	335	496	625	1054	4285	106
Van Buren	506	46915	......	380	459	24409	18397	363	11149
Wapello	486	43410	220	1028	1459	15267	15763	975	2532
Warren	524	44492	3	821	1496	4692	6882	11053	468
Washington	704	71523	104	56	134	21750	25561	6402	2240
Wayne	337	17975	73	2924	4288	4114	4736	4252	874
Webster	197	10477	......	2	14	58	110	16866	3
Winnebago	11	317	......	......	......	......	......	2932	......
Winneshiek	88	5036	16	221	420	8600	9227	21572	2123
Woodbury	20	1983	......	6	10	......	......	7408	......
Worth	41	2168	......	51	252	17	1	6434	44
Wright	55	2719	......	......	12	44	31	5664	......
Total	25796	2094557	14697	39436	58889	497460	537812	823153	107532

TABLE V.

EXHIBITING THE STATISTICS BY COUNTIES OF THE POTATO, ONION AND FLAX CROPS OF THE STATE OF IOWA FOR THE YEAR 1866.

COUNTIES.	No. acres Irish potatoes	No. bushels harvested.	No. bushels sweet potatoes.	No. bushels onions.	No. acres flax.	No. bushels seed harvested.	No. pounds lint.	No. gallons linseed oil.
Adair	72	5077	147	259		.....	.....	.....
Adams	91	5817	164	506	3	6	176	.....
Allamakee	1125	71582	4	1174	1	5	70	.....
Appanoose	310	17069	1494	3198	672	3254	753	.....
Audubon	29	2490	3	105	½	4	.....	.....
Benton	653	51424	418	1984	7	38	400	.....
Black Hawk	819	44028	130	2093	3	19	375	.....
Boone	292	22817	447	992	1	2	.....	.....
Bremer	610	36646	4	1235	25	117	18	.....
Buchanan	729	45793	28	1655	7	6	45	.....
Buena Vista	10	942	.....	12	.....	.....	.....	.....
Butler	351	34281	2	886	2	7	55	.....
Calhoun	23	1313	.....	63	.....	.....	.....	.....
Carroll	26	3014	.....	62	.....	.....	.....	.....
Cass	94	7348	108	340	.....	.....	.....	.....
Cedar	630	28424	550	10645	2597	15471	45	.....
Cerro Gordo	142	13040	.....	262	.....	.....	.....	.....
Cherokee	6	649	.....	7	.....	.....	.....	.....
Chickasaw	370	30784	.....	644	1116	3	15	.....
Clarke	247	13328	194	3396	18	77	630	.....

Clay	17	1386		11	½	4		
Clayton	1442	82919	5	2560	3	7	120	
Clinton	2398	64310	176	2925	44	227		3000
Crawford	62	4167		178	½	3		
Dallas	263	27229	667	1080	5	36		
Davis	461	23447	760	3477	382	1832	2606	
Decatur	352	11134	323	2374	27	99	786	
Delaware	882	50518	187	2506	1	5½	30	
Des Moines	710	40374	1767	2096	363	2193		
Dickinson	31	3140		36				
Dubuque	2266	64148	178	2315	29	126		
Emmett	42	3571		48	⅛			
Fayette	808	61703	2	1599	15	52	65	
Floyd	362	30243		1127	½	2		
Franklin	174	8937		1043				
Fremont	195	13346	64	987	3	5	10	
Greene	82	8091	72	438				
Grundy	155	14505	16	409	11	5	80	
Guthrie	133	15481	27	566	4	33		
Hamilton	230	9269		394	1	1	25	
Hancock	28	3117		46				
Hardin	535	41481	160	1697	7	7	35	
Harrison	207	16172	21	1187	½			
Henry	582	49209	2776	2610	485	2873	145	
Howard	447	37849	3	551	1	40	30	
Humboldt	87	8298		101	¼	4		
Ida	4	305		8				
Iowa	779	50691	327	2143	14	139	186	
Jackson	1236	51937	154	1639	¾	2¼		
Jasper	725	65622	1498	4466	3	4		
Jefferson	560	38789	3064	3278	114	505	1401	51

TABLE V.—Continued.

COUNTIES.	No. acres Irish potatoes.	No. bushels harvested.	No. bushels sweet potatoes.	No. bushels onions.	No. acres flax.	No. bushels seed harvested.	No. pounds lint.	No. gallons linseed oil.
Johnson	885	38135	793	1706	2879	22319	356075	65000
Jones	1345	37105	369	2366	½	1	......	......
Keokuk	521	29256	3095	4115	190	580	725	......
Kossuth	68	5051	......	52	......	......	......	......
Lee	977	70683	2301	1964	46	199	84	......
Linn	892	45085	811	2903	69	485	127	......
Louisa	438	30931	1011	1357	258	1637	80	......
Lucas	233	17494	776	1735	3	10	260	......
Lyon (not organized)	......	......	......	......	......	......	......	......
Madison	370	35577	2014	1349	7	28	563	1
Mahaska	545	51067	1291	3672	415	2209	4330	12000
Marion	673	59926	3524	3282	30	361	381	......
Marshall	554	49492	614	2851	24	188	......	......
Mills	191	15602	71	1278	......	......	......	......
Mitchell	387	38838	......	507	2	5	132	......
Monona	190	6389	6	168	½	......	20	......
Monroe	298	22551	1473	1738	141	598	416	......
Montgomery	61	4445	5	422	½	3	90	......
Muscatine	938	46586	2558	5215	993	2637	200	......
O'Brien	10	750	......	......	......	......	......	......

Osceola (not organized)								
Page	210	9378	234	1245	4	31	197	
Palo Alto	58	5582		17				
Plymouth	20	2480		208				
Pocahontas	63	4349		44				
Polk	656	63263	1441	3459	1	9	15	
Pottawattamie	226	17054	520	1076	1	2	100	
Poweshiek	405	29835	311	2214				
Ringgold	142	7203	143	562	14	284	12000	
Sac	31	2955		55				
Scott	3028	193727	1874	72206				
Shelby	55	5174		136	½			
Sioux	1	200						
Story	346	26528	283	1284	1	1½		
Tama	515	44977	97	1739	2	20	480	
Taylor	152	8426	931	1076	3	11	110	
Union	121	8448	223	797	5	8	335	
Van Buren	657	34285	2128	3792	347	1798	1230	
Wapello	512	43773	2197	2987	95	683	350	
Warren	515	51906	1663	3323	143	7	261	
Washington	552	34411	1153	2723	82	48	2679	
Wayne	206	10768	340	2065	88	523	300	
Webster	223	16277		524	72	5	80	
Winnebago	39	4245		54				
Winneshiek	1049	77584		1235	21	2	292	
Woodbury	66	5624	200	206		10		
Worth	93	9583		25	¼		40	
Wright	92	6426		135				
Total	42493	2666678	50390	213285	11906	61917	400053	80052

Note.—The amount for Chickasaw in the item of "acres of flax" is undoubtedly erroneous, but it is as officially reported from the county.—[Sec. of State.

TABLE VI.

EXHIBITING VARIOUS AGRICULTURAL STATISTICS, ARRANGED BY COUNTIES.

COUNTIES.	No. acres in all other crops.	No. fruit trees in bearing.	No. fruit trees not in bearing.	No. pounds grapes raised	No. gallons wine made.	No. pounds hops raised.	No. pounds tobacco raised.	No. acres planted for timber.	No. hives bees.	No. pounds honey taken.	No. pounds beeswax.
Adair	192	397	2036	182	7	4	1404	19	168	4227	116
Adams	75	196	4566	171	8	6	6480	52	189	5345	118
Allamakee	198	3395	32404	1248	148	749	4512	1½	1044	8134	424
Appanoose	315	14684	69585	3066	48½	201	11387	11	2048	34333	900
Audubon	61	20	618	11	8	12	185	8½	105	1620	71
Benton	259	6875	79980	1976	12	360	5018	613	862	5733	473
Black Hawk	504	7050	42179	2628	357	128	700	266	512	5122	382
Boone	16	2773	20779	500	45	89	4222	42	409	7784	312
Bremer	385	3515	21257	245	90½	192	1013	194	429	4584	219
Buchanan	567	4751	44640	1064	48½	388	3116	185	715	4662	233
Buena Vista	5	......	......	......	......	......	......	......	1	22	1
Butler	222	906	14859	105	1	1345	351	137	287	2745	150
Calhoun	......	6	709	......	......	11	387	1	13	52	12
Carroll	......	10	1280	......	......	......	125	8	7	111	......
Cass	19	126	2501	64	270	20	443	40	233	1795	65
Cedar	712	29877	94227	8526	240	837	3215	300	2786	11040	552
Cerro Gordo	260	469	2479	253	......	7	21	35	79	693	39
Cherokee	¼	6	......	......	2	40	......	......	......	......	......
Chickasaw	2055	679	7940	323	37	383	5874	30	360	4204	187
Clarke	355	7128	29914	1541	19	73	3772	49	773	18702	461

Clay	......	....	65	......	......	......	......	......	......	......	......
Clayton	3630	9364	86972	1020	391	5581	4295	73	1223	8619	407
Clinton	860	22721	107846	5892	998	571	9383	85	2060	13941	487
Crawford	11	2	11185	1	......	......	40	17	166	1457	93
Dallas	292	7365	27995	3944	55	92	4915	203	676	8921	535½
Davis	181	23226	52995	2528	10	956	13716	3	2428	32120	1470
Decatur	231	7972	35319	2365	58	57	12985	53	2152	31204	1329
Delaware	300	7489	54229	685	235	1459	3039	148	1110	7963	468
Des Moines	4667	114152	82306	113986	7393	554	4603	8	2149	14067	741
Dickinson	......	1	2161	10	......	......	......	......	......	......	......
Dubuque	868	24560	249169	20632	894	604	9061	3	1271	8896	557
Emmett	76	....	82	25	3	......	50	9	8	70	......
Fayette	1249	2857	33407	699	26	1008	4067	181	1071	8471	359
Floyd	35	626	12952	218	20	475	657	34	476	4463	240
Franklin	......	93	4745	......	......	......	......	59	7	......	......
Fremont	4274	3902	24945	75	6	......	996	151	679	10856	320
Greene	19	200	4522	106	6	70	1576	17	85	2050	123
Grundy	56	499	9168	107	4	10	478	170	24	183	9
Guthrie	14	1431	15899	503	52	325	1821	117	259	4294	81
Hamilton	398	233	6888	110	154	14	293	67	235	2804	182
Hancock	19	16	309	......	......	12	25	13	3	......	......
Hardin	195	3719	40148	423	5	154	2409	266	504	8287	183
Harrison	418	211	4138	50	130	202	1271	30	806	12856	390
Henry	447	82181	130469	31460	202	1012	14934	84	2810	17624	644
Howard	2429	563	53857	51	42	448	924	220	195	1166	69
Humboldt	155	46	1849	......	6	101	199	53	11	515	16
Ida	44	....	80	......	......	......	......	5	......	......	......
Iowa	2591	4824	36426	6511	491	424	8086	90	977	9467	815
Jackson	1272	20888	75755	6096	755	1269	9122	9	1995	18819	1166
Jasper	2315	7670	88290	2372	34	290	9554	179	1578	19721	728
Jefferson	950	59720	82792	32495	646	1466	17738	77	2742	18748	1712

TABLE VI.—Continued.

COUNTIES.	No. acres in all other crops.	No. fruit trees in bearing.	No. fruit trees not in bearing.	No. pounds grapes raised	No. gallons wine made.	No. pounds hops raised.	No. pounds tobacco raised.	No. acres planted for timber.	No. hives bees.	No. pounds honey taken.	No. pounds beeswax.
Johnson	244	26447	138734	38776	603	754	6358	356	2621	11415	688
Jones	5787	10704	68088	2857	227	11120	4201	579	1704	12232	639
Keokuk	282	21396	67199	7250	207	710	16698	644	2276	20348	786
Kossuth	.....	9	790	10	.....	8	62	19	13	275	.....
Lee	1895	113187	104507	65072	5633	584	10720	130	2741	22713	1028
Linn	395	16266	78907	10351	866	1225	5038	211	2384	8698	625
Louisa	877	35904	101077	3152	67	623	6721	29	2212	13118	602
Lucas	79	12646	37904	652	7	247	6032	306	1086	22659	503
Lyon (not organized)	.....	.....	.....	.....	.....	.....	.....	.....	.....	.....	.....
Madison	326	8275	49792	4968	4	121	6190	121	1319	25487	1015
Mahaska	1038	29997	72685	10739	106	670	15083	212	2649	30050	1052
Marion	4161	17953	54924	11121	49	315	18055	466	2469	39820	1356
Marshall	364	4366	61205	963	140	176	4084	4574	846	11102	436
Mills	121	3221	13699	120	903	.....	2856	144	583	8085	315
Mitchell	85	399	8355	25	291	467	815	11	340	2532	133
Monona	293	563	425	.....	2	100	27	98	280	11545	125
Monroe	658	10770	27733	6990	.....	224	7353	7	1485	24503	616
Montgomery	139	615	3622	.....	.....	.....	1380	4	205	3491	103
Muscatine	1287	44739	77848	19438	591	475	4786	18	1880	15704	498
O'Brien	.....	.....	.....	.....	.....	.....	.....	.....	.....	.....	.....

Osceola (not organized)	......	......	......	......	......	......	......	......	......	......	......
Page	145	2155	22236	513	5	16	3576	72	600	9359	396
Palo Alto	492	......	336	......	......	......	......	......	......	......	......
Plymouth	......	......	3	......	11	......	......	......	......	......	......
Pocahontas	19	......	1027	......	......	......	......	6	......	......	......
Polk	532	22655	80875	11936	172	286	7154	103	1586	23711	613
Pottawattamie	103	1582	11018	1325	30	45	945	154	313	4061	103
Poweshiek	329	5626	41634	928	14	134	4985	170	968	9907	165
Ringgold	145	1160	8632	204	3	10	4709	39	477	9482	97
Sac	38	......	126	......	10	......	50	1	7	65	7
Scott	402	48803	149410	28013	2455	4468	5349	178	1234	9817	1032
Shelby	21	240	777	20	1	......	333	2	96	1536	43
Sioux	2	......	......	..	4	......	......	......	......	......	......
Story	202	1488	34277	366	2	80	2750	77	624	8723	235
Tama	186	2840	49043	858	15	113	1885	185	729	7554	97
Taylor	177	1010	17669	156	......	17	3360	57	559	11225	180
Union	137	598	9985	615	17	6	2201	10	366	7355	214
Van Buren	508	57856	92195	16814	512	774	9295	6	2982	23000	983
Wapello	639	25827	79940	13413	1066	432	8441	29	2501	21747	964
Warren	1691	14106	65040	8510	349	691	7136	398	1846	34112	1061
Washington	3021	35282	91858	25203	954	760	10458	185	2846	13710	1003
Wayne	197	3040	25395	600	......	132	3888	59	1028	18149	303
Webster	1593	1727	16903	205	121	96	1945	14	327	5122	252
Winnebago	18	24	732	......	......	......	24	$\frac{1}{4}$	9	80	......
Winneshiek	210	2268	41069	1748	86	690	1374	14	738	4081	188
Woodbury	1	2	238	......	......	......	60	1	43	1232	15
Worth	16	11	843	......	......	83	50	6	......	......	......
Wright	64	25	2118	......	15	2	103	28	35	450	50
Total	63116	1075177	3629789	549179	29495	48653	385002	48774	85727	896745	36266

TABLE VII.

EXHIBITING THE STATISTICS OF FARM ANIMALS, &c., IN THE STATE OF IOWA, BY COUNTIES.

COUNTIES.	No. of hogs of all ages.	No. of cattle of all ages.	No. milch cows.	No. pounds butter made.	No. pounds cheese made.	No. work oxen.	No. sheep in 1866.	No. pounds wool shorn in 1866.	No. sheep in 1867.	No. horses of all ages.	No. mules and asses of all ages.	No. dogs.	Value of sheep killed by dogs.	Value of sheep killed by wolves.
Adair	2049	1879	647	39887	2826	88	3359	11105	3738	860	47	304	104	95
Adams	3028	2698	836	44280	6197	127	7639	24336	7037	1030	121	348	245	572
Allamakee	24956	15132	5527	336895	15213	1299	10439	36795	11657	4864	51	2501	741	1347
Appanoose	29202	15102	4714	277941	6876	765	36930	114828	43689	5597	417	1799	1311	805
Audubon	835	1528	451	20444	2437	40	2073	8209	1632	453	86	132	67	182
Benton	27962	16437	5627	359389	17969	324	19749	61339	20759	7056	162	1991	815	511
Black Hawk	14801	12597	5199	368945	14432	271	15945	59496	15332	5625	152	1782	469	269
Boone	12788	7542	2595	136844	5196	273	16129	62718	17588	3290	192	1125	1961	408
Bremer	10882	9992	3635	238272	2841	284	10032	33110	9943	3960	48	1248	436	300
Buchanan	14298	12607	4605	343449	14494	408	18449	62170	20734	4786	90	1547	1189	794
Buena Vista	58	262	66	3195	....	59	101	367	43	42	.....	20	4	.....
Butler	7801	8962	3001	200304	13730	251	8611	24760	6631	3461	80	916	283	159
Calhoun	473	586	211	15268	530	70	999	2672	888	243	6	81	38	3
Carroll	1097	784	243	10927	40	125	1551	6398	1499	233	3	89	127	95
Cass	3166	3618	1180	59457	13295	96	4879	14817	4701	1472	79	435	16	91
Cedar	49095	24854	8034	547822	10845	198	37084	124810	45773	9923	401	2301	1831	1228
Cerro Gordo	1651	2704	1149	46880	75848	76	2563	9300	2811	944	8	247	160	129
Cherokee	27	321	101	3792	....	33	10	30	10	70	6	33	.....	.....
Chickasaw	6083	8823	2971	213977	8350	490	9850	35001	8800	2735	55	833	666	597
Clarke	15198	7101	2164	117254	4272	197	17797	59067	20529	3081	185	1060	1495	721

Clay	106	483	125	7423	....	121	417	1159	63	104	3	56	......	36
Clayton	37696	20559	7743	506828	17862	1098	16715	56186	16284	8306	371	3390	1119	1596
Clinton	47726	30556	10548	718716	21734	154	13828	45903	15289	12618	377	3596	1441	1587
Crawford	1100	1943	502	20029	60	172	2595	9178	2725	523	36	107	58	223
Dallas	16232	9001	2719	156730	3724	227	19801	74553	23090	3906	430	1143	702	600
Davis	30739	16377	5068	269535	5409	471	41447	123621	45595	6614	981	2104	919	276
Decatur	15674	9757	3072	156973	5031	378	29135	94799	30965	3992	352	1307	989	396
Delaware	27696	18796	6766	448770	74231	454	18946	67792	22945	6988	188	2179	983	1512
Des Moines	38600	17459	6296	365453	3024	365	26278	84837	31630	8122	742	2840	897	662
Dickinson	104	545	192	9200	370	22	35	12	32	113	......	33	......	.....
Dubuque	42509	25754	10006	524093	46473	489	13758	50741	15842	9805	291	4032	922	1701
Emmett	180	1054	254	17240	2000	91	586	1997	954	186	5	48	18½	......
Fayette	21563	16473	6208	421827	24348	638	21406	82108	20392	5988	119	2001	1146	1824
Floyd	6303	6936	2368	162056	7040	210	9079	36179	13361	3284	87	786	692	729
Franklin	2500	2650	993	60336	5910	160	4439	17390	4099	1155	28	349	230	114
Fremont	18471	12074	3645	136251	6485	830	14059	40851	12608	3191	435	1242	752	1561
Greene	4142	2362	768	41372	811	132	6252	22515	5146	1058	40	336	278	66
Grundy	3221	3098	1090	59105	2365	73	6775	23998	6495	1467	25	414	317	157
Guthrie	10099	5186	1498	92820	1170	131	13654	49415	15094	2086	75	630	583	696
Hamilton	2617	3967	1346	79714	20298	187	12018	22623	6410	1422	56	3735	16	2
Hancock	227	504	177	9935	688	19	1063	3814	1000	216	1	52	99	......
Hardin	14377	8451	2961	181871	12453	241	13884	45852	12452	4354	85	1136	1742	1689
Harrison	10471	9415	2843	111730	12000	399	8234	28680	8549	4057	168	731	540	304
Henry	41381	16716	6654	386047	13050	308	52534	180112	62760	8937	482	2732	2226	377
Howard	4024	6116	2304	166807	13611	406	5403	17256	4492	1999	26	649	114	304
Humboldt	579	1504	505	34670	73032	137	2307	9394	1628	492	9	215	125	......
Ida	66	151	48	2850	140	15	3	9	33	38	2	13	......	......
Iowa	28565	16481	5392	324476	20330	860	20432	64942	19834	6040	230	1883	825	724
Jackson	45957	24915	9044	500061	35022	361	18865	66485	20133	9820	150	3483	1030	2433
Jasper	57115	16850	5558	343284	19074	481	51919	167464	55704	7727	565	2356	2526	996
Jefferson	37718	15789	6062	354302	8292	201	47678	161491	52068	8065	672	2534	2729	1003

TABLE VII.—CONTINUED.

COUNTIES.	No. of hogs of all ages.	No. of cattle of all ages.	No. milch cows.	No. pounds butter made.	No. pounds cheese made.	No. work oxen.	No. sheep in 1866.	No. pounds wool shorn in 1866.	No. sheep in 1867.	No. horses of all ages.	No. mules and asses of all ages.	No. dogs.	Value of sheep killed by dogs.	Value of sheep killed by wolves.
Johnson	50611	25706	8536	413392	45199	510	40756	141365	47686	9391	595	2690	1379	1228
Jones	43290	22146	7516	472605	51198	279	22624	81933	24019	8362	151	2430	1145	1242
Keokuk	38110	18529	5673	294732	16463	391	39304	130147	44410	7839	632	2663	2068	432
Kossuth	557	1708	524	21390	400	144	1513	3849	859	555	11	151	18	......
Lee	40084	22248	8145	424605	173283	199	33577	121083	39490	9486	940	3992	5704	1517
Linn	47711	26243	8972	561068	29798	284	33805	118641	36781	10396	401	2730	2354	1086
Louisa	33878	19142	5226	272113	15357	200	24501	82713	27189	7152	449	1839	1434	1828
Lucas	15453	8385	2801	139559	7490	228	18684	51436	18992	3108	248	1069	944	297
Lyon (unorganized)	......	......	......	......	......	......	......	......	......	......	......	......	......	......
Madison	23346	11302	3566	218559	7429	366	37109	126274	38233	4778	480	1421	1016	1455
Mahaska	41879	20259	6113	367638	14237	543	76825	282065	78166	8395	770	2467	1640	903
Marion	47808	19732	6127	339003	11503	497	34547	138769	39463	8490	681	2778	1648	182
Marshall	19959	10473	3843	273254	21291	197	34416	108451	24474	5466	117	1442	1562	814
Mills	11080	10621	3078	151785	7640	345	9047	31245	9931	3334	454	1150	409	235
Mitchell	3788	6899	2641	176976	14029	276	5008	14485	4790	2438	51	701	534	196
Monona	1404	3219	1138	26596	6739	239	3928	14805	11805	794	27	215	71	196
Monroe	21218	12093	3474	162258	3345	462	30802	88486	31877	4549	359	1614	815	391
Montgomery	3864	2657	844	38312	1620	174	4912	19174	6460	991	62	301	99	109
Muscatine	33000	19983	7312	417661	75286	154	20546	61128	19423	9118	580	2432	1809	571
O'Brien	10	50	25	400	200	10	......	......	......	30	3	4	......	......

Osceola (unorganized)														
Page	11857	8172	2609	123262	9231	313	14816	49407	12433	3091	382	1024	526	295
Palo Alto	224	1116	276	16368		91	117	471	70	155	2	71		
Plymouth	97	779	174	3640		136	47		65	120	6	30		
Pocahontas	274	848	274	18590	3650	114	2	8	12	152	2	89		
Polk	29172	16452	5768	289063	13879	252	25321	84970	28806	6818	562	2055	1683	336
Pottawattamie	4549	6424	2475	118390	13200	245	5935	15484	5585	2465	143	846	681	549
Poweshiek	19707	11391	3437	213414	20400	321	29118	101060	34920	4834	345	1299	1126	819
Ringgold	7451	4782	1471	85807	2847	153	10273	31678	13361	1999	159	658	269	552
Sac	340	649	210	10310	458	40	1070	3303	1067	277	1	67	39	190
Scott	42001	21503	9058	543703	31761	116	18211	58343	19236	10363	667	3977	1907	1177
Shelby	1598	1834	913	25605	400	88	3762	11607	3722	730	63	254	123	65
Sioux		17	10	75						7		4		
Story	9628	8170	2783	179864	10109	139	11672	37886	11260	3094	74	900	658	248
Tama	20144	12692	4275	378372	6500	750	21266	69209	18666	5503	128	1581	919	1002
Taylor	8601	5730	1776	93666	4221	210	9513	21102	10273	2105	187	638	237	289
Union	5087	3305	1041	66903	3383	141	9509	31551	11006	1474	91	449	405	342
Van Buren	36136	15689	5733	334660	19262	207	41352	134265	49065	7517	769	2165	1420	474
Wapello	36441	15922	5528	285980	4682	434	55699	138102	54886	6645	820	2686	3155	691
Warren	31523	16287	4775	274576	6113	378	37836	112401	37355	6684	454	1941	2205	500
Washington	41355	22240	6588	439664	25416	400	56301	186767	60997	8988	452	2511	1695	1113
Wayne	13921	9382	2902	146717	4296	355	23725	83418	25088	38014	322	1277	1142	1546
Webster	4982	5860	2012	114288	3801	516	11279	61634	10802	2366	43	733	709	29
Winnebago	288	1010	361	16506	500	142	665	1585	567	146	4	100	26	18
Winneshiek	20933	20149	7868	478321	15018	1221	16577	53399	19856	7306	102	2323	1204	2847
Woodbury	942	3987	941	24665	18052	306	1153	2766	945	594	9	191	6	
Worth	1162	3076	928	49115	2560	279	1583	4834	1818	483	5	143	8	12
Wright	1238	1856	608	33562	10190	96	2786	9402	1583	6055	14	202	12	5
Total	1620089	956169	326559	19192727	1403864	27246	1598226	5323385	1708958	425055	22037	125207	$82612	$ 5655

TABLE VIII.

EXHIBITING THE AGGREGATES OF THE SEVERAL ITEMS IN THE PRECEDING TABLES; AND COMPARING THEM WITH THOSE OF THE CENSUS OF 1865.

ITEMS.	1865.	1867.
Number of dwelling-houses	114351	155758
Number of white males	379746	463537
Number of white females	371379	433316
Total white population	751125	897325
Number of colored males	1804	2508
Number of colored females	1803	2203
Total colored population	3607	4715
Number entitled to vote	146427	181749
Number of militia	94734	125646
Number of foreigners not naturalized	10594	13503
Number between the ages of 5 and 21 years	293565	339618
Number of blind	*259	*412
Number of deaf and dumb	376	368
Number of insane	613	644
Number of miles railroad finished	793	1152
Number of colleges, academies, and universities	41	62
Number of students attending college	2337	3951
Number of acres land inclosed	5327053	8263174
Number of acres sorghum	21452	25796
Number of gallons syrup from sorghum	1443605	2094557
Number of pounds sugar from sorghum	8386	14697
Number of acres Hungarian grass	37894	39436
Number of tons hay from Hungarian grass	63698	58889
Number of acres tame grasses	302899	497460
Number of tons hay from tame grasses	225349	537812
Number of tons hay from wild grass	713119	823153
Number of bushels grass seed	62114	107532
Number of acres spring wheat	827487	983905
Number of bushels harvested	7175784	13912368
Number of acres winter wheat	116965	73425
Number of bushels harvested	1108781	723152
Number of acres oats	577540	504361
Number of bushels harvested	15928777	15861494
Number of acres corn	1727777	1992326
Number of bushels harvested	48471133	56928938
Number of acres rye	48992	35604
Number of bushels harvested	662388	492841
Number of acres barley	51804	48013
Number of bushels harvested	950696	1197729
Number of acres Irish potatoes	40198	42493
Number of bushels harvested	2730811	2666678
Number of bushels sweet potatoes	26222	50390
Number of bushels onions	207638	213285
Number of acres flax	12111	11906
Number of bushels seed harvested	75721	61917
Number of pounds lint	1112753	400053
Number of gallons linseed oil	890	80052
Number of acres in all other crops	202788	63116

* The number of blind in 1865 does not include the inmates of the State Asylum for the Blind at Vinton; the census of 1867, on the contrary, does include the inmates of that Institution.

TABLE VIII.—AGGREGATES—CONTINUED.

ITEMS.	1865.	1867.
Number of fruit trees in bearing	636458	1075177
Number of fruit trees not in bearing	2523905	3629789
Number of hogs of all ages	1037117	1620089
Number of cattle of all ages	901831	956169
Number of milch cows	310137	326559
Number of pounds butter made	14538216	19192727
Number of pounds cheese made	1000738	1403864
Number of work oxen	37717	27246
Number of sheep in 1864	1000541	....
Number of sheep in 1866	....	1598226
Number of pounds wool shorn in 1864	2813620	....
Number of pounds wool shorn in 1866	....	5323385
Number of sheep in 1867	....	1708958
Number of horses of all ages	316702	425055
Number of mules and asses of all ages	14303	22037
Number of dogs	86060	125207
Number of hives bees	87118	85727
Number of pounds honey taken	1128399	896745
Number of pounds beeswax	51434	36266
Number of pounds grapes raised	390409	549179
Number of gallons wine made	30779	29495
Number of pounds hops raised	27847	48653
Number of pounds tobacco raised	753626	385002
Number of acres planted for timber	20285	48774
Number of rods hedging	331741	663063
Number of bushels coal raised, 80 pounds per bushel	1666582	2483010
Value of minerals raised, not including coal	$31875	$320820
Value of manufactures	$7100465	$15957599
Value of agricultural implements, machinery, and wagons	$7707027	$11362402
Value of sheep killed by dogs	....	$82612
Value of sheep killed by wolves	....	$55655
Number of acres land assessed	....	28773400
Assessed value of lands and town lots	....	$189550825
Assessed value of personal property	....	$66966359
Total assessed valuation	....	$256517184

TABLE IX.

SHOWING THE AVERAGE YIELD OF CERTAIN AGRICULTURAL PRODUCTS IN THE SEVERAL COUNTIES OF THE STATE FOR THE YEAR **1866.**

COUNTIES.	Bushels spring wheat.	Bushels winter wheat.	Bushels oats.	Bushels corn.	Bushels rye.	Bushels barley.	Bushels Irish potatoes.	Gallons syrup from sorghum	Pounds wool per sheep.
Adair	15.13	15.00	32.36	24.29	12.50	.....	70.50	76.93	3.31
Adams	13 90	15.00	27.50	17.64	10.72	15.00	63.92	63 28	3.19
Allamakee	13 73	13.14	27.11	24.37	14.00	23.28	63 62	64.40	3.52
Appanoose	10.49	12.09	32.47	19.66	12.32	23.27	55.06	73.04	3.11
Audubon	16.22	....	18.34	12.89	.....	22.00	88.90	82.54	3.96
Benton	15.57	11.63	36.57	29.02	12.83	26.14	78.87	78.86	3.10
Black Hawk	15.67	10.00	41.74	24.91	15.00	22.81	53.75	62 34	3.73
Boone	12.88	12.45	33.25	28.30	19.94	28.75	78 14	77.37	3.89
Bremer	13.61	18.00	30.34	24.45	15.00	27.10	60.08	62.43	3 30
Buchanan	13.87	6.47	27.16	21.23	15.46	21.36	62.90	79 56	3.37
Buena Vista	18.90	.....	23 00	24.15	.....	.....	94.20	58.50	3.63
Butler	13.88	15.00	29.40	22.52	14.00	28.18	97.67	63.42	2.87
Calhoun	20.10	.....	40.30	29 52	.....	40.00	57.08	86.40	2.67
Carroll	17.43	.....	36.00	29.91	.....	25 00	115.93	101.38	4.12
Cass	17.32	26.00	34.83	20.44	.....	19.70	78.17	85 21	3.04
Cedar	13.69	7.74	32.20	30.41	15.93	23.96	45.12	96.30	3.37
Cerro Gordo	12.11	.....	29 22	21.13	.....	17.04	91.83	55 16	3.63
Cherokee	15.00	.....	30.00	11.70	.....	.....	108.17	52.46	3.00
Chickasaw	13.16	.....	26 49	17.94	20.00	19.88	83.20	64.32	3.57
Clarke	13.46	11.25	28 74	19 77	12.73	....	53.96	62.50	3.32
Clay	18.26	. ...	27.00	13.05	.....	.....	81.53	51 00	2.78
Clayton	15.24	8.52	26.68	28.40	15.70	26.20	57.50	111.24	3.36
Clinton	14.57	11.21	31.78	26 79	16.67	25.63	26.82	109.21	3.32
Crawford	22.20	.....	35.73	25.95	27.50	60.00	67.24	39.30	3.53
Dallas	13.88	9.00	34.49	33.53	13.78	25.30	103.53	43 49	3.76
Davis	7.27	11.22	27.24	18.15	11.17	72 00	50.86	66.79	2.98
Decatur	10 93	11.89	28.46	11 96	13.07	9.68	31.63	43.97	3.25
Delaware	14.51	6.00	31.52	22.66	16.52	25.04	57.27	74.50	3.57
Des Moines	10.69	9.03	29.91	32 90	12.72	21.56	56.85	90 26	3.23
Dickinson	15.82	.....	32.02	14 86	.....	30 00	101.30	33.50	.35
Dubuque	14.44	5.00	31.74	28.74	18.62	25.41	28.31	69.82	3.69
Emmett	16.54	.....	.20	23.95	.....	.....	85.02	38.60	3.40
Fayette	13 43	13.41	27.51	24.29	9.55	21.06	76.36	69.57	3.84
Floyd	12.11	8.00	26.38	22 56	14.05	17.33	83 54	56.88	3.98
Franklin	13.88	.....	26.87	23.33	....	7.36	51.36	49 58	3.91
Fremont	18.38	9.69	32.52	14.37	18.44	17.34	68.44	100.69	2.91
Greene	15 94	.....	37.06	23 36	8.08	15.00	98.67	97.58	3.60
Grundy	14 96	....	37.17	25 84	12.25	21.90	93.58	55 75	3 54
Guthrie	15.54	15.53	38.88	34.55	12.00	80.00	116.40	109.20	3.62

TABLE IX — AVERAGES — CONTINUED.

COUNTIES.	Bushels spring wheat.	Bushels winter wheat.	Bushels oats.	Bushels corn.	Bushels rye.	Bushels barley.	Bushels Irish potatoes.	Gallons syrup from sorghum.	Pounds wool per sheep.
Hamilton	13.20	12.84	35.80	23.16	12.00	23 00	40.30	60.24	1.88
Hancock	10.45	.....	36.43	17.90	.....	38.00	111.32	29.62	3.58
Hardin	15.20	.....	37.82	27 54	11.96	19.42	77.53	65.21	3 30
Harrison	20.40	14.37	40.94	28.92	18.00	25.55	78.12	73.40	3.48
Henry	9.41	10.52	31.11	36 03	10.54	18.85	84 55	97 07	3.42
Howard	10 48	.....	18.91	17.53	13.00	17.91	84.67	51.18	3.20
Humboldt	18.59	.....	37.60	31.78	.....	28.00	95.38	53.68	4.07
Ida	20.66	.....	43.65	16.68	.....	32.66	76.00	90.00	3.00
Iowa	14.85	7.52	35.77	33.41	16 28	28.16	65.07	94.04	3.18
Jackson	13.97	9 70	30.35	29.01	14.70	22.76	42.02	89.73	3.52
Jasper	18.69	8.47	36.15	40.00	15.49	31.70	90.51	93.65	3.22
Jefferson	9.44	9.73	28.81	34.08	12.82	19.93	69.26	102.54	3.39
Johnson	15.20	9 36	35.00	32.49	16.38	23.05	43.09	90.52	3.47
Jones	14.49	9.95	27.81	26.24	17.95	24.04	27.59	89.73	3.62
Keokuk	11.05	9.44	38.92	33.46	14.10	27.20	56.15	89.58	3.31
Kossuth	14.34	.....	25.76	15.92	.....	16.60	74.28	28.24	2.54
Lee	9.43	7.57	26.97	29.19	12.83	19.48	72.35	96.75	3.61
Linn	13.23	11.00	32.79	27 94	15.61	22.10	50.54	82.79	3 51
Louisa	11.27	11.85	30.98	36.63	13.21	19.89	70.62	99.89	3.38
Lucas	9.81	11.15	31.10	22.90	44.11	16.31	75.08	70.46	2.75
Lyon (not organized)	.....	.....	.....	.....	.....	.....	....	....	.....
Madison	15.46	11.62	31.34	23.48	13.41	42.00	96.15	83.21	3.40
Mahaska	13 00	11.28	34.08	39.08	14.58	19.76	93.70	109.58	3.67
Marion	12.89	9.95	31.61	37.28	14.15	20.45	89.04	95.20	4.01
Marshall	14.37	15 70	48.36	30.37	11.40	26.00	89.34	71.84	3.15
Mills	16.46	5.00	38 00	31.65	18 40	27.80	81.70	79.02	3.45
Mitchell	13.71	.....	30.89	20.91	9 37	22 88	100.36	58.94	2.89
Monona	23.71	.....	44.65	25.18	15.50	59.00	33.63	56.06	3.77
Monroe	9.72	12.04	24 56	24.29	14.27	16.30	75.67	59.83	2.87
Montgomery	14 00	14.67	34.00	26.44	9.70	20 00	72.87	77.17	3.90
Muscatine	12.78	7.61	35.10	32.64	14.79	26.78	49.67	101.09	2.97
O'Brien	20.00	.....	30.00	35.00	.....	.....	75.00	....	.....
Osceola (not organized)	.....	.....	.....	.....	.....	.....	....	....	.....
Page	10.55	15.00	28.98	17.96	12.62	13.40	93.78	54.14	3.33
Palo Alto	20.34	.....	27.70	13.44	.....	.....	96 24	71.15	4.02
Plymouth	22.38	.....	34.24	27.98	.....	30.75	124.00	70.00	.....
Pocahontas	15.70	.....	28.28	20.18	.....	.....	69.03	43.00	4.00
Polk	14.86	13.63	37 54	37.59	14.72	21.50	96.44	64.18	3.36
Pottawattamie	16.26	....	32.12	26.06	31.80	22.97	75.46	84.01	2.60
Poweshiek	15.33	12.60	35.18	36.22	17.41	19.25	73.66	88.23	3.47
Ringgold	11.19	8.00	27.00	11.55	10.50	18.00	50.72	42.00	3.08
Sac	22.75	....	33.61	21.55	.....	.....	95.32	58.64	3 09
Scott	14.65	10.07	29.03	32.87	16.46	27.37	63.98	112.52	3.20

TABLE IX.—AVERAGES—CONTINUED.

COUNTIES.	Bushels spring wheat.	Bushels winter wheat.	Bushels oats.	Bushels corn.	Bushels rye.	Bushels barley.	Bushels Irish potatoes.	Gallons syrup from sorghum.	Pounds wool ℔ sheep.
Shelby	18.19	.....	32 67	21.55	.....	.....	97.04	82.07	3.08
Sioux	12.88	....	4 00	20.00	.....	....	200.00	....	.....
Story	12.88	15.00	34.70	27.02	12.25	16.80	76.66	68.52	3.24
Tama	18.55	8.60	36.74	32 24	16.70	29.00	87.34	89.32	3.27
Taylor	12.06	5.04	27.17	16.60	15.12	.....	55.43	40.13	2.22
Union	11.36	11.07	29.72	17.00	13.30	10.00	69.82	57.18	3.32
Van Buren	8.00	8.93	29.36	27.11	12.15	17.25	52.19	92.72	3.25
Wapello	10.09	10.94	27.16	27.40	13.53	5.15	85.46	89.32	2.48
Warren	15.01	13.52	33.10	34.32	12.56	7.34	100.79	84.91	2 97
Washington	11.78	8.43	35.10	34.67	13.63	25.44	62.34	101.60	3.32
Wayne	6 60	11.88	31.38	16.83	13.00	20.00	52.27	53.34	3.51
Webster	17.12	.....	31.92	15.73	8.17	24.00	73.00	53.18	5.46
Winnebago	14.45	....	29.00	23.59	.....	9.31	108.84	28.82	2.38
Winneshiek	14.37	15 00	28.64	23.63	16.21	23.24	73.96	57.23	3.22
Woodbury	25 57	25.00	42 56	24.09	....	1.13	85.21	99.15	2.40
Worth	13.71	.....	30.87	20.25	.....	14.80	103.04	52.88	3.05
Wright	13.92	.....	33.46	24.54	4.00	17.22	69.84	49.44	3.37

TABLE X.

EXHIBITING THE STATISTICS OF ASSESSMENT, VALUATION, AND TAXATION, THE AMOUNT OF LAND INCLOSED, THE NUMBER OF DWELLING-HOUSES, AND THE TOTAL POPULATION, IN THE SEVERAL COUNTIES OF THE STATE.

COUNTIES.	Number of acres of land assessed.	Number of acres of land inclosed.	Assessed value of land per acre.	Assessed value of lands and town lots.	Assessed value of personal property.	Total valuation.	State tax at 2½ mills.	No. of dwelling-houses.	Total population.
Adair	358808	6034	$3.20	$1165724	$91732	$1257456	$3143.63	262	1594
Adams	259791	12388	2.99	814009	157584	971593	2428.98	390	2317
Allamakee	406163	117620	3.76	1781368	701231	2482599	6206.50	2762	16003
Appanoose	324648	95920	5.48	1916141	998507	2914648	7286.62	2072	13064
Audubon	121096	3429	3.02	376831	68122	444953	1112.38	139	790
Benton	459498	118226	5.72	3039932	997069	4037001	10092.50	2464	14772
Black Hawk	351138	98693	6.65	3208707	1034360	4243067	10607.67	2742	16036
Boone	304104	34147	4.61	1722223	522287	2244510	5611.27	1482	9861
Bremer	267115	70964	5.06	1589694	378937	1968631	4921.58	1586	9337
Buchanan	359104	96629	6.14	2701115	714605	3415720	8539.30	2090	12231
Buena Vista	141051	344	2.00	382102	5318	387420	968.55	29	151
Butler	360608	57167	4.00	1501213	303423	1804636	4511.59	1144	6542
Calhoun	297095	1619	2.69	802850	35790	838640	2096.60	114	546
Carroll	223680	2371	3.08	692356	43296	735652	1839.13	132	688
Cass	306452	13309	3.57	1155894	194268	1350162	3375.40	388	2479
Cedar	364916	177749	9.13	3635839	1325840	4961679	12404.20	2747	16076
Cerro Gordo	359642	13337	3.14	1157297	70679	1227967	3069.95	326	1988
Cherokee	59980	208	1.67	101925	11338	113263	283.16	40	209
Chickasaw	315022	47399	4.00	1346909	186535	1533444	3833.61	1048	6220

TABLE X.—CONTINUED.

COUNTIES.	Number of acres of land assessed.	Number of acres of land inclosed.	Assessed value of land per acre.	Assessed value of lands and town lots.	Assessed value of personal property.	Total valuation.	State tax at 2½ mills.	No. of dwelling-houses.	Total population.
Clarke	270478	45634	$4.16	$1233808	$502451	$1735259	$4338.15	1025	6244
Clay	......	751	......	......	......	......	......	58	369
Clayton	492294	172415	6.86	4367688	1341806	5709494	14273.72	3918	22879
Clinton	445078	228389	8.04	5188965	1668568	6857533	17143.83	4810	27234
Crawford	264382	5347	3.15	863522	55178	918700	2296.75	168	1070
Dallas	367404	34667	4.84	1884892	1194555	3059447	7648.62	1156	7538
Davis	315290	117096	5.68	1937633	1058512	2996145	7490.36	2101	13517
Decatur	339593	58141	4.00	1423811	423906	1847717	4619.28	1400	8501
Delaware	363137	156644	6.90	2829687	818150	3647837	9119.59	2670	14463
Des Moines	256846	126321	12.54	5234926	2504524	7739450	19348.62	4013	23444
Dickinson	2991	1435	2.05	6125	29051	30176	75.44	97	509
Dubuque	381650	169433	8.56	6992217	3971503	10763720	26909.30	6130	38860
Emmett	16134	1423	1.97	35987	45377	81364	203.41	114	708
Fayette	460035	128431	4.89	2425278	618340	3043618	7609.05	2492	14993
Floyd	323084	45460	4.04	1503780	320432	1824212	4560.53	1189	6731
Franklin	322809	12520	3.07	1001612	92954	1094566	2736.42	407	2321
Fremont	283199	44366	4.85	1537109	635332	2172441	5431.10	1148	7013
Greene	317851	10548	3.79	1278696	234846	1513542	3783.85	424	2353
Grundy	317692	20306	3.36	1070580	118735	1189315	2973.29	367	2119
Guthrie	333910	24115	4.01	1377978	287893	1665871	4164.48	654	3906

Hamilton	336915	15781	3.26	1183111	206656	1389767	3474.42	546	3154
Hancock	344890	1919	2.15	7737223	13593	750816	1877.04	63	357
Hardin	336921	64476	4.06	1470214	423090	1893304	4733 26	1721	9345
Harrison	355427	24811	5.37	1986494	605793	2529287	6480.72	1009	5836
Henry	265893	132534	9 25	3262542	1532095	4794637	11986.59	3374	20110
Howard	291000	3582	3.64	1140744	174664	1315408	3288 52	776	4401
Humboldt	156912	4842	2.46	388129	67512	455641	1139.10	237	1307
Ida	....	115	......	....	......	....	....	18	90
Iowa	389101	97789	5.93	2508182	1018185	3526367	8815.92	2090	12390
Jackson	397578	168152	6.88	3236131	1029533	4265664	10664.16	2575	19970
Jasper	449175	107596	6.29	3138455	1477605	4616060	11540 15	2639	16239
Jefferson	273326	121471	7.33	2263270	969544	3232814	8082.03	2811	16420
Johnson	388507	160821	8.78	4286661	1663771	5950432	14876.08	3634	21641
Jones	353740	158528	7.40	2865462	1143298	4008760	10021.90	2792	16228
Keokuk	369089	124118	6.22	2446444	1019170	3465614	8664.03	2611	15429
Kossuth	165829	4007	2.07	349474	46041	395515	988.78	259	1573
Lee	320609	164223	11.45	7246069	3009215	10255284	25638.21	5388	31417
Linn	448306	174320	8.76	5041544	1800913	6842457	17106 14	4148	24549
Louisa	247142	108619	7.11	1931939	907978	2839917	7099 79	2275	11885
Lucas	272285	45128	4.79	1507507	529974	2037481	5093.70	1213	7749
Lyon (not organized)	....	....	......	....	....	....	....	......	......
Madison	359173	64333	5.89	2225433	953738	3179171	7947.94	1562	9764
Mahaska	359686	141172	8.97	3687115	1828080	5515195	13787.99	3128	18693
Marion	354104	120276	7.54	2988429	1542771	4531200	11328.00	3556	20181
Marshall	330938	79230	6.37	2236598	924669	3161267	7903.17	2102	11513
Mills	258660	35950	5.00	1401810	709624	2111434	5278 58	1249	6994
Mitchell	286436	38947	4.10	1305574	308027	1613601	4034.00	1025	6150
Monona	303255	6937	3.29	1056502	143042	1199544	2998.86	281	1664
Monroe	270164	70218	6.56	1975525	833836	2809361	7023.40	1735	10208
Montgomery	173600	9363	3.16	577149	147827	724976	1812.44	344	2072
Muscatine	272567	149718	11.86	4186560	1711631	5898191	14745.48	6475	20699
O'Brien	112589	123	2.00	225178	3155	228333	570.83	7	20

TABLE X.—CONTINUED.

COUNTIES.	Number of acres of land assessed.	Number of acres of land inclosed.	Assessed value of land per acre.	Assessed value of lands and town lots.	Assessed value of personal property.	Total valuation.	State tax at 2½ mills.	No. of dwelling-houses.	Total population.
Osceola (not organized)	......	......	......	......	......	......	......	......	......
Page	335689	34191	$ 3.72	$1346141	$452426	$1798567	$4496.42	956	6025
Palo Alto	......	951	2 00	......	......	......	......	71	413
Plymouth	53813	675	2.00	107726	23847	131573	328.93	......	214
Pocahontas	250063	1424	2.00	500126	22352	522478	1306.19	87	453
Polk	362098	81801	8.80	5608883	1960423	7569306	18923.26	3436	22630
Pottawattamie	458427	22580	6.00	4412981	844391	5257372	13143.43	1571	8733
Poweshiek	356256	69417	6.03	2320714	944952	3270666	8176.66	1653	9888
Ringgold	343862	23130	3.30	1160390	214644	1375034	3437.58	610	3888
Sac	166361	2593	2.04	349875	30164	380039	950.10	103	595
Scott	284906	193381	12.74	6367323	2346496	8713819	21784 55	5638	34362
Shelby	208487	4616	3.20	675614	168616	844230	2110.57	204	1213
Sioux	175454	40	2 00	351858	3509	355367	888.42	4	18
Story	359241	40373	3.96	1507869	317841	1825710	4554.27	1111	6888
Tama	450773	77354	5.14	2548770	880989	3429759	8574.40	1891	11165
Taylor	380540	26941	3.11	1237861	544259	1782120	4455.30	706	4546
Union	271867	18271	3.33	947630	191690	1139320	2848 30	655	3010
Van Buren	305350	123684	8.07	2814693	1341458	4156151	10390.38	2780	16293

Wapello	272761	113821	7.81	3261505	1913062	5174567	12936 42	3213	18930
Warren	355408	83074	7.02	2715735	1064382	3780117	9450 29	2154	13162
Washington	357867	155347	7.37	3143992	1625421	4769413	11923.53	3005	17675
Wayne	333799	57974	4.32	1489661	439008	1928669	4821.67	1317	7657
Webster	438342	27117	3.08	1694430	289213	1983643	4959 11	1039	5631
Winnebago	244918	1429	2.00	491726	24166	515892	1289.73	128	785
Winneshiek	438027	179265	4.09	2090910	639724	2730634	6826 58	3438	19302
Woodbury	221233	3413	3.00	962369	256411	1218780	3046 95	346	1970
Worth	244639	7593	2.15	536630	79756	616386	1540.96	269	1543
Wright	346634	6832	2.19	764522	59095	823617	2059.04	231	1332
Total	28773400	8263174	......	$189550825	66966359	$256517184	$641292.88	155558	902040

NOTE.—The statistics of assessment, valuation, and taxation above have been obtained from the office of the Auditor of State, and are here inserted for purposes of reference and comparison.—[SECRETARY OF STATE.

TABLE XI.

SHOWING THE POPULATION OF THE SEVERAL COUNTIES OF IOWA AT EACH ENUMERATION SINCE THE ORGANIZATION OF THE TERRITORY OF WISCONSIN.

COUNTIES.	WIS. TERR.	IOWA TERRITORY.				STATE OF IOWA.											
	1836.	1838.	1840.	1844.	1846.	1847.	1849.	1850.	1851.	1852.	1854.	1856.	1859.	1860.	1863.	1865.	1867.
Adair											150	663	1011	984	900	1071	1594
Adams											339	1019	1413	1533	1638	1818	2317
Allamakee							227	777	1300	2000	4266	7709	10843	12237	13465	13957	16003
Appanoose					1300	948	1281	3131	3951	4243	6265	9075	11449	11931	11866	10748	13064
Audubon												283	365	454	388	510	790
Benton					297	312	312	673	753	1237	2623	6247	8063	8496	9561	11245	14772
Black Hawk										315	2514	5538	7095	8244	10014	12306	16036
Boone							419	756	890	1024	1678	3518	4018	4232	4607	5236	9861
Bremer										309	1095	3228	4336	4915	5404	7224	9337
Buchanan					149	250	406	519	1006	1023	2299	5125	6918	7906	8294	10037	12231
Buena Vista														57			151
Butler										73		2141	3504	3724	4142	5006	6542
Calhoun												119	136	147	170	224	546
Carroll												251	250	281	297	400	688
Cass											416	815	1489	1612	1623	1895	2479
Cedar		557	1225	2217	2862	2809	3183	3941	4084	4971	7643	9481	12175	12949	13274	14041	16076
Cerro Gordo												632	855	940	1007	1311	1988
Cherokee													85	58	20	64	209
Chickasaw										400	588	2651	3816	4336	4397	5355	6220
Clarke										549	1626	3978	5006	5427	5693	5716	6244
Clay														52			369
Clayton		274	1044	1200	1500	2176	3000	3873	5000	6318	9337	15187	18669	20728	21235	21922	22879
Clinton		445	800	1201	1300	1570	2044	2835	3001	3822	7306	13441	17395	18938	19821	22405	27234
Crawford												235	429	383	456	574	1070
Dallas						164	635	812	925	1216	2392	3991	4058	5244	5088	5886	7538

Davis	.....	.....	.....	2622	3400	4464	4939	7264	7454	7553	9787	11258	13323	13764	13959	13123	13517
Decatur	.....	.....	.....	.....	.....	.....	.....	965	1016	1184	3025	6229	8238	8677	8373	8052	8501
Delaware	.....	.....	171	300	781	1111	1300	1759	2000	2615	4637	8099	10024	11024	11667	12508	14463
Des Moines	6257	4605	5546	9109	9391	10071	11649	12914	14488	12575	16700	20198	20781	19611	21213	19894	23444
Dickinson	.....	.....	.....	.....	.....	.....	.....	.....	.....	.....	.....	.....	121	180	189	300	509
Dubuque	4274	2381	3056	4049	6030	7440	9185	10841	11000	12500	16662	25871	30581	31164	30839	33078	38860
Emmett	.....	.....	.....	.....	.....	.....	.....	.....	.....	.....	.....	.....	.....	105	.....	368	708
Fayette	.....	.....	.....	.....	.....	.....	.....	825	1200	2065	5042	8375	11391	12073	12739	13124	14992
Floyd	.....	.....	.....	.....	.....	.....	.....	.....	.....	.....	.....	2448	3458	3744	4018	4886	6731
Franklin	.....	.....	.....	.....	.....	.....	.....	.....	.....	.....	.....	780	1159	1309	1448	1899	2321
Fremont	.....	.....	.....	.....	.....	.....	.....	1244	1600	2044	3006	3368	4327	5074	4778	5698	7013
Greene	.....	.....	.....	.....	.....	.....	.....	.....	.....	.....	.....	1089	1424	1374	1416	1659	2353
Grundy	.....	.....	.....	.....	.....	.....	.....	.....	.....	.....	.....	435	680	793	1024	1332	2119
Guthrie	.....	.....	.....	.....	.....	.....	.....	.....	222	300	772	2149	2754	3058	3205	3249	3906
Hamilton	.....	.....	.....	.....	.....	.....	.....	.....	.....	.....	.....	.....	655	1699	1602	2023	3154
Hancock	.....	.....	.....	.....	.....	.....	.....	.....	.....	.....	.....	.....	121	179	240	292	357
Hardin	.....	.....	.....	.....	.....	.....	.....	.....	.....	300	1259	4033	3323	5440	5376	6813	9345
Harrison	.....	.....	.....	.....	.....	.....	.....	.....	.....	.....	1065	1900	3132	3621	3663	4265	5836
Henry	.....	3058	3784	6017	6875	6759	7229	8707	8915	9633	10159	15395	16299	18701	16780	17816	20110
Howard	.....	.....	.....	.....	.....	.....	.....	.....	.....	.....	.....	444	3017	3168	3382	3871	4401
Humboldt	.....	.....	.....	.....	.....	.....	.....	.....	.....	.....	.....	.....	519	332	394	606	1307
Ida	.....	.....	.....	.....	.....	.....	.....	.....	.....	.....	.....	.....	38	43	.....	.....	90
Iowa	.....	.....	.....	.....	.....	435	600	822	1000	1323	2307	4873	7098	8029	8544	10258	12390
Jackson	.....	881	1452	2000	4767	4639	5677	7210	7597	8231	12166	14077	17710	18493	19158	19097	19970
Jasper	.....	.....	.....	.....	.....	560	1223	1288	1492	1674	3466	7490	9195	9883	10627	12095	16239
Jefferson	.....	.....	2780	5694	6000	8463	8825	9997	10081	10225	11117	13305	14478	15038	14649	14772	16420
Johnson	.....	237	1504	2949	3000	3387	4010	4474	5061	5788	8467	14457	16900	17573	17184	18778	21641
Jones	.....	241	475	1112	1758	1779	2140	3007	3400	4201	6075	9835	13475	13306	13495	14376	16228
Keokuk	.....	.....	.....	.....	.....	2918	3953	4822	5105	5306	7299	10646	12329	13271	13412	13996	15429
Kossuth	.....	.....	.....	.....	.....	.....	.....	.....	.....	.....	.....	377	310	416	365	694	1573

TABLE XI.—Continued.

COUNTIES.	Wis. Terr.	Iowa Territory.				State of Iowa.											
	1836.	1838.	1840.	1844.	1846.	1847.	1849.	1850.	1851.	1852.	1854.	1856.	1859.	1860.	1863.	1865.	1867.
Lee	......	2839	6095	9830	12860	13231	15000	18783	17625	20360	22590	27273	31242	29232	28523	28063	31417
Linn	......	205	1385	2643	3411	3954	4762	5444	6160	6890	10802	14702	17720	18947	18700	20754	24549
Louisa	......	1180	1925	3238	3644	3648	4155	5067	5100	5476	7341	9568	10805	10370	10673	10948	11885
Lucas	......	......	......	......	......	......	......	471	1025	1046	1921	4408	5287	5766	6257	6352	7746
Lyon (unorgan-[ized)	......	......	......	......	......	......	......	......	......	......	......	......	......	......	......	......	......
Madison	......	......	......	......	......	......	701	1174	1492	1832	3122	5508	7071	7339	7934	8214	9764
Mahaska	......	......	......	......	2942	3774	5559	5986	6758	7479	9093	13050	14515	14816	16249	17082	18693
Marion	......	......	......	......	1360	2350	3797	5412	5809	6289	9315	14060	16167	16813	17318	18719	20181
Marshall	......	......	......	......	......	......	......	338	454	710	1607	4460	5713	6015	7550	8759	11513
Mills	......	......	......	......	......	......	......	......	......	1463	2171	310[illegible]	4381	4481	6287	5218	6994
Mitchell	......	......	......	......	......	......	......	......	......	......	......	1911	3291	3409	3375	4176	6150
Monona	......	......	......	......	......	......	......	......	......	......	222	459	885	832	931	1096	1664
Monroe	......	......	......	386	400	1222	2000	2886	3125	3430	4577	6860	8377	8612	9322	9435	10208
Montgomery	......	......	......	......	......	......	......	......	......	......	233	872	1094	1256	1218	1535	2072
Muscatine	......	1247	1942	2882	1485	3010	4516	5773	6170	6812	9555	12569	15503	16444	16089	17241	20699
O'Brien	......	......	......	......	......	......	......	......	......	......	......	......	......	8	......	......	20
Osceola (unor-[ganized)	......	......	......	......	......	......	......	......	......	......	......	......	......	......	......	......	......
Page	......	......	......	......	......	......	......	551	534	636	1148	1964	3674	4419	4662	5211	6025
Palo Alto	......	......	......	......	......	......	......	......	......	......	......	......	131	132	142	216	413
Plymouth	......	......	......	......	......	......	......	......	......	......	......	......	112	148	93	105	214
Pocahontas	......	......	......	......	......	......	......	......	......	......	......	......	126	103	12[illegible]	215	453
Polk	......	......	......	......	1301	1792	4214	4444	6000	5939	5368	9417	11238	11625	12956	16473	22630
Pottawattamie	......	......	......	......	......	......	6552	7828	5758	5057	3060	3498	5012	4968	4737	5388	8733
Poweshiek	......	......	......	......	......	......	443	615	742	915	1953	4460	5338	5668	6370	7796	9388
Ringgold	......	......	......	......	......	......	......	......	......	......	......	1472	2507	2923	3039	3089	3888
Sac	......	......	......	......	......	......	......	......	......	......	......	251	269	246	234	304	595

Scott	......	1252	2193	2750	3000	3652	4837	5987	6016	8628	12671	21521	25861	25959	26327	28474	34362
Shelby	......	......	......	......	......	......	......	......	......	......	328	456	784	818	828	900	1213
Sioux	......	......	......	......	......	......	......	......	......	......	......	......	......	10	......	......	18
Story	......	......	......	......	......	......	......	......	......	214	836	2868	3826	4051	4368	5918	6888
Tama	......	......	......	......	......	......	......	......	......	262	1163	3520	5346	5285	7027	7882	11165
Taylor	......	......	......	......	......	......	......	204	393	479	891	2079	3468	3590	3757	4299	4546
Union	......	......	......	......	......	......	......	......	......	80	81	806	1993	2012	2420	2528	3010
Van Buren	......	3174	6166	9019	9870	10203	11577	12269	13000	12753	13843	15921	15879	17081	15862	15599	16292
Wapello	......	......	......	2814	4422	5660	7255	8479	8500	8888	10521	13246	15060	14518	16729	18794	18930
Warren	......	......	......	......	......	......	649	943	1193	1488	4446	8000	9150	10281	10932	11150	13162
Washington	......	283	1571	3120	3483	3518	4434	4991	5079	5881	7560	11113	13366	14235	15003	15739	17675
Wayne	......	......	......	......	......	......	......	341	500	794	1665	4182	5860	6409	6522	6327	7657
Webster	......	......	......	......	......	......	......	......	......	372	907	3088	2596	2504	2858	3772	5631
Winneshiek	......	......	......	......	......	182	300	546	800	1523	3315	7506	12211	13942	15421	15421	19303
Winnebago	......	......	......	......	......	......	......	......	......	......	......	......	188	168	204	298	785
Woodbury	......	......	......	......	......	......	......	......	......	......	170	2000	1100	1119	1106	1295	1970
Worth	......	......	......	......	......	......	......	......	......	......	......	......	759	756	895	1143	1543
Wright	......	......	......	......	......	......	......	......	......	......	......	427	632	653	693	908	1332
Total	10531	22859	43114	75152	97588	116651	152988	191982	204774	230713	326013	519055	638775	674913	701732	754699	902040

NOTE.—Calhoun county was originally called Fox county; Lyon was called Buncombe; Monroe, Kishkehosh; Washington, Slaughter; and Woodbury, Wahkaw. Hamilton was created as Risley county, and subsequently formed a part of Webster. Humboldt county, originally erected under that name, was afterwards divided between Kossuth and Webster; more recently, the territory which had been annexed to Kossuth, with the northern half of that detached to Webster, was re-erected into the county of Humboldt. The northern part of Kossuth county was at first Bancroft county, which, with the northern half of Humboldt was united with Kossuth in 1855; subsequently the territory obtained from Humboldt was again detached. Webster county was at first called Yell county, which in 1855 was united with Risley and two tiers of townships in Humboldt to form Webster; in 1857, Hamilton county was detached, and also one tier of townships to Humboldt.

ALPHABETICAL LIST OF POST-OFFICES IN THE STATE NOVEMBER 1, 1867.

Names of Post-offices.	Counties.	Names of Post-offices.	Counties.
Abingdon	Jefferson	Belle Plaine	Benton
Ackley	Hardin	Bellevue	Jackson
Adel	Dallas	Belmond	Wright
Adelphi	Polk	Belvidere	Monona
Afton	Union	Bennington	Marion
Agency City	Wapello	Benson Grove	Winnebago
Agricola	Mahaska	Benton	Mills
Ainsworth	Washington	Bentonsport	Van Buren
Albany	Davis	Berlin	Hardin
Albia	Monroe	Bertram	Linn
Albion	Marshall	Bethel	Fayette
Alden	Hardin	Bethlehem	Wayne
Algona	Kossuth	Big Grove	Pottawattamie
Allamakee	Allamakee	Bigler's Grove	Harrison
Allen's Grove	Scott	Big Mound	Lee
Allison	Dubuque	Big Rock	Scott
Alton	Dallas	Birmingham	Van Buren
Ames	Story	Blairsburg	Hamilton
Amish	Johnson	Blairstown	Benton
Amity	Scott	Blakesburg	Wapello
Anamosa	Jones	Bloomfield	Davis
Andrew	Jackson	Blue Grass	Scott
Aplington	Butler	Bluffton	Winneshiek
Apple Grove	Polk	Bon Accord	Johnson
Arbor Hill	Adair	Bonaparte	Van Buren
Arcola	Monona	Boone	Dallas
Argo	Lucas	Boonsboro	Boone
Armstrong's Grove	Emmett	Border Plains	Webster
Ashland	Wapello	Botany	Shelby
Atalissa	Muscatine	Botavia	Jefferson
Atlanta	Buchanan	Bottom	Monona
Attica	Marion	Bowen's Prairie	Jones
Auburn	Mahaska	Boyer River	Crawford
Augusta	Des Noines	Boylan's Grove	Butler
Aurora	Keokuk	Bradford	Chickasaw
Avon	Polk	Brandon	Buchanan
		Brighton	Washington
Bach Grove	Wright	Bristol	Worth
Baden	Keokuk	Brookfield	Clinton
Badger Hill	Tama	Brooklyn	Poweshiek
Baker	Jefferson	Brookville	Jefferson
Ballyclough	Dubuque	Brownsville	Mitchell
Bangor	Marshall	Brush Creek	Fayette
Bankston	Dubuque	*Buck Creek	Bremer
Barclay	Black Hawk	Buck Horn	Mahaska
Barryville	Delaware	Buckingham	Tama
Bartlett	Fremont	Buena Vista	Clinton
Beacon	Mahaska	Buffalo	Scott
Bear Grove	Guthrie	Buffalo Fork	Kossuth
Bedford	Taylor	Buffalo Grove	Buchanan
Beetrace	Appanoose	Burgess	Clinton
Belfast	Lee	Burke	Benton
Belgrove	Butler	Burlington	Des Moines
Belinda	Lucas	Burr Oak	Winneshiek
Belle Fontaine	Mahaska	Burr Oak Springs	"

* Not in the lists in the preceding pages, having been reported to the Census Board or otherwise ascertained since those pages were printed.

Alphabetical List of Post offices—Continued.

Names of Post-offices.	Counties.	Names of Post-offices.	Counties.
Busti	Howard	Clanton	Madison
Butler	Keokuk	Clarence	Cedar
Butler Center	Butler	Clarinda	Page
Butlerville	Tama	Clarksville	Butler
		Clay	Washington
Cairo	Louisa	Clayford	Jones
Cal[a]mus	Clinton	Clay's Grove	Lee
Caldwell	Appanoose	Clayton	Clayton
Caledonia	Ringgold	Clayton Center	"
Calhoun	Harrison	Clear Creek	Allamakee
Calmer	Winneshiek	Clear Lake	Cerro Gordo
Caloma	Marion	Clermont	Fayette
Camanche	Clinton	Clifton	Louisa
Cambria	Wayne	Clinton	Clinton
Cambridge	Story	Clio	Wayne
Campton	Delaware	Clyde	Jasper
Canton	Jackson	Coal Creek	Keokuk
Cardiff	Mitchell	Coalton	Monroe
Carl	Adams	Coldwater	Franklin
Carlisle	Warren	Colesburg	Delaware
*Carroll City	Carroll	Colfax	Jasper
Carrollton	"	College Springs	Page
Carr's Point	Montgomery	Colo	Story
Carson's Point	Boone	Columbia	Marion
Cascade	Dubuque	Columbus City	Louisa
Cassady's Corner	Boone	Communia	Clayton
Castalia	Winneshiek	Competine	Wapello
Castana	Monona	Comstock's Station	"
Castle Grove	Jones	Confidence	Wayne
Castleville	Buchanan	Cono	Iowa
Cedar Bluffs	Cedar	Conover	Winneshiek
Cedar Falls	Black Hawk	Coon Rapids	Carroll
Cedar Rapids	Linn	Cooperville	Wapello
Cedar Valley	Black Hawk	Copi	Johnson
Cedarville	Washington	Cora	Fremont
Center	Page	Correctionville	Woodbury
Center Point	Linn	Corydon	Wayne
Centerville	Appanoose	Cottage	Hardin
Central City	Linn	Cottage Hill	Dubuque
Ceres	Clayton	Cottonville	Jackson
Cessford	Cedar	Council Bluffs	Pottawattamie
Chandler	Keokuk	Council Hill	Clayton
Chapin	Franklin	Cox Creek	"
Chariton	Lucas	Crawfordsville	Washington
Charles City	Floyd	Crescent City	Pottawattamie
Charleston	Lee	Cresco	Howard
Charlotte	Clinton	Cross	Ringgold
Chatham	Buchanan	Croton	Lee
Chattanooga	Dallas	Crystal	Tama
Chelsea	Tama		
Chequest	Davis	Dahlonega	Wapello
Cherokee	Cherokee	Dairy	Washington
Chickasaw	Chickasaw	Dakota	Humboldt
Chillicothe	Wapello	Dale City	Guthrie
Christiansburg	"	Dallas	Marion
Cincinnati	Appanoose	Dalmanutha	Guthrie

* Not in the list in the preceding pages, having been reported to the Census Board since those pages were printed.

Alphabetical List of Post-offices—Continued.

Names of Post-offices.	Counties.	Names of Post-offices.	Counties.
Danforth	Johnson	Elkport	Clayton
Danville	Des Moines	Elk River	Clinton
Davenport	Scott	Ellington	Hancock
Davis Creek	Washington	Ellsworth	Madison
*Dayton	Bremer	Elm Springs	Butler
Dayton Center	Chickasaw	Elon	Allamakee
Decatur	Decatur	Elvira	Clinton
Decorah	Winneshiek	Ely	Marion
Deep River	Poweshiek	Emmett	Emmett
Deerfield	Chickasaw	Emmettsburg	Palo Alto
Delanti	Hardin	English Settlement	Marion
Delaware	Delaware	Enterprise	Black Hawk
Delhi	Delaware	Epworth	Dubuque
Denison	Crawford	Estella	Ringgold
Denmark	Lee	Estherville	Emmett
Dennis	Appanoose	Eugene	Ringgold
*Denver	Bremer	Eveland Grove	Mahaska
Derrinane	Dubuque	Exira	Audubon
Des Moines	Polk		
De Witt	Clinton	Fairbank	Buchanan
Dixon	Scott	Fairfax	Linn
Dodge	Guthrie	Fairfield	Jefferson
Dodgeville	Des Moines	Fairport	Muscatine
Doran	Mitchell	Fairview	Jones
Dorchester	Allamakee	Farley	Dubuque
Doud's Station	Van Buren	Farmersburg	Clayton
Douglas	Fayette	Farmers' Creek	Jackson
Dover	Lee	Farmersville	Mahaska
Downey	Cedar	Farmington	Van Buren
Drakeville	Davis	Fayette	Fayette
Dry Creek	Linn	Fern Valley	Palo Alto
Dubuque	Dubuque	Festina	Winneshiek
*Dunlap	Harrison	Fillmore	Dubuque
Durango	Dubuque	Flemingville	Linn
Durant	Cedar	Flint	Mahaska
Dutch Creek	Washington	Florence	Benton
Dyersville	Dubuque	Floris	Davis
		Floyd	Floyd
Eagle	Bremer	Fontanelle	Adair
Eagle Grove	Wright	Foote	Iowa
Earlville	Delaware	Forest City	Winnebago
East Melrose	Monroe	Forest Home	Poweshiek
East Nodaway	Adams	Foreston	Howard
Eastport	Fremont	Forestville	Delaware
Eatonville	Howard	Fort Atkinson	Winneshiek
Eddyville	Wapello	Fort Dodge	Webster
†Eden	Fayette	Fort Madison	Lee
Edenville	Marshall	Fort Plain	Warren
Edinburg	Jones	Frankfort	Montgomery
Edna	Cass	Franklin Center	Lee
Egypt	Mills	Franklin Grove	Page
Eldora	Hardin	Frank Pierce	Johnson
Eldorado	Fayette	Frankville	Winneshiek
Elgin	Fayette	Frederica	Bremer
Elkader	Clayton	Frederick	Monroe
Elkhart	Polk	Fredericksburg	Chickasaw

* Not in the list in the preceding pages, having been reported to the Census Board since those pages were printed.

† Eden post-office is also printed as in Clinton county on page 16.

Alphabetical List of Post-offices—Continued.

Names of Post-offices.	Counties.	Names of Post-offices	Counties.
Fredonia	Louisa	Half Way Prairie	Monroe
Freedom	Lucas	Hamburg	Fremont
Freeport	Winneshiek	Hamilton	Marion
Fremont	Mahaska	Ham in	Woodbury
French Creek	Allamakee	Hamlin's Grove	Audubon
Freyburg	Wright	Hammondsburg	Warren
Fuller's Mills	Jones	Hampton	Franklin
Fulton	Jackson	Hardin	Allamakee
Funk's Mills	Decatur	Hardin City	Hardin
		Harlan	Shelby
Galesburg	Jasper	Harper's Ferry	Allamakee
Garden Grove	Decatur	Harris Grove	Harrison
Garibaldi	Keokuk	Harrison	"
Garnavillo	Clayton	Hartford	Warren
Garry Owen	Jackson	Hartland	Worth
Gaston	Fremont	Hawleyville	Page
Gem	Clayton	Hazel Green	Delaware
Geneseo	Cerro Gordo	Hebron	Adair
Geneva	Franklin	Helena	Tama
Genoa	Wayne	Henderson's Prairie	Fayette
Genoa Bluffs	Iowa	Hesper	Winneshiek
Georgetown	Monroe	Hesperian	Webster
Germanville	Jefferson	Hibbsville	Appanoose
Giard	Clayton	High Lake	Emmett
Gilbert	Scott	Highland	Clayton
Gilbertsville	Black Hawk	Highland Grove	Jones
Given	Mahaska	High Point	Decatur
Glasgow	Jefferson	Holiday	Adair
Glenwood	Mills	Holt	Taylor
Glidden	Carroll	Home	Van Buren
Goldfield	Wright	Homer	Hamilton
Gosport	Marion	Homestead	Iowa
Grand Mound	Clinton	Hook's Point	Hamilton
Grand River	Wayne	Hopeville	Clarke
Grandview	Louisa	Hopewell	Mahaska
Grant	Montgomery	Hopkinton	Delaware
Grant City	Sac	Horton	Bremer
Granville	Mahaska	Howard	Howard
Gravity	Taylor	Howard Center	"
Great Oak	Palo Alto	Howardville	Floyd
Greeley	Delaware	Hudson	Black Hawk
Green Bay	Clarke	Humboldt	Humboldt
Greencastle	Jasper	Huron	Des Moines
Greenfield	Adair		
Greenvale	Dallas	Iconium	Appanoose
*Greenwood	Kossuth	Ida	Ida
Greenwood	Polk	Illinois Grove	Marshall
Grinnell	Poweshiek	Illyria	Fayette
Grove City	Cass	Independence	Buchanan
Grove Creek	Jones	Indianapolis	Mahaska
Grove Hill	Bremer	Indianola	Warren
Grundy Center	Grundy	Ingart Grove	Ringgold
Gurley	Cass	Ingham	Franklin
Guthrie Center	Guthrie	Inland	Cedar
Guttenberg	Clayton	Ioka	Keokuk
		Iola	Marion

* As reported to this office from Algona. It is probably incorrect. Greenwood post-office is in Polk county.

Alphabetical List of Post-offices—Continued.

Names of Post-offices.	Counties.	Names of Post offices.	Counties.
Ion	Allamakee	Lawrenceburg	Warren
Iowa Center	Story	Lebanon	Van Buren
Iowa City	Johnson	Le Claire	Scott
Iowa Falls	Hardin	Legrand	Marshall
Iowaville	Van Buren	Leighton Station	Mahaska
Iron Hill	Jackson	Leo	Fayette
Irvington	Kossuth	Leon	Decatur
		*Leroy	Bremer
Jacksonville	Chickasaw	Lester	Black Hawk
Janesville	Bremer	†Letts	Louisa
Jeddo City	Harrison	Lewis	Cass
Jefferson	Dubuque	Lewisburg	Wayne
Jeffersonville	Lee	Liberty	Clarke
Jenks	Taylor	Liberty Center	Warren
Jerome	Appanoose	Libertyville	Jefferson
Jessup	Buchanan	Lima	Fayette
Johnson	Jones	Lime Creek	Cerro Gordo
Jollyville	Lee	Lime Springs	Howard
Jone	Iowa	Lincoln	Polk
		Linden	Dallas
Kasson	Madison	Linton	Des Moines
Kendrick	Greene	Lisbon	Linn
Keokuk	Lee	Lithopolis	Hardin
Keosauqua	Van Buren	Little Sioux	Harrison
Kier	Buchanan	Little Turkey	Chickasaw
Kilbourne	Van Buren	Livingston	Appanoose
Kimball	Jasper	Lockridge	Jefferson
King	Dubuque	Locust Lane	Winneshiek
Kingston	Des Moines	Logan	Harrison
Kirkville	Wapello	Lott's Creek	Humboldt
Kniffin	Wayne	Louden	Cedar
Knoxville	Marion	Loveland Mills	Pottawattamie
Kossuth	Des Moines	‡Lovilia	Monroe
Kossuth Center	Kossuth	Lowell	Henry
Koszta	Iowa	Low Moor	Clinton
		Lucerne	Wayne
Lacelle	Clarke	Ludlow	Allamakee
Lacey	Muscatine	Luni	Wright
Lacona	Warren	Lybrand	Allamakee
Ladora	Iowa	Lycurgus	Allamakee
Lafayette	Linn	§Lynn	Warren
Lagrange	Lucas	Lynnville	Jasper
Lake City	Calhoun	Lyons	Clinton
Lake Mills	Winnebago	Lytle City	Iowa
Lakin's Grove	Hamilton		
Lamotte	Jackson	Macedonia	Pottawattamie
Lancaster	Keokuk	McGregor	Clayton
Langworthy	Jones	Macksville	Guthrie
Lansing	Allamakee	Madison	Jones
La Porte	Clarke	Magnolia	Harrison
La Porte City	Black Hawk	Malcom	Poweshiek
Last Chance	Lucas	Manchester	Delaware
Lattners	Dubuque	Manteno	Shelby
La Vega	Des Moines	Manti	Fremont

* Not in the list in the preceding pages, having been reported to the Census Board since those pages were printed

† Incorrectly printed "Letis" on page 38.

‡ Incorrectly printed "Lovilla" on page 45.

§ Printed "Lima" on page 57 from erroneous information.

Alphabetical List of Post-offices—Continued.

Names of Post-offices.	Counties.	Names of Post-offices.	Counties.
Mapleton	Monona	Mt. Zion	Van Buren
Maquoketa	Jackson	Muscatine	Muscatine
Marble Rock	Floyd		
Marengo	Iowa	Nantrille	Black Hawk
Marietta	Marshall	Nashua	Chickasaw
Marion	Linn	National	Clayton
Marshall	Henry	Necot	Linn
Marshalltown	Marshall	Nelson	Mitchell
Martinsburg	Keokuk	Nemora	Johnson
Maysville	Franklin	Nevada	Story
Mason City	Cerro Gordo	Nevinville	Adams
Masonville	Delaware	Newark	Marion
Massillon	Cedar	New Buda	Decatur
Maxfield	Bremer	Newburg	Mitchell
Mechanicsville	Cedar	New Hampton	Chickasaw
Memory	Taylor	New Hartford	Butler
Memphis	Appanoose	New Jefferson	Greene
Mennon	Marion	New Liberty	Scott
Mentor	Bremer	New London	Henry
Merrimac	Jefferson	New Oregon	Howard
Middle River	Madison	New Philadelphia	Story
Middletown	Des Moines	New Port Center	Johnson
Mill	Fayette	New Providence	Hardin
Milledgeville	Appanoose	New Sharon	Mahaska
Milleray	Dubuque	Newton	Jasper
Millersburg	Iowa	New Vienna	Dubuque
Mill Grove	Poweshiek	New Virginia	Warren
Mill Rock	Jackson	New York	Wayne
Millville	Clayton	Nine Eagles	Decatur
Milpine	Muscatine	Nishna	Pottawattamie
Milton	Van Buren	Nora Springs	Floyd
Mineral Ridge	Boone	Norris	Marshall
Minerva	Marshall	North	Madison
Missouri Valley	Harrison	Northfield	Des Moines
Mitchell	Mitchell	North Liberty	Johnson
*Mitchellville	Polk	North McGregor	Clayton
Modail	Harrison	Northville	Greene
Moffitt's Grove	Guthrie	North Washington	Chickasaw
Moingona	Boone	Northwood	Worth
Monmouth	Jackson	Norwalk	Warren
Monona	Clayton	Nugent's Grove	Linn
Monroe	Jasper	Numa	Appanoose
Montana	Boone		
Monterey	Davis	Oakfield	Audubon
Montezuma	Poweshiek	Oakland Valley	Franklin
Monticello	Jones	Oak Springs	Davis
Montrose	Lee	Oasis	Johnson
Moravia	Appanoose	Ogden	Dubuque
Morning Sun	Louisa	Ohio	Madison
Moscow	Muscatine	Okoboji	Dickinson
Mt. Auburn	Benton	Ola	Lucas
Mt. Ayr	Ringgold	Old Mission	Winneshiek
Mt. Hope	Delaware	Onawa City	Monona
Mt. Joy	Scott	Oran	Fayette
Mt. Pleasant	Henry	Orange	Clinton
Mt. Sterling	Van Buren	Orford	Tama
Mt. Vernon	Linn	Orleans	Appanoose

* Printed "Mitchell" on page 48 from erroneous information.

Alphabetical List of Post-offices—Continued.

Names of Post-offices.	Counties.	Names of Post-offices.	Counties.
Orono	Muscatine	Point Palestine	Story
Osage	Mitchell	Point Pleasant	Hardin
Osborne	Howard	Polk City	Polk
Osceola	Clarke	Port Allen	Louisa
Oskaloosa	Mahaska	Port Louisa	"
Osprey	Monroe	Port Richmond	Wapello
Ossian	Winneshiek	Postville	Allamakee
Oswego	Warren	Prairieburg	Linn
Otho	Webster	Prairie City	Jasper
Otisville	Franklin	Prairie Creek	Poweshiek
Oto	Woodbury	Prairie Grove	Clarke
Otranto	Mitchell	Prairie Hill	Boone
Otsego	Fayette	Prairie Mills	Muscatine
Ottawa	Clarke	Primrose	Lee
Otter Creek	Jackson	Princeton	Scott
Otterville	Buchanan	Promise City	Wayne
Ottumwa	Wapello	Prospect Hill	Linn
Owen's Grove	Cerro Gordo	Pulaski	Davis
Oxford Mills	Jones	Putnam	Fayette
Ozark	Jackson		
		Quasqueton	Buchanan
Palestine	Johnson	Queen City	Adams
Palmyra	Warren	Quincy	"
Palo	Linn		
Palo Alto	Louisa	Randall	Hamilton
Panora	Guthrie	Rapids	Boone
Paris	Linn	Redding	Ringgold
Parkersburg	Butler	Redfield	Dallas
Parrish	Des Moines	Red Oak	Cedar
Pedee	Cedar	Red Oak Junction	Montgomery
Pella	Marion	Red Rock	Marion
Peoria	Mahaska	Reeder's Mills	Harrison
Peoria City	Polk	Riceville	Mitchell
Peosta	Dubuque	Richfield	Fayette
Peru	Madison	Richland	Keokuk
*Peterson	Clay	Richmond	Washington
Pierceville	Van Buren	Ridgedale	Polk
Pierce's Point	Dallas	Riley	Clarke
Pike	Muscatine	Ringgold	Ringgold
Pilot Grove	Lee	Rippey	Greene
Pilot Mound	Boone	Rising Sun	Polk
Pilot Rock	Cherokee	Riverside	Boone
Pin Oak	Dubuque	Robin	Benton
Pittsburg	Van Buren	Rochester	Cedar
Platteville	Taylor	Rock	Cerro Gordo
Pleasant Grove	Des Moines	Rockdale	Dubuque
Pleasant Hill	Cedar	Rockford	Floyd
Pleasant Plain	Jefferson	Rock Grove City	Floyd
Pleasant Prairie	Muscatine	Rolfe	Pocahontas
†Pleasant Valley	Scott	‡Rolley	Jackson
Pleasantville	Marion	Rose Grove	Hamilton
Plum Hollow	Fremont	Rose Mount	Warren
Plymouth	Cerro Gordo	Rosette	Cedar
Plymouth Rock	Winneshiek	Rossville	Allamakee
Point Isabel	Wapello	Round Grove	Scott

* Not in the list in the preceding pages.
† Printed "Valley City" on page 52.
‡ Printed "Rolly" on page 31.

Alphabetical List of Post-offices—Continued.

Names of Post-offices.	Counties.
Russell	Lucas
Sabula	Jackson
Sac City	Sac
Saint Ansgar	Mitchell
Saint Charles	Madison
Saint Clair	Monona
Saint Donatus	Jackson
Saint John	Harrison
Saint Paul	Lee
Salem	Henry
Salina	Jefferson
Sand Spring	Delaware
Sandusky	Lee
Sandysville	Warren
Saratoga	Howard
Savannah	Davis
Sawana	Clayton
Saylorville	Polk
Sciola	Montgomery
Scotch Grove	Jones
Scott Center	Fayette
Seaton	"
Sedgwick	Decatur
Selma	Wayne
Seneca	Kossuth
Seventy-eight	Johnson
Sharon	Warren
Shellrock	Butler
Shellrock Falls	Cerro Gordo
Shellsburg	Benton
Sherman	Poweshiek
Sherrill's Mound	Dubuque
Shobe's Grove	Franklin
Shueyville	Johnson
Siam	Taylor
Sidney	Fremont
Sigel	Clayton
Sigourney	Keokuk
Simpson	Adams
Sioux City	Woodbury
Sisley's Grove	Linn
Smithland	Woodbury
Smyrna	Clarke
Snyder	Dallas
Soda Bar	Palo Alto
Solon	Johnson
South English	Keokuk
South Flint	Des Moines
Spillville	Winneshiek
Spirit Lake	Dickinson
Spragueville	Jackson
Spring Brook	Jackson
Spring Creek	Tama
Springdale	Cedar
Springfield	Keokuk
Spring Grove	Linn
*Spring Lake	Bremer
Spring Valley	Decatur
Springville	Linn
Springwater	Winneshiek
Staceyville	Mitchell
Stapleton	Chickasaw
Starr	Marion
State Center	Marshall
Stellapolis	Iowa
Sterling	Jackson
Stiles	Davis
Story City	Story
Strawberry Point	Clayton
Summerset	Warren
Summitville	Lee
Sumner	Bremer
Sunnyside	Buchanan
Swanton	Butler
Swede Point	Boone
Sweetland Center	Muscatine
Sylvan Retreat	Humboldt
Syracuse	Bremer
Tabor	Fremont
Tallahoma	Lucas
Talleyrand	Keokuk
Tama City	Tama
Tarkio	Page
Taylorsville	Fayette
Terrehaute	Decatur
Thompsonville	Monroe
Timber Creek	Marshall
Tipton	Cedar
Tipton Grove	Hardin
Tivoli	Dubuque
Toledo	Tama
Toolsboro	Louisa
Toronto	Clinton
Tower Hill	Delaware
Trenton	Henry
Tripoli	Bremer
Troy	Davis
Troy Mills	Linn
Tyro	Poweshiek
Tyrone	Monroe
Ulster	Floyd
Union	Hardin
Union City	Union
Union Grove	Page
Union Hill	Ringgold
Union Mills	Mahaska
Union Prairie	Allamakee
Uniontown	Delaware
Unionville	Appanoose
Unity	Benton
Upper Grove	Hancock

* Not in the list of post offices in Bremer county as printed on page 8.

Alphabetical List of Post-offices—Continued.

Names of Post-offices.	Counties.	Names of Post-offices.	Counties.
Upton	Van Buren	West Branch	Cedar
Urbana	Benton	West Dayton	Webster
Utica	Van Buren	Western College	Linn
		Westerville	Decatur
Valiska	Montgomery	West Fork	Monona
Valley	Washington	West Grove	Davis
Valley City	Scott	West Irving	Tama
Valley Farm	Linn	West Liberty	Muscatine
Van Buren	Jackson	West Mitchell	Mitchell
Vandalia	Jasper	West Point	Lee
Venus	Madison	West Prairie	Linn
Vernon	Van Buren	West Union	Fayette
Vernon Springs	Howard	What Cheer	Keokuk
Victor	Iowa	Wheatland	Clinton
Vienna	Marshall	Wheeler's Grove	Pottawattamie
Village Creek	Allamakee	Wheeling	Marion
Vincennes	Lee	White Cloud	Mills
Vinton	Benton	White Oak	Mahaska
Viola	Linn	White Pigeon	Keokuk
Virginia Grove	Louisa	Whitesboro	Harrison
Volga City	Clayton	Whitneyville	Cass
Volney	Allamakee	Wickliffe	Jackson
		Williamston	Chickasaw
Wacousta	Humboldt	Willoughby	Butler
Wadaloup	Grundy	Wilson Grove	Fayette
Wagner	Clayton	Wilton	Muscatine
Wahaghbonsy	Mills	Winchester	Van Buren
Walcott	Scott	Windham	Johnson
Walnut City	Appanoose	Windsor	Fayette
Walnut Fork	Jones	Winfield	Henry
Walnut Grove	Scott	Winterset	Madison
Waltham	Tama	Winthrop	Buchanan
Wapello	Louisa	Wolf Creek	Tama
Wapsa	Linn	Woodbine	Harrison
Ward	Mills	Woodbridge	Cedar
Ward's Corners	Buchanan	Woodbury	Woodbury
Warren	Lee	*Woodville	Winneshiek
Warsaw	Wayne	Wooster	Jefferson
Washington	Washington	Worth	Boone
Wassonville	Washington	Worthington	Dubuque
Waterford	Jackson	Wyoming	Jones
Waterloo	Black Hawk		
Waterville	Allamakee	Xenia	Dallas
Waubeck	Linn		
Waucoma	Fayette	Yankee Settlement	Clayton
Waudena	Fayette	Yatesville	Calhoun
Waukon	Allamakee	Yatton	Washington
Waverly	Bremer	Yazoo	Harrison
Webster	Keokuk	York	Delaware
Webster City	Hamilton	York Prairie	Cedar
Weller	Monroe	Yough	Boone
Wells's Mills	Appanoose		
Welton	Clinton	Zoar	Cedar
Wentworth	Mitchell	Zurich	Jones
West Bend	Palo Alto		

* Woodville is also printed as in Jasper county, on page 33 from erroneous information.

NOTE.—The above list of post-offices, which in another form appears in the Census Returns, was obtained from the Clerks of the District Court, and also from Postmasters at county-seats, of the latter of whom about eighty responded to circulars sent, asking the desired information.

OFFICIAL REGISTER FOR THE YEAR 1868.

STATE GOVERNMENT.

William M. Stone, Marion county, Governor.
George J. North, Polk county, Private Secretary to the Governor.
Benjamin F. Gue, Webster county, Lieutenant-Governor.
The above persons will be succeeded, about January 16, by the following:
Samuel Merrill, Clayton county, Governor.
———————, Clayton county, Private Secretary to the Governor.
John Scott, Story county, Lieutenant-Governor.

Ed Wright, Cedar county, Secretary of State.
Wm. H. Fleming, Clinton county, Deputy.
John A. Elliott, Mitchell county, Auditor of State.
Samuel A. Ayres, Polk county, Deputy.
Samuel E. Rankin, Washington county, Treasurer of State.
Isaac Brandt, Polk county, Deputy.
Cyrus C. Carpenter, Webster county, Register of State Land Office.
John M. Davis, Johnson county, Deputy.
D. Franklin Wells, Johnson county, Superintendent of Public Instruction.
Lewis J. Coulter, Linn county, Clerk, and *ex officio* State Librarian.
Francis W. Palmer, State Printer.
James S. Carter, State Binder.

THE JUDICIARY.

SUPREME COURT.

John F. Dillon, Scott county, Chief Justice.
Chester C. Cole, Polk county, Judge.
George G. Wright, Van Buren county, Judge.
Joseph M. Beck, Lee county, Judge.
Charles Linderman, Page county, Clerk.
Henry O'Connor, Muscatine county, Attorney-General.
Edward H. Stiles, Wapello county, Reporter of the Decisions.

DISTRICT COURTS.

JUDGES.

Francis Springer, Louisa county, 1st judicial district.
Harvey Tannehill, Appanoose county, 2d judicial district.
James G. Day, Fremont county, 3d judicial district.
Henry Ford, Harrison county, 4th judicial district.
Hugh W. Maxwell, Warren county, 5th judicial district
Ezekiel S. Sampson, Keokuk county, 6th judicial district.
J. Scott Richman, Muscatine county, 7th judicial district.
James H. Rothrock, Cedar county, 8th judicial district.
James Burt, Dubuque county, 9th judicial district.
Milo McGlathery, Fayette county, 10th judicial district.
Daniel D. Chase, Hamilton county, 11th judicial district.
William B. Fairfield, Floyd county, 12th judicial district.

DISTRICT ATTORNEYS.

Joshua Tracy, Des Moines county, 1st judicial district.
James B. Weaver, Davis county, 2d judicial district.
Charles E. Millard, Mills county, 3d judicial district.
Orson Rice, Dickinson county, 4th judicial district.
Samuel D. Nichols, Guthrie county, 5th judicial district.
Moses A. McCoid, Jefferson county, 6th judicial district.
Lyman Ellis, Clinton county, 7th judicial district.
C. R. Scott, Jones county, 8th judicial district.
Mathew M. Trumbull, Black Hawk county, 9th judicial district.
L. O. Hatch, Allamakee county, 10th judicial district.
John H. Bradley, Marshall county, 11th judicial district.
John E. Burke, Bremer county, 12th judicial district.

The terms of the officers of the Twelfth judicial district will expire on the 1st day of January, 1869; those of the others on the 1st day of January, 1871.

THE MILITIA.

The Governor, Commander-in-Chief.
Brigadier-General Nathaniel B. Baker, Clinton county, Adjutant and Inspector General, Acting Quartermaster-General, and acting as Paymaster-General.
Lieut.-Col. William F. Sapp, Pottawattamie county, Aide-de-Camp.
Lieut.-Col. Samuel L. Glasgow, Wayne county, Aide-de-Camp.
Lieut.-Col. George Cowie, Washington, D. C., Aide-de-Camp.
Lieut.-Col. Frank Sutton, Special Aide-de-Camp.
Lieut.-Col. George J. North, special Aide-de-Camp.

The officers of the Governor's staff are appointed by the Governor, and hold office during his pleasure

TWELFTH GENERAL ASSEMBLY.

Convenes at the Capitol, Des Moines, Monday, January 13, 1868.

SENATE.

Dists.	COUNTIES.	SENATORS.	POST-OFFICES.
1	Lee	*Nathaniel G. Hedges	Keokuk
	Lee	*Joseph Hollman	Fort Madison
2	Van Buren	*Eliab Doud	Doud's Station
3	Davis	‖Henry C. Traverse	West Grove
4	Appanoose	‖Madison M. Walden	Centerville
5	Wayne, Lucas, Clarke	William Hartshorn	Corydon
6	Monroe	Edward M. Bill	Albia
7	Decatur, Ringgold	Isaac W. Keller	Mount Ayr
8	Taylor, Page, Adams, Union, Montgomery	Napoleon B. Moore	Clarinda
9	Pottawattamie, Mills, Cass, Fremont	Jefferson P. Casady	Council Bluffs
10	Des Moines	†Charles L. Matthies	Burlington
11	Henry	*Theron W. Woolson	Mount Pleasant
12	Jefferson	Abial R. Pierce	Lockridge
13	Wapello	†Augustus H. Hamilton	Ottumwa
14	Louisa	*James M. Robertson	Columbus City
15	Washington	‖Granville G. Bennett	Washington
16	Muscatine	*John A. Parvin	Muscatine
17	Keokuk	†John C. Johnson	Richland
18	Mahaska	John R. Needham	Oskaloosa
19	Marion	§Thomas McMillan	English Settlement
20	Warren	‖George E. Griffith	Indianola
21	Madison, Adair, Guthrie, Dallas	*Joseph R. Reed	Adel
22	Scott	*Andrew M. Larimer	LeClaire
	Scott	‡William W. Cones	Davenport
23	Clinton	*John Henry Smith	Camanche
24	Cedar	William P. Wolf	Tipton
25	Johnson	Samuel H. Fairall	Iowa City
26	Iowa, Poweshiek	Matthew Long	Stellapolis
27	Jasper	*John Meyer	Newton
28	Polk	*Jonathan W. Cattell	Des Moines
29	Jackson	L. B. Dunham	Maquoketa
30	Jones	*Sewell S. Farwell	Monticello
31	Linn	Robert Smyth	Mount Vernon
32	Benton, Tama	James Chapin	Vinton
33	Marshall, Hardin	Wells S. Rice	Marshalltown
34	Dubuque	§F. M. Knoll	Dubuque
	Dubuque	*Benjamin B. Richards	Dubuque
35	Delaware	Joseph Grimes	Colesburg
36	Buchanan, Bremer	William G. Donnan	Independence
37	Clayton	Homer E. Newell	McGregor
38	Fayette	William Larrabee	Clermont
39	Franklin, Butler, Grundy, Cerro Gordo	Marcus Tuttle	Clear Lake
40	Black Hawk	*James B. Powers	Cedar Falls
41	Allamakee	‖L. E. Fellows	Lansing
42	Winneshiek	*H. C. Bulis	Decorah

* Elected in 1865. † Elected in 1866 to fill vacancies. ‡ Elected in 1867 to fill vacancy. § Re-elected. ‖ Members of the House of Representatives 11th General Assembly.

List of Senators—Continued.

Dists.	COUNTIES.	SENATORS.	POST OFFICES.
43	Floyd, Mitchell, Howard, Chickasaw	§John G. Patterson	Charles City
44	Boone, Hamilton, Story, Greene,	Isaac J. Mitchell	Boonsboro
45	Worth, Winnebago, Kossuth, Emmett, Dickinson, Clay, Palo Alto, Hancock, Wright, Humboldt, Pocahontas, Sac, Buena Vista, Calhoun, Webster	Theodore Hawley	Fort Dodge
46	Harrison, Shelby, Audubon, Carroll, Crawford, Monona, Woodbury, Ida, Cherokee, Plymouth, Sioux, O'Brien	*Addison Oliver	Onawa City

*Elected in 1865. §Re-elected.

Mr. Needham was a member of the Senate in the 4th and 5th General Assemblies, and as Lieutenant-Governor presided in the Senate of the 9th General Assembly. Mr. Cattell was a Senator in the 6th and 7th General Assemblies, Mr. Woolson in the 9th and 10th, and Mr. Parvin in the 10th.

HOUSE OF REPRESENTATIVES.

Dists.	COUNTIES.	REPRESENTATIVES.	POST-OFFICES.
1	Lee	Gibson Browne	Keokuk
	Lee	C. C. Bauder	Primrose
	Lee	William Werner	West Point
2	Van Buren	*Joel Brown	Birmingham
	Van Buren	Seth Craig	Keosauqua
3	Davis	*J. M. Garrett	Troy
	Davis	William G. Wilson	Mt. Pleasant or Stiles.
4	Appanoose	Brannock Phillips	Unionville
5	Wayne	William Glasgow	Promise City
6	Decatur	H. W. Peck	Decatur City
7	Des Moines	†Robert Allen	Dodgeville
	Des Moines	A. G. Adams	Burlington
8	Henry	John P. Grantham	Mt. Pleasant
	Henry	Jacob Hart	Mt. Pleasant
9	Jefferson	John Hayden	Libertyville
	Jefferson	A. R. Fulton	Fairfield
10	Wapello	*Charles Dudley	Agency City
	Wapello	Samuel T. Caldwell	Eddyville
11	Monroe	A. A. Ramsay	Albia
12	Lucas	Samuel D. Wheeler	Chariton
13	Clarke	Barclay Burrows	Osceola
14	Page	Joseph Cramer	Clarinda
15	Fremont	Charles O. Dewey	Sidney
16	Mills	John Y. Stone	Glenwood
17	Louisa	Albert Ellis	Cairo
18	Washington	Joseph D. Miles	Crawfordsville
	Washington	M. Goodspeed	Lexington
19	Keokuk	†John Morrison, jr.	Butler
	Keokuk	William Hartsock	South English

* Sat in the 11th General Assembly.
† Elected in 1866 to fill vacancy, and re-elected in 1867.

List of Representatives—Continued.

Dists.	COUNTIES.	REPRESENTATIVES.	POST-OFFICES.
20	Mahaska	Charles Stanley	Oskaloosa
	Mahaska	Thomas Ballinger	Farmersville
21	Marion	Edmund Meachem	Attica
	Marion	Banner G. Bowan	Pella
22	Warren	Mark A. Dashiell	Hartford
23	Madison	Benjamin F. Murray	Winterset
24	Pottawattamie	Lysander W. Babbitt	Council Bluffs
25	Muscatine	*Samuel McNutt	Muscatine
	Muscatine	*R. M. Burnett	Muscatine
26	Johnson	John P. Irish	Iowa City
	Johnson	Jacob Y. Blackwell	Iowa City
27	Iowa	Abraham Bolton	Homestead
28	Poweshiek	Leonard F. Parker	Grinnell
29	Jasper	Merritt W. Atwood	Newton
30	Polk	John A. Kasson	Des Moines
	Polk	Joshua H. Hatch	Des Moines
31	Dallas	Le Roy Lambert	Redfield
32	Scott	*M. J. Rohlfs	Davenport
	Scott	Charles Kelley	LeClaire
	Scott	M. C. Davis	Davenport
33	Clinton	Aylett R. Cotton	Lyons
	Clinton	Charles G. Trusdell	Clinton
	Clinton	Charles E. Leffingwell	Wheatland
34	Jones	*John Russell	Wyoming
	Jones	*John McKean	Anamosa
35	Cedar	William S. Chase	West Liberty
	Cedar	C. P. Sheldon	Tipton
36	Jackson	L. W. Stuart	Monmouth
	Jackson	John A. Tritz	St. Donatus
37	Linn	Adam Perry	Western
	Linn	William B. Leach	Cedar Rapids
38	Benton	John W. Traer	Vinton
39	Tama	James Wilson	Wolf Creek
40	Marshall	Ben W. Johnson	Marshalltown
41	Dubuque	*Thomas S. Wilson	Dubuque
	Dubuque	R. B. Lockwood	Worthington
	Dubuque	John B. Longueville	King
	Dubuque	Dennis Donovan	Ballyclough
42	Delaware	Cummings Sanborn	Earlville
43	Buchanan	*Phineas C. Wilcox	Independence
44	Black Hawk	George Ordway	Waterloo
45	Hardin	*Thomas B. Knapp	Iowa Falls
46	Clayton	Horace Hamilton	National
	Clayton	James Newbury	Strawberry Point
	Clayton	P. G. Baily	Hardin
47	Fayette	Aaron Brown	Fayette
	Fayette	Curtis R. Bent	West Union
48	Bremer	D. P. Walling	Tripoli
49	Chickasaw	William Tucker	Chickasaw
50	Allamakee	*P. G. Wright	Ludlow
	Allamakee	George R. Miller	Rossville
51	Winneshiek	*Horace B. Williams	Hesper
	Winneshiek	Jeremiah T. Atkins	Frankville
52	Boone	Jackson Orr	Montana
53	Story	James Hawthorn	Nevada

* Sat in the 11th General Assembly. Mr. McNutt was also a member of the 10th General Assembly, and Mr. Russell of the 9th and 10th.
† Elected in 1866 to fill vacancies, and re-elected in 1867.

List of Representatives—Continued.

Dists.	COUNTIES.	REPRESENTATIVES.	POST-OFFICES.
54	Floyd	*Wilberforce P. Gaylord	Rock Grove City
55	Harrison, Shelby	Joseph H. Smith	Magnolia
56	Mitchell, Howard	*J. H. Brown	Cresco
57	Sioux, O'Brien, Buena Vista, Cherokee	Eli Johnson	Cherokee
58	Dickinson, Emmett, Clay, Palo Alto	Roderick A. Smith	Okoboji
59	Cerro Gordo, Winnebago, Worth, Kossuth	Charles W. Tenney	Plymouth
60	Woodbury, Ida, Sac, Plymouth	Eugene Criss	Sac City
61	Wright, Hamilton, Franklin, Hancock	John D. Hunter	Webster City
62	Webster, Pocahontas, Calhoun, Humboldt	Samuel Rees	Fort Dodge
63	Monona, Crawford, Carroll	Stephen Tillson	Onawa City
64	Greene, Guthrie, Audubon	Henry C. Rippey	New Jefferson
65	Ringgold, Taylor	†Leonard T. McCoun	Bedford
66	Adair, Cass, Montgomery	G. F. Kilburn	Fontanelle
67	Butler, Grundy	James A. Guthrie	Shellrock
68	Adams, Union	N. W. Rowell	Afton

* Sat in the 11th General Assembly.
† Elected in 1866 to fill vacancy, and re-elected in 1867.

PUBLIC INSTITUTIONS.

STATE UNIVERSITY OF IOWA,

IOWA CITY, JOHNSON COUNTY.

Established, 1847.

BOARD OF TRUSTEES.

The Governor, *ex-officio* President.

Lewis W. Ross, Pottawattamie county; term expires 1868.

Rush Clark, Johnson county; term expires 1868.

R. M. Burnett, Muscatine county; term expires 1870.

H. C. Bulis, Winneshiek county; term expires 1870.

Coker F. Clarkson, Grundy county; term expires 1870.

Christian W. Slagle, Jefferson county; term expires 1870.

Samuel J. Kirkwood, Johnson county; term expires 1868.

N. R. Leonard, President *pro tem.* of the Faculty, *ex-officio* Trustee.

William J. Haddock, Secretary of the Board.
William Crum, Treasurer of the Board.

The Trustees of the State University are elected by the General Assembly for four years. The Treasurer and Secretary are chosen by the Board of Trustees, and hold office during the pleasure of that body. The Board also elects a President and the requisite number of professors and tutors.

ASYLUM OF THE BLIND,

VINTON, BENTON COUNTY.

Established at Iowa City in 1853. *Removed to Vinton, August,* 1862.

BOARD OF TRUSTEES.

James McQuinn, Benton county, term expires in 1870: President of the Board.
Elijah Sells, Benton county; term expires in 1868.
James Chapin, Benton county; term expires in 1868: Treasurer of the Board.
John H. Dysart, Tama county; term expires in 1870.
Charles H. Conklin, Benton county; term expires in 1870.
James L. Geddes, Principal of the Institution, *ex-officio* Trustee; term as member of the Board expires in 1868: Secretary of the Board.

Mrs. N. A. Morton, Matron.

The Trustees of the Asylum of the Blind are chosen by the General Assembly for the term of four years. The Board elects its own officers, and chooses the Principal, Matron, Teachers, &c., of the Asylum, and from the employees selects a Steward.

INSTITUTION OF THE DEAF AND DUMB.

Established at Iowa City, Johnson County, January 31, 1855. *Permanently located at Council Bluffs, Pottawattamie County, July* 4, 1866.*

BOARD OF TRUSTEES.

The Governor.
N. H. Brainerd, Johnson county, appointed September 24, 1863.
Thomas M. Banbury, Johnson county, appointed in 1864.
Milton B. Cochran, Johnson county, appointed February 10, 1866.
Thomas J. Cox, Johnson county, appointed March 1, 1867, by the Governor, to fill vacancy.
Ed Wright, Cedar county, Secretary of State.

* The Institution remains at Iowa City, awaiting the erection of the buildings at Council Bluffs.

D. Franklin Wells, Johnson county, Superintendent of Public Instruction.
Benjamin Talbot, Principal of the Institution.

—

Mrs. Mary B. Swan, Matron.

—

The Trustees of the above Institution are appointed by the Governor and Senate for four years; vacancies occurring during the recess of the General Assembly are filled by the Governor till the next session of that body. The Board elects one of its own members Treasurer; it also chooses the Principal, Matron, and other officers, &c., of the Institution, and from the employees chooses a Steward.

—

COMMISSIONERS *under the Act of April 3, 1866, to locate the Institution at Council Bluffs.*

Thomas Officer, Pottawattamie county.
Caleb Baldwin, " "
Dr. E. Honn, " "

IOWA HOSPITAL FOR THE INSANE.

MOUNT PLEASANT, HENRY COUNTY.

—

Established in 1855.

—

BOARD OF TRUSTEES.

Maturin L. Fisher, Clayton county, term expires July 4, 1872.
Martin L. Edwards, Henry county, term expires July 4, 1868.
Luke Palmer, Des Moines county, term expires July 4, 1870.
J. Monroe Shaffer, Jefferson county, term expires July 4, 1868.
John R. Needham, Mahaska county, term expires July 4, 1872.
Andrew W. McClure, Henry county, term expires July 4, 1870.
Benjamin Crabb, Washington county, term expires July 4, 1872.

—

Mark Ranney, M. D., Superintendent.
Martin L. Edwards, Treasurer.

—

The Trustees of the "Iowa Hospital for the Insane" are elected by the General Assembly for the term of six years. The Board holds an annual meeting on the first Wednesday of December, at which time the President and Secretary of the Board are elected. The Board also appoints the Medical Superintendent, the Matron, and one or more Assistant Physicians.

STATE AGRICULTURAL COLLEGE AND MODEL FARM,

STORY COUNTY.

Established March 31, 1858.

BOARD OF TRUSTEES.

The President of the College *ex-officio* President of the Board. Office now vacant.
The Governor.
Peter Melendy, Black Hawk county.
J. Wilson Williams, Des Moines county.
James D. Wright, Lucas county.
Hugh M. Thomson, Scott county.
John Russell, Jones county.
Benjamin F. Gue, Webster county.
B. O. Stevenson, Adams county.
J. C. Cusey, Humboldt county.
Thomas K. Brooks, Polk county.
Theron A. Morgan, Keokuk county.
R. W. Humphrey, Floyd county.
John Garber, Clayton county.

John Russell, Jones county, J. Wilson Williams, Des Moines county, James D. Wright, Lucas county,	Building Committee.

C. A. Dunham, Des Moines county, Superintendent of the College building.
Hugh M. Thomson, Scott county, Superintendent of Agricultural College Farm and *ex-officio* Secretary of the Board of Trustees.
L. P. Sherman, Polk county, Treasurer.

The Trustees are elected by the General Assembly for the term of four years. The terms of one-half the above named Trustees will expire on the 1st day of May, 1868, and of the other half two years later. The Board of Trustees meets annually on the second Monday of January, at which time the Treasurer is elected. The Board appoints the Superintendent of Agricultural College Farm during its pleasure, and has the power to elect a "President for the State Agricultural College and Farm," &c.

IOWA SOLDIERS' ORPHANS' HOME.

HOMES AT DAVENPORT, SCOTT COUNTY, CEDAR FALLS, BLACK HAWK COUNTY AND GLENWOOD, MILLS COUNTY.

Established as a State Institution in 1866.

BOARD OF TRUSTEES.

Jonathan W. Cattell, Polk county, President.
Pearl P. Ingalls, Polk county.
Thomas E. Corkhill, Des Moines county.
John A. Parvin, Muscatine county.
P. G. Wright, Allamakee county.
N. H. Brainerd, Johnson county.
James B. Powers, Black Hawk county.

The Trustees of the "Iowa Soldiers' Orphans' Home" are elected by the General Assembly for the term of two years. The terms of office of the above named Trustees expire on the 2d day of April, 1868.

THE PENITENTIARY OF THE STATE.

FORT MADISON, LEE COUNTY.

Established February 25, 1839.

Martin Heisey, Des Moines county, Warden.
James H. Reynolds, Deputy Warden.
Charles Hillis, Clerk.
William Reinick, Chaplain.
Augustus W. Hoffmeister, Physician.

The Warden is elected by joint ballot of the General Assembly at each regular session. He appoints the Clerk, Deputy Warden, Chaplain, and Guards; and with the concurrence of the Governor appoints the Physician; and on the nomination of the latter appoints the Steward.

MISCELLANEOUS.

DIRECTORS OF THE STATE BANK OF IOWA.

IOWA CITY, JOHNSON COUNTY.

Established July 29, 1858.

Edward T. Edginton, Lucas county.
George M. Woodbury, Marshall county.
One vacancy.

BANK COMMISSIONERS UNDER THE GENERAL BANKING LAW.

Created July 29, 1858.

Thomas A. Graham, Tama county.
William Bickford, Jefferson county.
Philip Viele, Lee county.

The Bank Commissioners, as well as the Directors of the State Bank of Iowa are chosen by the General Assembly, the former in joint convention, every two years. Both offices are now merely nominal, as the State Bank has ceased to exist, and there has never been any bank established under the general banking law.

COMMISSIONERS OF LEGAL INQUIRY.

William H. Seevers, Mahaska county.
Jacob Butler, Muscatine county, appointed by the Governor September 13, 1866, to fill vacancy.
One vacancy.

The Commissioners of Legal Inquiry are appointed by the Governor and Senate every sixth year. A full Commission was appointed April 2d, 1866.

GEOLOGICAL SURVEY.

Charles A. White, Johnson county, State Geologist.

Gustavus Hinrichs, Johnson county, Chemist of the Survey.

O. H. St. John, Black Hawk county, Assistant Geologist.

The State Geologist was appointed by Chapter 73, Acts 11th General Assembly, and his term of service will continue until April 2, 1868, and until his successor is appointed. He appoints his Assistant and the Chemist of the Survey.

COUNTY GOVERNMENT.

TABLE SHOWING THE NAMES OF THE COUNTY JUDGES, CLERKS OF THE DISTRICT COURT, TREASURERS, AND RECORDERS, WITH THE COUNTY-SEATS OF THE SEVERAL COUNTIES.

COUNTIES.	COUNTY-SEATS.	COUNTY JUDGES.	CLERKS OF THE DISTRICT COURT.	TREASURERS.	RECORDERS.
Adair	Fontanelle	A. S. Taylor	William B. Hall	James C. Gibbs	Wesley Taylor
Adams	Quincy	S. H. Bugbee	John Bixby	Walter E, McDuffee	Walter E. McDuffee
Allamakee	Waukon	M. B. Hendrick	Giles P. Eells	H. H. Stillwell	Patrick Ryder
Appanoose	Centerville	Samuel M. Moore	Kelita P. Morrison	Charles W. Bowen	Samuel M. Moore
Audubon	Exira	Amherst Heath	Albert I. Brainard	A. B. Houston	H. F. Andrews
Benton	Vinton	George W. Gilchrist	Buren R. Sherman	James H. Shutts	Frederick Lyman
Black Hawk	Waterloo	Daniel W. Foote	Gustavus A. Eberhart	Romain A. Whitaker	James W. McClure
Boone	Boonsboro	Minor M. King	Henry R. Wilson	George E. Jones	Alonzo J. Barkley
Bremer	Waverly	Oren F. Avery	Henry C. Moore	William V. Lucas	Edward C. Dougherty
Buchanan	Independence	William H. Barton	Edward Brewer	Lewis A. Main	Thomas J. Marinus
Buena Vista	Prairieville	Richard Ridgway	Abner Bell	Hubbard Sanderson	James George
Butler	Butler Center	A. J. Tompkins	James W. Davis	John F. Wright	J. H. Hale
Calhoun	Lake City	Henry W. Sprague	William H. Fitch	Samuel T. Hutchisson	George G. Gray
Carroll	Carrollton	Thomas Elwood	Wm. Henry Price	William Gilley	Thomas Elwood
Cass	Lewis	Luther L. Alexander	William Waddell	Wilkins Warwick	Henry Temple
Cedar	Tipton	J. C. Betts	Sylvanus Yates	Edwin H. Pound	Jesse James
Cerro Gordo	Mason City	George E. Frost	B. F. Hartshorn	Thomas G. Emsley	Charles M. Adams
Cherokee	Cherokee	George W. Banester	Elisha Kingsbury	Carlton Corbett	Luther Phipps
Chickasaw	New Hampton	George A. Hamilton	Chester O. Case	William W. Birdsall	Benjamin E. Morton
Clarke	Osceola	James Rice	Allen H. Burrows	William G. Kennedy	Harvey H. Hess
Clay	Peterson	Peter M. M[o]ore.	Samuel W. Dubois	David N. Coats	Christian Kirchner
Clayton	Elkader	C. A. Dean	Henry S. Granger	J. C. Vaupel	William D. Crook
Clinton	De Witt	George B. Young	Noel B. Howard	Robert Williams	Joseph D. Fegan
Crawford	Denison	J. D. Miracle	Andrew D. Molony	Morris McHenry	Thomas Dobson

LIST OF COUNTY OFFICERS.—Continued.

COUNTIES.	COUNTY-SEATS.	COUNTY JUDGES.	CLERKS OF THE DISTRICT COURT.	TREASURERS.	RECORDERS.
Dallas	Adel	Jeremiah Perkins	John R. Joy	John Maulsby	Jeremiah Perkins
Davis	Bloomfield	William Van Benthusen	Erasmus W. Tatlock	Henry Nulton	Ambrose H. Hill
Decatur	Decatur City	Robert Kinnear	Edward K. Pitman	Samuel C. Thompson	William W. Ellis
Delaware	Delhi	J. B. Boggs	Eli O. Clemans	Joseph M. Holbrook	William H. H. Blanchard
Des Moines	Burlington	John C. Powers	William Garrett	William Horner	Samuel Pollock
Dickinson	Spirit Lake	Samuel Pillsbury	Albert A. Mosher	Thomas Wyckoff	Alexander Jenkins
Dubuque	Dubuque	Stephen Hempstead	H. A. Rooney	Arthur McCann	Warner Lewis
Emmett	Estherville	Charles Jarvis	Howard Graves	D. M. L. Bemus	Howard Graves
Fayette	West Union	H. N. Hawkins	Joseph Hobson	James Stewart	Edwin H. Kinyon
Floyd	Charles City	Abner Root	John V. W. Montague	Hervey Wilbur	Gustavus B. Eastman
Franklin	Hampton	W. W. Day	R. S. Benson	George Beed	James H. Beed
Fremont	Sidney	Alexander Wilson	John C. Shockley	Giles Cowles	D. G. Bodenhamer
Greene	New Jefferson	Harry Potter	I. D. Howard	Gillum S. Tolliver	Thomas G. Stiles
Grundy	Grundy Center	Albert F. Willoughby	James M. Comstock	E. H. Beckman	Albert F. Willoughby
Guthrie	Panora	Wm. Elliott	Wm. Maxwell	George W. Harlan	Howard Brown
Hamilton	Webster City	Isaiah Doane	Michael Sweeney	John Eckstein	Isaiah Doane
Hancock	Ellington	George W. Elder	James M. Elder	Henry N. Brockway	Lambert B. Bailey
Hardin	Eldora	Ellis Parker	Richard F. Ripley	Lucius E. Campbell	Samuel S. Waldo
Harrison	Magnolia	Benjamin Bonney	John W. Stocker	Augustin W. Ford	Henry C. Harshbarger
Henry	Mt. Pleasant	John B. Drayer	Thomas A. Bereman	Columbus V. Arnold	Horton J. Howard
Howard	New Oregon	Darius O. Preston	Aaron Kimball	M. M. Moon	William H. Patterson
Humboldt	Dakota City	Jared M. Snyder	Andrew W. McFarland	Charles Bergk	Charles Bergk
Ida	Ida	Obed Waterman	W. J. Wagoner	J. H. Moorehead	Ebenezer Comstock
Iowa	Marengo	Isaac Goodin	William G. Springer	Charles Baumer	Charles V. Gardner
Jackson	Andrew	J. S. Darling	E. J. Holmes	James A. Bryan	Benj. Van Steenburg
Jasper	Newton	Orlando C. Howe	John A. Seaton	Josiah B. Eyerly	John C. Wilson
Jefferson	Fairfield	Thomas Morgan	William Long	L. P. Vance	David B. Miller

Johnson......	Iowa City.......	James Cavanagh.......	Fernando H. Lee.......	Archibald C. Younkin..	Joseph S. Lodge........
Jones.........	Anamosa........	Davis McCarn..........	Jacob C. Dietz.	Lawrence Schoonover..	James S. Perfect ... ...
Keokuk	Sigourney.......	William McLoud.......	Joseph Andrews........	John J. Howard.... ...	James E. Woods........
Kossuth.....	Algona....	Lewis H. Smith........	James L. Paine....	Jerome E. Stacy.... ...	Harvey M. Taft........
Lee	Fort Madison....	Edmund Jaeger.........	Charles Doerr...... ...	A. C. Roberts..........	Noble Warwick .. ....
Linn	Marion	A. B. Dumont..........	Andrew J. McKean....	Richard T. Wilson.....	John J. Daniels........
Louisa	Wapello....	William G. Allen......	John Hale............	Whitney S. Kremer ...	John A. Brown.........
Lucas........	Chariton	Robert McCormick....	Nelson B. Gardner.....	James B. Custer........	Robert McCormick ....
Lyon.........	Not organized...	....	....	....	....
Madison......	Winterset	Thomas C. Gilpin......	Miller R. Tidrick.......	William L Leonard....	Oziah A. Moser........
Mahaska......	Oskaloosa	Samuel Thompson.....	Charles P. Searle.......	James A. Young........	John Larmer..........
Marion.......	Knoxville......	Joseph Brobst....	George Kruck....... ..	Edward Baker.	Allen Hamrick.........
Marshall	Marshalltown ...	Truman A. Lampman..	James L. Williams.....	Harry A. Gerhart......	A. J. Cooper...........
Mills.....	Glenwood........	D. M. Mitchell.........	H. A. Copeland.........	William H. Taft........	Jason M. Powell........
Mitchell	Mitchell.........	Amos S. Faville........	Calvin S. Prime........	Charles Sweney........	Garrett S. Needham....
Monona	Onawa.........	Elijah Peake..........	Herbert E. Morrison....	John E. Selleck.......	John E. Selleck........
Monroe	Albia...........	George Hickenlooper...	Joseph T. Young	Harrison Hickenlooper.	James Coen...........
Montgomery..	Red Oak Junction	W. G. Ewing.........	William W. Merritt.....	Wayne Stennett........	W. G. Ewing..........
Muscatine.....	Muscatine......	Henry H. Benson.......	John W. Jayne........	Robert F. Thompson....	Wilford M. Kennedy...
O'Brien	O'Brien.........	Archibald Murray......	John Moore..........	Chester W. Inman.....	Archibald Murray......
Osceola.....	Not organized...	....	....	....	....
Page..........	Clarinda....	John R. Morledge......	Jacob Butler........ ..	Henry Dorsey....	Ancil B. Cramer.......
Palo Alto	Soda Bar...	John M. Hefley........	James H. Underwood...	James P. White	Allen Barker..........
Plymouth	Melbourne..	A. E. Rea..............	A. C. Sheetz..........	John Henry Morf... ..	Henry Snider..........
Pocahontas...	Milton..........	Samuel N. Harris.......	William D. McEwen....	William H. Hait.......	E. C. Brown..........
Polk	Des Moines.....	John B. Miller.........	Harry H. Griffiths......	Charles G. Lewis	Irving N. Thomas......
Pottawa'tamie	Council Bluffs...	Hardin Jones..........	Edward F. Burdick....	William Porterfield	William G. Crawford...
Poweshiek ...	Montezuma	Lucian C. Blanchard....	John W. Cheshire......	Sylvester Bates.........	John Hall.............
Ringgold	Mount Ayer.....	John T. Williams......	Thomas Ross..........	Charles W. Dake.......	Warren R. Turk........
Sac..........	Sac City........	David Carr Early.	Wm. H. Hobbs.........	R. Ellis................	Nathan W. Condron....
Scott.........	Davenport	Theodore D. Eagal. ...	John Galligan..........	Levy S. Viele	James Thorington......

LIST OF COUNTY OFFICERS.—CONTINUED.

COUNTIES.	COUNTY-SEATS.	COUNTY-JUDGES.	CLERKS OF THE DISTRICT COURT.	TREASURERS.	RECORDERS.
Shelby	Harlan	Nathan Lindsey	Alfred M Louis	Milo H. Adams	John P. Gish
Sioux	Calliope	R. D. Fought	Bartlett M. Morse	Andrew J. Brown	David Carroll
Story	Nevada	Rothens H. Mitchell	Joseph A. Fitchpatrick	Thomas C. Davis	Samuel Bates
Tama	Toledo	Thomas J. Free	David D. Appelgate	James H. Struble	Jacob Yeiser, jr.
Taylor	Bedford	R. B. Kinsell	Elisha T. Smith	Ezekiel Rose	Daniel Underwood
Union	Afton	Joshua F. Bishop	G. W. Beymer	Ira Seeley	Orrin E. Davis
Van Buren	Keosauqua	Alexander Brown	John A. Miller	Joshua S. Sloan	Edwin Goddard
Wapello	Ottumwa	James S. Porter	Leonidas M. Godley	William J. Ross	Daniel W. Tower
Warren	Indianola	John D. Ingalls	Charles McKay	Paris P. Henderson	Miles W. Judkins
Washington	Washington	Samuel Bigger	Christopher T. Jones	Robert Glasgow	William R. Jeffrey
Wayne	Corydon	Martin Read	E. W. Fullerton	Benjamin S. Jones	A. R. Meredith
Webster	Fort Dodge	James R. Strow	Wilson Lumpkin	Jonathan Hutchinson	David H. Taylor
Winnebago	Forest City	Samuel Tennis	E. D. Hinman	R. Clark	H. S. Botsford
Winneshiek	Decorah	E. Cutler, jr.	Dan. Lawrence	George N. Holway	John E. Powers
Woodbury	Sioux City	J. H. Snider	F. J. Lambert	B. F. Smith	A. Groninger
Worth	Northwood	John U. Perry	Horace V. Dwelle	Duncan McKercher	Duncan McKercher
Wright	Grant	John L. Morse	George A. McKay	Charles A. Overbaugh	R. K. Eastman

TABLE SHOWING THE SHERIFFS, SURVEYORS, SUPERINTENDENTS OF COMMON SCHOOLS, CORONERS, AND DRAINAGE COMMISSIONERS OF THE SEVERAL COUNTIES OF THE STATE.

COUNTIES.	SHERIFFS.	SURVEYORS.	SUPERINTENDENTS OF COMMON SCHOOLS.	CORONERS.	DRAINAGE COMMISSIONERS.
Adair	Abner Root	S. W. Pryor	C. J. Bowman	Lemuel Lewis	
Adams	William Bixler	Abel A. Nolan	B. Wiesner	James P. Campbell	Zachary Lawrence
Allamakee	Robert Bathan	Henry Dayton	Theodore Nachtway	John Farrell	G. L. Miller
Appanoose	Henry H. Wright	J. J. Wall	L. N. Judd	Beverly A. Joiner	
Audubon	John Huntley	P. I. Whitted	B. G. Dodge	B. Muermen	B. B. Beers
Benton	Henry M. Wilson	James A. Brown	Amos Dean	Moses Denman	
Black Hawk	William F. Brown	E. A. Snyder	Seymour Gookins	George W. Dickenson	
Boone	George W. Crooks	J. B. Torbert	Harrison Selby	Lewis Davis	Jacob Stull
Bremer	Charles M. Kingsley	Harry S. Hoover	J. Ransom Hall	G. W. Nash	
Buchanan	John A. Davis	J. W. Myers	Sylvester G. Pierce	Hiram H. Hunt	
Buena Vista	Olans H. Dahl	F. W. Suckow	O. H. Starle	M. Steen	Theodore Steen
Butler	Lyman L. Smith	O. W. McIntosh	George Graham	E. W. Metzger	E. D. Button
Calhoun	William Miles	Seldon H. Richardson	Jonathan Bishop	Daniel Lowe	James Fluce
Carroll	James H. Colclo	J. F. H. Sugg	John K. Deal	A. P. Willson	
Cass	Victor M. Bradshaw	Albert Wakefield	H G. Smith	Oliver Mills	Horace Littlefield
Cedar	John D. Shearer	Martin G. Miller	E. L. Bassett	William H. Hammond	Robert Gower
Cerro Gordo	A. M. Thompson	Charles McNany	Nathan Bass	Gabriel Pence	D. Dougherty
Cherokee	Samuel T. Miller	Joel H. Davenport	George E. Fisher	Silas B. Parkest	John Doak
Chickasaw	James A. Albertson	H. H. Patter	J. C. Johnson	William Everingham	Julius H. Powers
Clarke	Eben. M. Ledgerwood	Abraham C. Rarick	Jesse L. Adkins	Jonas Smith	
Clay	David Watts	Peter M. Mo[o]re	Romanzo A. Coats	Joseph L. Crozier	J. W. Brockschink
Clayton	James Davis	M. E. Smith	W. A. Preston	H. D. Bro[w]nson	
Clinton	Robert Hogle	Benjamin B. Hart	Richard J. Crouch	Daniel McNeil	W. W. A. Huntington
Crawford	Benjamin Clough	Morris McHenry	Henry C. Laub	David McWilliams	
Dallas	John M. Byers	Thomas C. Walsh	Amos Dilley	Macklin E. Coons	G. L. Robertson
Davis	Daniel Bradbury	John E. F. Patterson	John W. Young	Ed. Grinstead	
Decatur	George Woodbury	Samuel Sears	Samuel Bowman	M. D. Miller	
Delaware	William Williams	Hezekiah G. Doolittle	F. W. Dunham	D. Trumbull	
Des Moines	James H. Latty	Charles Handeler	Thomas J. Trulock	William A. Haw	J. Wilson Williams

LIST OF COUNTY OFFICERS—Continued.

COUNTIES.	SHERIFFS.	SURVEYORS.	SUPERINTENDENTS OF COMMON SCHOOLS.	CORONERS.	DRAINAGE COMMISSIONERS.
Dickinson	W. S. Beers	W. F. Pillsbury	John Smith	....	....
Dubuque	William D. Bucknam	John T. Everett	J. J. E. Norman	J. O'Hea Cantillon	J. Gilmore
Emmett	Giles W. Robbins	L. S. Williams	A. C. Rasmussen	A. Ordway	Nels Peterson
Fayette	Jacob Swank	H. J. Ingersoll	A. M. Felts	Lewis Armstrong	....
Floyd	David M. Ferguson	Edwin Klintop	Henry O. Pratt	Benjamin F. Wright	....
Franklin	Albert Pickering	S. H. Vankirk	L. B. Raymond	J. K. Addis	B. H. Gibbs
Fremont	William Martin	Eldred Huff	G. W. Hoop	J. A. Kelly	John Copeland
Greene	Clinton DeWitt	James L. Perry	M. B. McDuffie	James Thornton	....
Grundy	Charles H. Clark	John J. Schuber	Lorenzo D. Tracy	E. B. Lamb	Joseph F. Walker
Guthrie	Joseph W. Cummins	James W. Nation	James L. Grandstaff	Henry C. Cox	Ira P. Wetmore
Hamilton	John McMiller	William T. Wright	W. J. Covil	Jesse R. Burgess	Hewitt Ross
Hancock	J. H. Beadle	James Crow	C. Boughton	Sewell Whitcombe	John Christie, sen
Hardin	Nelson Gibbs	Judd Bradley	J. M. Boyd	S. P. Smith	T. H. Quiggle
Harrison	Albert J. Cutler	J. Z. Hunt	Charles H. Holmes	Matthew Winter	Job Ross
Henry	William T. Spearman	James Hanks	Joseph McCarty	William Bird	....
Howard	Jerry F. Powell	P. N. Glathart	Timothy W. Lee	J. J. Clemmer	....
Humboldt	Henry C. Cusey	T. Elwood Collins	Eber Stone	A. N. Coffin	John Bartholomew
Ida	A. J. Teal	A. J. Teal	Matthew G. Aldrich	C. L. Crain	....
Iowa	John M. Richardson	John L. Williams	William R. Akers	William K. Miller	....
Jackson	Morris S. Allen	A. C. Simpson	T. C. Phelan	James W. Eckles	James Clark
Jasper	James M. Rodgers	Charles C. Turner	Sanford J. Moyer	David S. Stover	....
Jefferson	Jacob S. Gantz	I. H. Crumley	David Herron	J. Monroe Shaffer	....
Johnson	Samuel P. McCaddon	Edward Worden	George S. Hampton	Charles A. Vogt	....
Jones	Orrin B. Crane	Daniel L. Blakeslee	James R. Stillman	V. C. Williston	....
Keokuk	John T. Parker	Joel Crossman	A. J. Kane	A. C. Robison	....
Kossuth	John M. Pinkerton	Henry Durant, jr	John Reed	George W. Paine	....

Lee	John A. Bishop	George Berry	William G. Kent	Henry Schevers	
Linn	John G. Hayzlett	George A. Gray	Zarah B. Ellsberry	Mowry Farnum	
Louisa	Edwin B. Lacey	William C. Blackstone	J. B. Porter	George Presbury	
Lucas	Gaylord Lyman	Wilson R. Larimer	William H. Maple	John C. Miller	
Madison	Jonas F. Brock	P. G. Andrews	H. W. Hardy	J. H. Mack	
Mahaska	James W. Hinesley	Nathaniel Caven	Jeremiah F. Everett	George W. Norton	Nathaniel Caven
Marion	J. P. Vincent	John Caruthers	(Not reported)	Henry Keefer	
Marshall	T. C. McCracken	William Bremner	Thomas J. Wilson	William B. Waters	
Mills	Ezra B. Samson	David Templeton	L. S. Williams	D. F. Eakin	D. B. Herrington
Mitchell	William Ramsdell	Nelson Rood	Alva Bush	L S. Hart, jr	G. S. Johnson
Monona	William A. Grow	Charles H. Holbrook	J. S. Maughlin	Richard Stebbins	Delos M. Dimmick
Monroe	Alexander McDonald	John N. Massey	J. W. H. Griffin	Elijah T. Knight	
Montgomery	Hiram G. McMillan	E. P. Milner	E. H. Burris	J. M. Hewitt	
Muscatine	Abraham E. Keith	John A. Mathewson	Robert H. McCampbell	John Beard	Gamaliel Olds
O'Brien	C. Chesley	Daniel W. Inman	Chester W. Inman	H. H. Waterman	R. B. Crego
Osceola					
Page	George W. Burns	Thomas J. Garnett	James A. Woods	James W. Scott	
Palo Alto	John McFarland	Ben Franklin	D. W. Spaldin		
Plymouth	J. P. Riley	A. C. Sheetz	A. C. Sheetz	Andrew Black	
Pocahontas		Oscar Strong	James J. Brace	J. N. Johnson	
Polk	Peter H. Van Slyck	Jule Bausman	Cyrus A. Mosier	Madison Young	James Brundige
Pottawattamie	Perry Reel	Richard Kaywood	E. W. Bennett	Berthold Hahn	
Poweshiek	Nicholas Carr	Thomas J. Drain	S. Jay Buck	William S. Green	
Ringgold	John A. Lesan	Albert G. Beall	Henry H. Ross	James A. Drake	
Sac	J. S. Tiberghien	Charles Wilson	William P. Drewry	R. G. Platt	Eugene Criss.
Scott	Gustav Schnitger	Thomas Murray	John Gallagher	G. Hoepfner	
Shelby	Thomas Chatburn	Abraham Rubendall	Barney Hensdall	Martin Polland	William Howlett, jr.
Sioux	R. D. Fought	A. Scott	Bartlett M. Morse	A. St. Clair	A. Scott
Story	Henry F. Murphey	Madison C. Allen	Franklin D. Thompson		Adolphus Rood
Tama	Knight Dexter.	C. W. Hyatt	J. R. Stewart	Nathan Fisher	W. S. Turbett
Taylor	Martin V. King	D. W. Lamb	W. B. Snow	W. S. Hamilton	

LIST OF COUNTY OFFICERS—CONTINUED.

COUNTIES.	SHERIFFS.	SURVEYORS.	SUPERINTENDENTS OF COMMON SCHOOLS.	CORONERS.	DRAINAGE COMMISSIONERS.
Union	Milton Carter	Frederick Sommer	A. Robbins	C. T. Hyde	
Van Buren	John C. McCrary	Ira Claflin	George B. Walker	L. W. Thornburg	
Wapello	Thomas Bedwell	John Grant	S. L. Burnham	Ansel L. Chamberlin	
Warren	Elbert J. Kuhn	Levi Reeves	Julius C. Clarke	Archibald Payne	
Washington	Abram Bunker	C. C. Paulk	Isaiah G. Moore	Robert W. McElroy	
Wayne	William M. Littell	Burris Moore	W. H. H. Rogers	Nathan Brown	
Webster	Jacob Waltz	George S. Killam	Daniel A. Weller	Francis Brewer	Daniel W. Prindle
Winnebago	M. K. Landrue	Augustus Oulman	C. A. Steadman	G. P. Smith	Wm. Lackore
Winneshiek	A. Skofstad	Ebenezer Baldwin	John M. Wedgewood	Cyrus McKay	
Woodbury	George W. Kingsnorth	John C. Watts	M. Tingley	O. G. Fisher	S. R. Day
Worth	William H. Perkins	Lemuel Dwelle	James Keeler	Simon Kustad	James D. Kendall
Wright	William Hulse	John C. Morris	Wm. M. D. Van Velsor	R. E. Train	

IOWA IN XLTH CONGRESS.

SENATORS FROM IOWA.

James Harlan, Mt. Pleasant; term expires March 4, 1873.
James W. Grimes, Burlington; term expires March 4, 1871.

REPRESENTATIVES FROM IOWA.

James F. Wilson, Fairfield, 1st district.
Hiram Price, Davenport, 2d district.
William B. Allison, Dubuque, 3d district.
William Loughridge, Oskaloosa, 4th district.
Grenville M. Dodge, Council Bluffs, 5th district.
Asahel W. Hubbard, Sioux City, 6th District.

FEDERAL OFFICERS IN IOWA.

JUDICIAL.

Samuel F. Miller, Keokuk, Associate Justice of the Supreme Court of the United States, and Presiding Judge of the Eighth Circuit of the United States.

James M. Love, Ottumwa, Judge of the U. S. District of Iowa.

Wiliam G. Woodward, Muscatine, Clerk of the U. S. Circuit Court.

John C. Burns, Dubuque, Clerk of the U. S. District Court.

George W. Clark, Indianola, U. S. Marshal.
Alexander Bowers, Des Moines, Deputy.
Harry H. Fulton, Keokuk, Deputy.
P. M. Crawford, Dubuque, Deputy.
Fitzroy Sessions, Cedar Falls, Deputy.

REGISTERS IN BANKRUPTCY.

John Bruce, Keokuk, 1st Congressional District.
Milton M. Price, Davenport, 2d Congressional District.
Willis Drummond, McGregor, 3d Congressional District.
Daniel Anderson, Albia, 4th Congressional District.
John Mitchell, Des Moines, 5th Congressional District.
Charles W. Lowrie, Boonsboro, 6th Congressional District.

U. S. COMMISSIONERS.

William G. Woodward, Muscatine, appointed November, 1862.
John L. Harvey, Dubuque, appointed November, 1862.
Stephen Sibley, Des Moines, appointed November, 1862.
H. B. Ten Eyck, Keokuk, appointed November, 1862.
John N. Rogers, Davenport, appointed November, 1862.
D. C. Bloomer, Council Bluffs, appointed November, 1862.
Micajah Williams, Oskaloosa, appointed November, 1862.
Richard Ambler, Mt. Pleasant, appointed November, 1862.
George Frazee, Burlington, appointed November, 1862.
Henry B. Hendershott, Ottumwa, appointed, 1862.
H. P. Scholte, Pella, appointed November, 1862.
Charles W. Simmons, Boonsboro, appointed November, 1862.
William G. Hammond, Des Moines, appointed November, 1862.
Henry Hospers, Marion county, appointed June 5, 1863.
James B. Powers, Cedar Falls, appointed June 8, 1865.
Walter I. Hayes, Clinton, appointed May, 1867.
Thomas Sargent, Fort Dodge, appointed May, 1867.
Daniel M. Harris, Panora, appointed May, 1867.
William T. Smith, Oskaloosa, appointed May, 1867.
Harvey J. Skiff, Powshiek county, appoiuted May, 1867.
Daniel F. Ellsworth, Hardin county, appointed May, 1867.
John Currier, Sioux City, appointed May, 1867.
John S. Stacy, Anamosa, appointed May, 1867.
George Woodbury, Decatur county, appointed May, 1867.
John A. Hull, Boonsboro, appointed May, 1867.
Rush Clark, Iowa City, appointed May, 1867.
James H. Shields, Dubuque, appointed October 26, 1867.

Benjamin W. Poor, Dubuque, appointed October 26, 1867.
* Franklin Wilcox, ———— appointed October 26, 1867.
*John Rogers, Keokuk county; appointed October 26, 1867.
*John N. W. Rumple, Iowa county; appointed October 26, 1867.
*Sanford Harned, Keokuk county; appointed October 26, 1867.

MASTER IN CHANCERY.

William G. Woodward, Muscatine county; appointed November 17, 1862.

INTERNAL REVENUE.

ASSESSORS.

James B. Weaver, 1st collection district; office at Bloomfield.
George Meason, 2d collection district; office at Muscatine.
Lucius L. Huntley, 3d collection district; office at Dubuque.
John Connell, 4th collection district; office at Toledo.
Cole Noel, 5th collection district; office at Adel.
Thomas H. Benton, jr., 6th collection district; office at Marshalltown.

COLLECTORS.

William W. Belknap, 1st collection district; office at Keokuk.
James Armstrong, 2d collection district; office at Davenport.
David B. Henderson, 3d collection district; office at Dubuque.
Alonzo J. Pope, 4th collection district; office at Sigourney.
Lampson P. Sherman, 5th collection district; office at Des Moines.
Albert Head, 6th collection district; office at New Jefferson.

* Commissions not yet issued.

PENSION AGENTS.

David B. Wilson, Fairfield.
M. Mobley, Dubuque.
James D. Thompson, Des Moines.

The office at Fairfield does the pension business of the following counties: those in the 1st Congressional district; those in the 4th do. except Benton, Jasper, Marion, and Tama; and Muscatine in the 2d do.

The office at Dubuque does the pension business for the following counties: those in the 2d Congressional district, except Muscatine; those in the 3d do.; Benton and Tama, in the 4th do.; and Black Hawk, Butler, Cerro Gordo, Franklin, Grundy, and Worth in the 6th district.

The Des Moines office does the pension business for the remainder of the State.

LIST OF NEWSPAPERS AND PERIODICALS PUBLISHED IN THE STATE, DEC. 1, 1867.

COUNTIES.	NAMES OF PUBLICATIONS.	WHERE PUBLISHED.	HOW OFTEN PUBLISHED.	CHARACTER.
Adair	The Adair County Register	Fontanelle	Weekly	Republican
Adams	Adams County Gazette	Quincy	Weekly	Republican
Allamakee	The Lansing Mirror	Lansing	Weekly	Republican
Allamakee	Weekly Chronicle	Lansing	Weekly	Neutral
Appanoose	The Loyal Citizen	Centerville	Weekly	Republican
Benton	Vinton Eagle	Vinton	Weekly	Republican
Benton	Belle Plaine Transcript	Belle Plaine	Weekly	Republican
Benton	The Benton County News	Vinton	Weekly	Neutral
Black Hawk	The Cedar Falls Gazette	Cedar Falls	Weekly	Republican
Black Hawk	Waterloo Courier	Waterloo	Weekly	Republican
Boone	The Montana Standard	Montana	Weekly	Republican
Boone	The Boone County Advocate	Boonsboro	Weekly	Republican
Bremer	Bremer County Phœnix	Waverly	Weekly	Republican
Bremer	Democratic News	Waverly	Weekly	Democrat
Buchanan	Buchanan County Bulletin and Guardian	Independence	Weekly	Republican
Buchanan	*Conservative	Independence	Weekly	Democrat
Butler	*Gazette	Clarksville	Weekly	Republican
Cass	Cass County Messenger	Lewis	Weekly	Republican
Cedar	The Tipton Advertiser	Tipton	Weekly	Republican
Cedar	Mechanicsville Journal	Mechanicsville	Weekly	
Cerro Gordo	Cerro Gordo Republican	Mason City	Weekly	Republican
Chickasaw	New Hampton Courier	New Hampton	Weekly	Republican
Chickasaw	The Weekly Nashua Post	Nashua	Weekly	Republican
Clarke	Clarke County Sentinel	Osceola	Weekly	Republican
Clayton	The Clayton County Journal	Elkader	Weekly	Republican
Clayton	North Iowa Times	McGregor	Weekly	Democrat
Clayton	Weekly McGregor News	McGregor	Weekly	Republican
Clinton	Lyons Weekly Mirror	Lyons	Weekly	Republican
Clinton	Clinton Semi-Weekly Herald	Clinton	Semi-weekly	Republican
Clinton	The DeWitt Observer	DeWitt	Weekly	Republican

LIST OF NEWSPAPERS AND PERIODICALS—CONTINUED.

COUNTIES.	NAMES OF PUBLICATIONS.	WHERE PUBLISHED.	HOW OFTEN PUBLISHED.	CHARACTER.
Clinton	*Lyons Advocate	Lyons	Weekly	Democrat
Clinton	*Iowa Volkszeitung*	Lyons	Weekly	"People's Party."
Crawford	Denison Review	Denison	Weekly	Republican
Dallas	The Dallas Weekly Gazette	Adel	Weekly	Republican
Davis	Weekly Union Guard	Bloomfield	Weekly	Republican
Decatur	The Leon Pioneer	Leon	Weekly	Democrat
Delaware	Delaware County Union	Manchester	Weekly	Republican
Des Moines	Burlington Hawk-Eye	Burlington	Daily, Semi-Weekly, and Weekly	Republican
Des Moines	Gazette and Argus	Burlington	Daily and Weekly	Democrat
Des Moines	Weekly National Merchant	Burlington	Weekly	Commercial
Des Moines	*Die Iowa Tribune*	Burlington	Tri-Weekly and Weekly	"People's Party."
Dubuque	*National Demokrat*	Dubuque	Weekly	Democrat
Dubuque	The Dubuque Times	Dubuque	Daily and Weekly	Republican
Dubuque	Dubuque Herald	Dubuque	Daily and Weekly	Democrat
Dubuque	*Iowa Staatszeitung*	Dubuque	Weekly	Republican
Fayette	The Fayette County Union	West Union	Weekly	Democrat
Fayette	*Leader	Clermont	Weekly	Republican
Fayette	North Iowa Observer	Fayette	Weekly	Republican
Floyd	Hildreth's Charles City Intelligencer	Charles City	Weekly	Republican
Franklin	Franklin Reporter	Hampton	Weekly	Republican
Fremont	The American Union	Sidney	Weekly	Democrat
Fremont	Fremont Weekly Times	Hamburg	Weekly	Republican
Greene	New Jefferson Era	New Jefferson	Weekly	Republican
Guthrie	Guthrie County Ledger	Panora	Weekly	Democrat
Guthrie	Guthrie Vedette	Panora	Weekly	Republican
Hamilton	The Hamilton Freeman	Webster City	Weekly	Republican
Hardin	Iowa Falls Sentinel	Iowa Falls	Weekly	Republican
Hardin	The Eldora Ledger	Eldora	Weekly	Republican
Harrison	The Western Star	Magnolia	Weekly	Republican

Henry	Mt. Pleasant Journal	Mt. Pleasant	Weekly	Republican
Henry	The Free Press	Mt. Pleasant	Weekly	Republican
Henry	The Salem Excelsior	Salem	Weekly	Republican
Howard	*Plaindealer		Weekly	Democrat
Howard	Cresco Times	Cresco	Weekly	Republican
Humboldt	Humboldt True Democrat	Springvale	Weekly	Republican
Iowa	Progressive Republican	Marengo	Weekly	Republican
Iowa	*Citizen	Marengo	Weekly	Democrat
Jackson	Maquoketa Excelsior	Maquoketa	Weekly	Republican
Jackson	The Bellevue Journal	Bellevue	Weekly	Republican
Jackson	*Sabula Gazette	Sabula	Weekly	Republican
Jasper	Jasper Free Press	Newton	Weekly	Republican
Jasper	The Jasper Weekly Republican	Newton	Weekly	Republican
Jefferson	The Fairfield Ledger	Fairfield	Weekly	Republican
Jefferson	The Home Visitor	Fairfield	Weekly	Republican
Jefferson	The Iowa Democrat	Fairfield	Weekly	Democrat
Johnson	Iowa City Republican	Iowa City	Weekly	Republican
Johnson	The State Press	Iowa City	Weekly	Democrat
Johnson	The Annals of Iowa	Iowa City	Quarterly	Historical
Jones	The Anamosa Eureka	Anamosa	Weekly	Republican
Jones	Monticello Express	Monticello	Weekly	Republican
Keokuk	Sigourney Weekly News	Sigourney	Weekly	Republican
Kossuth	The Upper Des Moines	Algona	Weekly	Republican
Lee	Gate City	Keokuk	Daily and Weekly	Republican
Lee	Fort Madison Plaindealer	Fort Madison	Weekly	Republican
Lee	The Constitution	Keokuk	Daily and Weekly	Democrat
Lee	*Der Keokuk Telegraph*	Keokuk	Weekly	Democrat
Linn	The Cedar Valley Times	Cedar Rapids	Weekly	Republican
Linn	The Marion Register	Marion	Weekly	Republican
Linn	*The Marion Patriot	Marion	Weekly	
Louisa	Wapello Republican	Wapello	Weekly	Republican
Lucas	The Chariton Patriot	Chariton	Weekly	Republican
Lucas	Chariton Democrat	Chariton	Weekly	Democrat

LIST OF NEWSPAPERS AND PERIODICALS—Continued.

COUNTIES.	NAMES OF PUBLICATIONS.	WHERE PUBLISHED.	HOW OFTEN PUBLISHED.	CHARACTER.
Madison	The Winterset Madisonian	Winterset	Weekly	Republican
Mahaska	The Weekly Oskaloosa Herald	Oskaloosa	Weekly	Republican
Mahaska	The Democratic Conservator	Oskaloosa	Weekly	Democrat
Mahaska	The Temperance Gem	Oskaloosa	Monthly	Temperance
Mahaska	The Central Iowa Citizen	Oskaloosa	Weekly	Republican
Marion	The Marion County Democrat	Knoxville	Weekly	Democrat
Marion	Pella Blade	Pella	Weekly	Republican
Marion	Iowa Voter	Knoxville	Weekly	Republican
Marion	*De Pella Gazette*	Pella	Weekly	Republican
Marshall	The Marshall County Times	Marshalltown	Weekly	Republican
Marshall	Marshall County Advance	Marshalltown	Weekly	Democrat
Mills	The Glenwood Opinion	Glenwood	Weekly	Republican
Mitchell	The North Iowan	Osage	Weekly	Republican
Mitchell	Mitchell County Press	Mitchell	Weekly	Republican
Monona	The Monona County Gazette	Onawa	Weekly	Republican
Monroe	The Weekly Albia Union	Albia	Weekly	Republican
Muscatine	Muscatine Journal	Muscatine	Daily, Tri-weekly, and Weekly	Republican
Muscatine	Muscatine Courier	Muscatine	Daily and Weekly	Democrat
Muscatine	The Wilton Chronicle	Muscatine	Weekly	....
Page	The Page County Herald	Clarinda	Weekly	Republican
Polk	Iowa State Register	Des Moines	Daily and Weekly	Republican
Polk	Iowa Statesman	Des Moines	Daily and Weekly	Democrat
Polk	Iowa Homestead	Des Moines	Weekly	Agricultural
Polk	Iowa Instructor and School Journal	Des Moines	Monthly	Educational
Polk	The Temperance Platform	Des Moines	Bi-weekly	Temperance
Polk	The Western Jurist	Des Moines	Bi-monthly	Legal
Pottawattamie	The Council Bluffs Bugle	Council Bluffs	Weekly	Democrat
Pottawattamie	Council Bluffs Nonpareil	Council Bluffs	Daily and Weekly	Republican
Poweshiek	The Montezuma Republican	Montezuma	Weekly	Republican
Ringgold	The Ringgold Record	Mount Ayr	Weekly	Republican

Scott	Davenport Gazette	Davenport	Daily and Weekly	Republican
Scott	*Der Demokrat*	Davenport	Daily and Weekly	"People's Party."
Scott	Davenport Democrat	Davenport	Daily and Weekly	Democrat
Scott	Le Claire Register	Le Claire	Weekly	Republican
Scott	The True Radical	Davenport	Weekly	"People's Party."
Scott	The Western Soldier's Friend	Davenport	Monthly	Republican
Story	The Story County Ægis	Nevada	Weekly	Republican
Tama	Tama County Union	Tama City	Weekly	
Tama	Tama County Republican	Tama City	Weekly	Republican
Tama	The Orford Leader	Orford	Weekly	Republican
Taylor	The Iowa South-West	Bedford	Weekly	Republican
Union	The Weekly Afton Tribune	Afton	Weekly	Republican
Van Buren	Keosauqua Republican	Keosauqua	Weekly	Republican
Van Buren	Bentonsport Signal	Bentonsport	Weekly	Democrat
Wapello	Ottumwa Courier	Ottumwa	Daily and Weekly	Republican
Wapello	The Eddyville Transcript	Eddyville	Weekly	Republican
Wapello	Ottumwa Democratic Mercury	Ottumwa	Daily and Weekly	Democrat
Warren	Weekly Visitor	Indianola	Weekly	Republican
Washington	The Washington County Press	Washington	Weekly	Republican
Washington	The Record	Washington	Weekly	Republican
Wayne	Corydon Monitor	Corydon	Weekly	Republican
Webster	The Iowa North-West	Fort Dodge	Weekly	Republican
Winneshiek	The Decorah Republican	Decorah	Weekly	Republican
Winneshiek	The Winneshiek Register	Decorah	Weekly	Republican
Woodbury	The Sioux City Register	Sioux City	Weekly	Democrat
Woodbury	The Sioux City Journal	Sioux City	Weekly	Republican

NOTE.—The names of the papers in the above list have been taken from the first page headings, except those marked thus *, copies of which were not at hand. The names in italics are of those printed in the German language, except "*De Pella Gazette*," which is printed in the Dutch language.

APPENDIX.

The matter contained in the following pages, comprising a list of executive, judicial, and legislative officers of the Territory and State from the organization of Iowa Territory, July 3, 1838, to the 1st of January, 1868, together with other information, has been prepared in the office of the Secretary of State from the records of that office and other reliable sources; and was gotten up for the purpose of preserving the information thus collected in a compact and convenient form for official reference hereafter. The Census Board, believing it would be of interest and use to the public generally, have requested its publication. Accordingly, it is here inserted as an Appendix to the Census Report.

ED WRIGHT, Secretary of State.

HISTORICAL MEMORANDA.

The territory embraced in the present State of Iowa is a part of what is commonly called the "Louisiana Purchase," which, as is known, includes all that portion of our national possessions west of the Mississippi river, excepting Texas and the territory since obtained from Mexico and from Russia. This immense domain, known in the treaties as the "Colony or Province of Louisiana," was originally taken possession of by France, which nation divided with England, Spain and Russia the entire continent of North America. In 1763, at the close of what is known in our history as the "Old French War," and in Europe as the "Seven-years War," France parted with her share of the continent: Great Britain retaining Canada and the regions to the northward, which she had conquered during the war; while Spain obtained, by cession, the territory west of the Mississippi. On the 1st of October, 1800, Spain, by the treaty of St. Idlefonso, retroceded this territory to France. By the treaty of April 30, 1803, France ceded it to the United States; in consideration of which the former government was to receive the sum of $11,250,000, and the liquidation of certain claims held by citizens of the United States against France, not exceeding in amount $3,750,000.

By act of Congress, approved October 31, 1803, the President was authorized to take possession of the territory and provide for it a temporary government. By another act of the same session, approved March 26, 1804, the newly acquired country was divided, October 1, 1804, into the territory of "Orleans" (south of the thirty-third parallel north latitude) and the District of "Louisiana," which latter was placed under the authority of the officers of Indiana Territory. On the 4th of July, 1805, under act of Congress, approved March 3, 1805, the "District of Louisiana" was organized into a territory of the same name, with a government of its own, in which condition it remained until 1812. On the 30th of April, in that year, the territory of Orleans became a State of the Union, under the name of "Louisiana;" and on the first Monday in December, by virtue of an act approved June 4, 1812, the territory of Louisiana was reorganized and called the "Territory of Missouri." By an act of Congress approved March 2, 1819, which took effect July 4, "Arkansaw Territory" was formed, comprising the present State of Arkansas and the country to the westward. By a joint resolution, approved March 2, 1821, the "State of Missouri," being a part of the territory of that name, was admitted into the Union.

By act of Congress, approved June 28, 1834, the territory "bounded on the east by the Mississippi river, on the south by the State of Missouri," &c., was made a part of the territory of Michigan. On the 3d day of July, 1836, Wisconsin territory, embracing within its limits the present States of Iowa, Minnesota, and Wisconsin, was taken from that of Michigan, and given a separate government. On the 3d day of July, 1838, by virtue of an act of Congress, approved June 12, 1838, the territory of IOWA was constituted; including, in addition to the present State, the greater part of what is now Minnesota, and extending northward to the British line.

By act of Congress, approved March 3d, 1845, provision was made for the admission of Iowa into the Union, with boundaries extending on the north to the parallel of latitude passing through the mouth of the Mankato or Blue Earth river, and on the west only to 17° 30′ west from Washington, corresponding very nearly to the existing line between Ringgold and Union counties, on the one hand, and Taylor and Adams on the other. The Constitutional Convention of 1844 had adopted much more extensive boundaries even than those of the present State, the northwestern line extending from the mouth of the Big Sioux or Calumet river direct to the St. Peter's river where the Watonwan river (according to Nicollet's map) enters the same; thence down the main channel of said river to the main channel of the Mississippi river; and thence down the Mississippi, embracing within the proposed limits some of the richest portions of the present State of Minnesota. The reduction of these boundaries by Congress being quite distasteful to the people, the whole thing was rejected at a popular election. In 1846, Congress proposed new boundary lines, which were embodied in the Constitution adopted that year; the State retaining the Missouri slope, but submitting to a material reduction of its pretensions on the north, its western line in that direction, however, being extended to the Big Sioux river. The Constitution with these modified boundaries having been accepted by the people, the STATE OF IOWA was formally admitted into the Union on the twenty-eighth day of December, in the year of our Lord one thousand eight hundred and forty-six, as the twenty-ninth State in the Confederacy.

REGISTER OF THE TERRITORY OF IOWA.

TERRITORIAL OFFICERS.

GOVERNORS.

Robert Lucas, appointed 1838.
John Chambers, appointed 1841.
James Clarke, appointed November, 1845.

SECRETARIES.

William B. Conway, appointed 1838; died in office, November, 1839.
James Clarke, appointed 1839.
O. H. W. Stull, appointed 1841.
Samuel J. Burr, appointed 1843.
Jesse Williams, appointed 1845.

TERRITORIAL AUDITORS.

Office created January 7, 1840.

Jesse Williams, appointed January 14, 1840.
William L. Gilbert, appointed January 23, 1843; reappointed February 27, 1844.
Robert M. Secrest, appointed 1845.

TERRITORIAL TREASURERS.

Office created February 23, 1839.

Thornton Bayless, appointed January 23, 1839.
Morgan Reno, appointed 1840.

TERRITORIAL AGENTS.

Office created January 14, 1841.

Jesse Williams, appointed January 15, 1841.
John M. Colman, appointed in 1842; reappointed February 15, 1843, and February 12, 1844.
Anson Hart, appointed 1844 or 1845.
Office abolished May 29, 1845.

SUPERINTENDENT OF PUBLIC INSTRUCTION.

Office created February 12, 1841.

William Reynolds, appointed in 1841.
Office abolished March 19, 1842.

COMMISSIONERS TO LOCATE THE SEAT OF GOVERNMENT AT IOWA CITY.

Under Act approved January 21, 1839.

Chauncey Swan, appointed February 20, 1839.
John Ronalds, appointed February 20, 1839.
Robert Ralston, appointed February 20, 1839.
Legislated out of office January 14, 1841.

JUDICIARY OF IOWA TERRITORY.

SUPREME COURT.

Charles Mason, Chief Justice, 1838 to 1846.
Joseph Williams, Associate Justice, 1838 to 1846.
Thomas S. Wilson, Associate Justice, 1838 to 1846.
Thornton Bayless, Clerk, 1838 to ——.
George S. Hampton, Clerk, —— to 1846.
Eastin Morris, Reporter, 1843 to 1846.

REPRESENTATION IN CONGRESS.

DELEGATES.

William W. Chapman; in the XXVth and XXVIth Congresses.
Francis Gehon.*
Augustus C. Dodge; in the XXVIIth, XXVIIIth, and XXIXth Congresses.

* Elected in 1839, but appears never to have acted as delegate.

LEGISLATIVE.

FIRST LEGISLATIVE ASSEMBLY.

Convened at Burlington, November 12, 1838. *Adjourned January* 25, 1839.

COUNCIL.

COUNTIES REPRESENTED.	NAMES OF MEMBERS.
Lee	Jesse B. Browne
Van Buren	J. Keith, E. A. M. Swazy
Des Moines	Arthur Inghram, Robert Ralston, George Hepner.
Henry	Jesse D. Payne, L. B. Hughes
Muscatine, Louisa, Slaughter	James M. Clark
Cedar, Johnson, Jones, Linn	Charles Whittlesey
Scott and Clinton	Jonathan W. Parker
Dubuque, Jackson, Clayton	Warner Lewis, Stephen Hempstead

Jesse B. Browne, elected President November 13.
B. F. Wallace, elected Secretary November 13.

HOUSE OF REPRESENTATIVES.

COUNTIES REPRESENTED.	NAMES OF MEMBERS.
Lee	William Patterson, Hawkins Taylor, Calvin J. Price, James Brierly
Van Buren	James Hall, Gideon S. Bailey, Samuel Parker
Des Moines	James W. Grimes, George Temple, Van B. Delashmutt, Thomas Blair, George H. Beeler*
Henry	William G. Coop, William H. Wallace, Asbury B. Porter
Muscatine, Louisa, Slaughter	John Frierson, William L. Toole, Levi Thornton, S. Clinton Hastings
Cedar, Johnson, Jones, Linn	Robert G. Roberts
Scott and Clinton	Laurel Summers, Jabez A. Burchard, jr.†
Dubuque, Jackson, Clayton	Chauncey Swan, Andrew Bankson, Thomas Cox, Hardin Nowlin

William H. Wallace, elected Speaker November 13.
Joseph T. Fales, elected Chief Clerk November 13.

* Qualified and took his seat November 21, as successor to Cyrus S. Jacobs, deceased.
† Obtained his seat November 22; the House on that day deciding in his favor, and against Samuel R. Murray, who had up till that time occupied the seat.

SECOND LEGISLATIVE ASSEMBLY.*

Convened at Burlington, November 4, 1839. *Adjourned January* 17, 1840.

COUNCIL.

COUNTIES REPRESENTED.	NAMES OF MEMBERS.
Lee	Jesse B. Browne
Van Buren	J. Keith, E. A. M. Swazy
Des Moines	Arthur Inghram, Robert Ralston, George Hepner.
Henry	Jesse D. Payne, L. B. Hughes
Muscatine, Louisa †Slaughter.	James M. Clark
Cedar, Jones, Linn, Johnson	Charles Whittlesey
Scott and Clinton	Jonathan W. Parker
Dubuque, Jackson, Clayton.	Warner Lewis, Stephen Hempstead

Stephen Hempstead, elected President November 7.
B. F. Wallace, elected Secretary November 5.

HOUSE OF REPRESENTATIVES.

COUNTIES REPRESENTED.	NAMES OF MEMBERS.
Lee	William Patterson, Edward Johnston, Alfred Rich, Joshua Owen
Van Buren	James Hall, Gideon S. Bailey, Uriah Biggs
Des Moines	William R. Ross, Shepherd Leffler, L. N. English, Isaac Fleenor, Joseph C. Hawkins
Henry and Jefferson	William G. Coop, Jacob L. Myers, John B. Lash.
Muscatine and Johnson	S. Clinton Hastings, T. T. Clark
Louisa and Washington	Daniel Brewer, Jacob Mintun
Cedar, Jones, and Linn	George H. Walworth
Scott and Clinton	Laurel Summers, Joseph M. Robertson
Jackson	Thomas Cox
Dubuque, Clayton, &c	Edward Langworthy, Loring Wheeler, James Churchman

Edward Johnston, elected Speaker November 4.
Joseph T. Fales, elected Chief Clerk November 4.

*An extra session of this Assembly was held at Burlington, July 13, 1840, pursuant to an act of the Legislative Assembly, approved January 11, 1840.

† Now called Washington.

THIRD LEGISLATIVE ASSEMBLY.

Convened at Burlington, November 2, 1840. *Adjourned January* 15, 1841.

COUNCIL.

COUNTIES REPRESENTED.	NAMES OF MEMBERS.
Lee	Jesse B. Browne, Edward Johnston
Van Buren	James Hall, Gideon S. Bailey
Des Moines	J. C. Hawkins
Henry	William H. Wallace
Jefferson	William G. Coop
Louisa and Washington	Francis Springer
Muscatine and Johnson	S. Clinton Hastings
Cedar, Jones, and Linn	George Greene
Scott and Clinton	Jonathan W. Parker
Jackson, Dubuque, Delaware, Clayton, &c	M. Bainbridge, Joseph S. Kirkpatrick

M. Bainbridge, elected President November 3.
B. F. Wallace, elected Secretary November 3.

HOUSE OF REPRESENTATIVES.

COUNTIES REPRESENTED.	NAMES OF MEMBERS.
Lee	James Brierly, Daniel F. Miller, John Box
Van Buren	Isaac N. Lewis, John Whitaker, William Steele
Des Moines	Shepherd Leffler, Milton D. Browning, Alfred Hebard, Robert Avery, David Hendershott
Henry	John B. Lash, Asbury B. Porter, Paton Wilson
Jefferson	Alexander A. Wilson
Louisa	William L. Toole
Washington	Simon P. Teeple
Muscatine	Thomas M. Isett
Johnson	Henry Felkner
Cedar, Jones, and Linn	George H. Walworth, Harmon Van Antwerp
Scott and Clinton	Laurel Summers, Joseph M. Robertson
Jackson	Thomas Cox
Dubuque, Delaware, Clayton, &c	Edward Langworthy, Timothy Mason

Thomas Cox, elected Speaker November 3.
Joseph T. Fales, elected Chief Clerk November 3.

FOURTH LEGISLATIVE ASSEMBLY.

Convened at Iowa City, December 6, 1841. *Adjourned February* 18, 1842.

COUNCIL.

COUNTIES REPRESENTED.	NAMES OF MEMBERS.
Lee	Jesse B. Browne, Edward Johnston
Van Buren	James Hall, Gideon S. Bailey
Des Moines	*Shepherd Leffler
Henry	William H. Wallace
Jefferson	William G. Coop
Louisa and Washington	Francis Springer
Muscatine and Johnson	S. Clinton Hastings
Cedar, Jones, and Linn	George Greene
Scott and Clinton	Jonathan W. Parker
Jackson, Dubuque, Delaware, Clayton, &c	M. Bainbridge, Joseph S. Kirkpatrick

J. W. Parker, elected President December 7.
J. W. Woods, elected Secretary December 7.

HOUSE OF REPRESENTATIVES.

COUNTIES REPRESENTED.	NAMES OF MEMBERS.
Lee	William Patterson, E. S. McCulloch, Henry S. Campbell
Van Buren	John M. Whitaker, Uriah Biggs, Oliver Weld
Des Moines	Alfred Hebard, Isaac Leffler, David E. Blair, George Hepner, James M. Morgan
Henry	Asbury B. Porter, Paton Wilson, Simeon Smead.
Jefferson	Richard Quinton
Louisa	William L. Toole
Washington	Thomas Baker
Muscatine	Samuel Holliday
Johnson	Henry Felkner
Cedar, Jones, and Linn	Samuel P. Higginson, Thomas Denson
Scott and Clinton	Joseph M. Robertson, James Grant
Jackson	James K. Morse
Dubuque, Delaware, Clayton, &c.	Warner Lewis, C. H. Booth

Warner Lewis, elected Speaker December 7.
Joseph T. Fales, elected Chief Clerk December 7.

* Elected to fill vacancy.

FIFTH LEGISLATIVE ASSEMBLY.

Convened at Iowa City, December 5, 1842. *Adjourned February* 17, 1843.

COUNCIL.

COUNTIES REPRESENTED.	NAMES OF MEMBERS.
Lee	William Patterson, Robert M. G. Patterson
Van Buren	John D. Elbert, James H. Jenkins
Des Moines	Shepherd Leffler
Henry	William H. Wallace
Jefferson	Joseph B. Teas
Louisa and Washington	Francis Springer
Muscatine and Johnson	Pleasant Harris
Cedar, Jones, and Linn	John P. Cook
Scott and Clinton	Robert Christie
Jackson, Dubuque, Delaware, Clayton, &c.	Thomas Cox, Francis Gehon

John D. Elbert, elected President December 7.
Joseph T. Fales, elected Secretary December 7.

HOUSE OF REPRESENTATIVES.

COUNTIES REPRESENTED.	NAMES OF MEMBERS.
Lee	James Brierly, E. S. McCulloch, Wm. Steele.
Van Buren	Isaac N. Lewis, Rickey D. Barton, Samuel Swearingen
Des Moines	David E. Blair, Geo. Hepner, James M. Morgan, Abner Hackleman, David J. Sales
Henry	Paton Wilson, Evan Jay, Thomas McMillan
Jefferson	John W. Culbertson
Louisa	Joseph Newell
Washington	David Bunker
Muscatine	Err Thornton
Johnson	Henry Felkner
Cedar and Jones	George H. Walworth, John C. Berry
Scott	Joseph M. Robertson
Clinton	Eli Goddard
Jackson	Ansel Briggs
Dubuque, Delaware, Clayton, &c.	Thomas Rogers, Frederick Andros

James M. Morgan, elected Speaker December 6.
B. F. Wallace, elected Chief Clerk December 6.

SIXTH LEGISLATIVE ASSEMBLY.*

Convened at Iowa City, December 4, 1843. *Adjourned February* 16, 1844.

COUNCIL.

COUNTIES REPRESENTED.	NAMES OF MEMBERS.
Lee	William Patterson, Robert M. G. Patterson
Van Buren	John D. Elbert, James H. Jenkins
Des Moines	Shepherd Leffler
Henry	William H. Wallace
Jefferson	Joseph B. Teas
Louisa and Washington	Francis Springer
Muscatine and Johnson	Pleasant Harris
Cedar, Jones, and Linn	John P. Cook
Scott and Clinton	Robert Christie
Jackson, Dubuque, Delaware, Clayton, &c	Thomas Cox, Francis Gehon

Thomas Cox, elected President January 11, on the forty-first ballot—Francis Springer acting as President *pro tem.* till that time.

B. F. Wallace, elected Secretary December 7.

HOUSE OF REPRESENTATIVES.

COUNTIES REPRESENTED.	NAMES OF MEMBERS.
Lee	James Brierly, William Steele, Joseph Roberts
Van Buren	Josiah H. Bonney, Sam'l Borland, Jas. M. Wray.
Des Moines	Alfred Hebard, Abner Hackleman, James W. Grimes, John Johnson, John D. Wright
Henry	Paton Wilson, Hamilton Robb, Wm. Thompson.
Jefferson	John W. Culbertson
Louisa	George W. McCleary
Washington	Thomas Baker
Muscatine	Edward E. Fay
Johnson	James P. Carleton
Cedar, Jones, and Linn	George H. Walworth, Robert Smythe
Scott	Gilbert C. R. Mitchell
Clinton	John Brophy
Jackson	John Foley
Dubuque, Delaware, Clayton, &c.	Thomas Rogers, Hardin Nowlin

James P. Carleton, elected Speaker December 5.

Joseph T. Fales, elected Chief Clerk December 5.

* An extra session of this Assembly was held at Iowa City June 16, 1844, pursuant to an act of the Assembly approved February 15, 1844.

FIRST CONSTITUTIONAL CONVENTION.

Convened at Iowa City, October 7, 1844. *Adjourned November* 1, 1844.

COUNTIES REPRESENTED.	NAMES OF MEMBERS.
Lee	Charles Staley, Alexander Kerr, David Galland, Calvin J. Price, James Marsh, John Thompson, Henry M. Salmon, O. S. X. Peck
Des Moines	James Clarke, Henry Robinson, John D. Wright, Shepherd Leffler, Andrew Hooten, Enos Lowe, John Ripley, George Hepner
Van Buren	Elisha Cutler, jr., John Davidson, Paul Brattain, David Ferguson, Gideon S. Bailey, John Hale, jr., Thomas Charlton
Jefferson	Robert Brown, Hardin Butler, Sulifand S. Ross, James I. Murray, Samuel Whitmore
Henry	Joseph C. Hawkins, George Hobson, John H. Randolph, Jonathan C. Hall, Joseph D. Hoag.
Washington	Wm. R. Harrison, Enoch Ross, Caleb B. Campbell.
Louisa	John Brookbank, Wm. L. Toole, Wright Williams.
Muscatine	Jonathan E. Fletcher, Ralph P. Lowe, Elijah Sells.
Johnson	Robert Lucas, Samuel H. McCrory, Henry Felkner.
Linn	Thomas J McKean, Samuel W. Durham, Luman M. Strong
Cedar	Samuel A. Bissell, James H. Gower
Scott	James Grant, Andrew W. Campbell, Ebenezer Cook
Clinton	Lyman Evans, Ralph R. Benedict
Jones	John Taylor
Jackson	Joseph S. Kirkpatrick, William Morden, Richard B. Wyckoff
Wapello	William H. Galbraith, William W. Chapman
Davis	J. C. Blankinship, Samuel W. McAtee
Keokuk	Richard Quinton
Mahaska	Van B. Delashmutt, Stephen B. Shelledy
Dubuque, Delaware, Black Hawk, and Fayette	Francis Gehon, Edward Langworthy, Theophilus Crawford, Stephen Hempstead, Samuel B. Olmstead, Michael O'Brien.

Shepherd Leffler, elected President October 7.
George S. Hampton, elected Secretary October 7.

The constitution adopted by this convention was rejected by the people at an election held on the 4th day of August, 1845, there being 7,235 votes cast "for the constitution," and 7,656 votes cast "against the constitution."

SEVENTH LEGISLATIVE ASSEMBLY.

Convened at Iowa City, May 5, 1845. *Adjourned June* 11, 1845.

COUNCIL.

COUNTIES.	NAMES OF MEMBERS.
Lee	James Brierly, John Thompson
Van Buren, Davis, Appanoose	Paul Brattain, Henry M. Shelby
Des Moines	Shepherd Leffler
Henry	John Stephenson
Jefferson, Wapello, and *Kishkekosh	William G. Coop
Louisa, Washington, Keokuk, Mahaska, &c	Enoch Ross
Muscatine and Johnson	S. Clinton Hastings
Cedar, Linn and Jones	William Abbe
Scott and Clinton	Laurel Summers
Jackson, Dubuque, Delaware, Clayton, &c	Stephen Hempstead, Philip B. Bradley

S. Clinton Hastings, elected President May 7.
John F. Kinney, elected Secretary May 7.

HOUSE OF REPRESENTATIVES.

COUNTIES REPRESENTED.	NAMES OF MEMBERS.
Lee	Jacob Huner, Charles Stewart, James Anderson.
Van Buren	Frederick Hancock, George Montague, George W. Lester
Des Moines	James M. Morgan, John Johnson, Ebenezer W. Davis, George Chandler, Richard Noble
Henry	Norton Munger, Samuel D. Woodworth, Charles Clifton
Jefferson, Wapello, and *Kishkekosh	Reuben R. Harper
Louisa	George W. McCleary
Washington, Keokuk, Mahaska, &c	Stephen B. Shelledy
Muscatine	Abraham T. Banks
Johnson	Hugh D. Downey
Cedar, Linn and Jones	Joseph K. Snyder, John Taylor
Scott	Joseph M. Robertson
Clinton	Shubaee Coy
Jackson	James Leonard
Dubuque, Delaware, Clayton, &c	David S. Wilson, Samuel Murdock

James M. Morgan, elected Speaker May 6.
William Thompson, elected Chief Clerk May 6.

*Now called Monroe.

EIGHTH LEGISLATIVE ASSEMBLY.

Convened at Iowa City, December 1, 1845. *Adjourned January* 19, 1846.

COUNCIL.

COUNTIES REPRESENTED.	NAMES OF MEMBERS.
Lee	James Brierly, John Thompson
Van Buren, Davis, and Appanoose	Paul Brattain, Henry M. Shelby
Des Moines	Shepherd Leffler
Henry	John Stephenson
Jefferson, Wapello, and Kiskkekosh	William G. Coop
Louisa, Washington, Keokuk, Mahaska, &c	Enoch Ross
Muscatine and Johnson	S. Clinton Hastings
Cedar, Linn, and Jones	William Abbe
Scott and Clinton	Laurel Summers
Jackson, Dubuque, Delaware, Clayton, &c	Stephen Hempstead, Philip B. Bradley

Stephen Hempstead, elected President December 3.
John F. Kinney, elected Secretary December 3.

HOUSE OF REPRESENTATIVES.

COUNTIES REPRESENTED.	NAMES OF MEMBERS.
Lee	Jacob Hunter, Wm. Patterson, Jesse B. Browne
Van Buren	Frederick Hancock, George W. Lester, David Ferguson
Des Moines	James M. Morgan, John D. Wright, John Ripley, Archibald McMichael, Joshua Holland
Henry	Norton Munger, Samuel D. Woodworth, Charles Clifton
Jefferson, Wapello, and *Kishkekosh	Joseph Flink
Louisa	George W. McCleary
Washington, Keokuk, Mahaska, &c	Stephen B. Shelledy
Muscatine	Abraham T. Banks
Johnson	Hugh D. Downey
Cedar, Linn and Jones	Joseph K. Snyder, John Taylor
Scott	Joseph M. Robertson
Clinton	Shubael Coy
Jackson	Thomas Graham
Dubuque, Delaware, Clayton, &c	David S. Wilson, Samuel Murdock

George W. McCleary, elected Speaker December 2.
William Thompson, elected Chief Clerk December 2.

*Now called Monroe.

SECOND CONSTITUTIONAL CONVENTION.

Convened at Iowa City, May 4, 1846. *Adjourned May* 19, 1846.

COUNTIES REPRESENTED.	NAMES OF MEMBERS.
Lee	David Galland, Josiah Kent, George Berry
Des Moines	Enos Lowe, Shepherd Leffler, George W. Bowie.
Van Buren	Thomas Dibble, Erastus Hoskins, Wm. Steele
Jefferson	Sullifand S. Ross, William G. Coop
Henry	George Hobson, Alvin Saunders
Davis	John J. Selman
Appanoose and Monroe	Wareham G. Clark
Wapello	Joseph H. Hedrick
Iowa, Marion, Polk, and Jasper	John Conrey
Mahaska	Stephen B. Shelledy
Keokuk	Sanford Harned
Washington	Stewart Goodrell
Louisa	John Ronalds
Muscatine	J. Scott Richman
Johnson	Curtis Bates
Linn and Benton	Socrates H. Tryon
Cedar	Samuel A. Bissell
Scott	James Grant
Clinton	Henry P. Haun
Jackson	William Hubbell
Jones	Sylvester G. Matson
Clayton	David Olmstead
Dubuque, Delaware, Buchanan, Fayette, Black Hawk	Thomas McCraney, Francis K. O'Ferrall

Enos Lowe, elected President May 4.
William Thompson, elected Secretary May 4.

The constitution adopted by this convention was sanctioned by the people at an election held on the 3d day of August, 1846, there being 9,492 votes cast "for the constitution," and 9,036 votes cast "against the constitution." This constitution was presented to Congress in December, 1846, and on the 28th of the same month an act was passed for the admission of Iowa into the Union. The first election for State officers was held on the 26th day of October, 1846, pursuant to proclamation of Governor James Clarke, when Ansel Briggs was elected Governor, Elisha Cutler, jr., Secretary of State, Joseph T. Fales, Auditor, and Morgan Reno, Treasurer.

REGISTER OF THE STATE OF IOWA.

OFFICERS OF THE STATE GOVERNMENT.

GOVERNORS.

Ansel Briggs, Jackson county; elected October 26, 1846; oath of office administered December 3, by Chief Justice Mason.

Stephen Hempstead, Dubuque county; elected August 5, 1850; oath of office administered December 4, by Chief Justice Williams.

James W. Grimes, Des Moines county; elected August 3, 1854; oath of office administered December 9, 1854, by Maturin L. Fisher, President of the Joint Convention.

Ralph P. Lowe, Lee county; elected October 13, 1857; oath of office administered January 14, 1858, by Chief Justice Wright.

Samuel J. Kirkwood, Johnson county; elected October 11, 1859; oath of office administered January 11, 1860, by Chief Justice Wright.

Samuel J. Kirkwood, Johnson county; re-elected October 8, 1861; oath of office administered January 15, 1862, by Chief Justice Baldwin.

William M. Stone, Marion county; elected October 13, 1863; oath of office administered January 14, 1864, by Chief Justice Wright.

William M. Stone, Marion county; re-elected October 10, 1865; oath of office administered January 11, 1866, by Lieut.-Governor Eastman.

Samuel Merrill, Clayton county; elected October 8, 1867.

LIEUTENANT-GOVERNORS.

Office created September 3, 1857, *by the New Constitution.*

Oran Faville, Mitchell county; elected October 13, 1857; qualified January 14, 1858.

Nicholas J. Rusch, Scott county; elected October 11, 1859; qualified January 11, 1860.

John R. Needham, Mahaska county; elected October 8, 1861; qualified January 15, 1862.

Enoch W. Eastman, Hardin county; elected October 13, 1863; qualified January 14, 1864.

Benjamin F. Gue, Webster county; elected October 10, 1865; qualified January 11, 1866.

John Scott, Story county; elected October 8, 1867.

SECRETARIES OF STATE.

Elisha Cutler, jr., Van Buren county; elected October 26, 1846; qualified December 5.

Josiah H. Bonney, Van Buren county; elected August 7, 1848; qualified December 4.

George W. McCleary, Johnson county; elected August 5, 1850; qualified December 2.

George W. McCleary, Johnson county; re-elected August 2, 1852; bond approved December 4.

George W. McCleary, Johnson county; re-elected August 7, 1854; qualified December 4.

Elijah Sells, Muscatine county; elected August 4, 1856; qualified December 1.

Elijah Sells, Muscatine county; re-elected October 12, 1858; second term commenced January 3, 1859.

Elijah Sells, Muscatine county; re elected November 6, 1860; third term commenced January 7, 1861.

James Wright, Delaware county; elected October 14, 1862; term of office commenced January 5, 1863.

James Wright, Delaware county; re-elected November 8, 1864; second term commenced January 2, 1865.

Ed Wright, Cedar county; elected October 9, 1866; term of office commenced January 7, 1867.

AUDITORS OF STATE*

Joseph T. Fales, Des Moines county; elected October 26, 1846; qualified December 4.

Joseph T. Fales, Des Moines county; re-elected August 7, 1848; bond approved March 5, 1849.

William Pattee, Bremer county; elected August 5, 1850; bond approved December 2.

William Pattee, Bremer county; re-elected August 2, 1852; bond approved December 8.

Andrew J. Stevens, Polk county; elected August 7, 1854; qualified December 4; resigned in 1855.

John Pattee, Bremer county; appointed by the Governor, September 13, 1855; bond approved September 22.

John Pattee, Bremer county; elected August 4, 1856; qualified December 2.

Jonathan W. Cattell, Cedar county; elected October 12, 1858; term of office commenced January 3, 1859.

Jonathan W. Cattell, Cedar county; re-elected November 6, 1860; second term commenced January 7, 1861.

Jonathan W. Cattell, Cedar county; re-elected October 14, 1862; third term commenced January 5, 1863.

John A. Elliott, Mitchell county; elected November 8, 1864; term of office commenced January 2, 1865.

John A. Elliott, Mitchell county; re-elected October 9, 1866; second term commenced January 7, 1867.

* This officer was styled "Auditor of Public Accounts," in the former Constitution of the State.

TREASURERS OF STATE.*

Morgan Reno, Johnson county; elected October 26, 1846; qualified December 18.

Morgan Reno, Johnson county; re-elected August 7, 1848; bond approved January 11, 1849.

Israel Kister, Davis county; elected August 5, 1850; qualified December 2.

Martin L. Morris, Polk county; elected August 2, 1852; qualified December 4.

Martin L. Morris, Polk county; re-elected August 7, 1854; qualified December 4.

Martin L. Morris, Polk county; re-elected August 4, 1856; qualified December 1.

John W. Jones, Hardin county; elected October 12, 1858; term of office commenced January 3, 1859.

John W. Jones, Hardin county; re-elected November 6, 1860; second term commenced January 7, 1861.

William H. Holmes, Jones county; elected October 8, 1862; term of office commenced January 5, 1863.

William H. Holmes, Jones county; re-elected November 8, 1864; second term commenced January 2, 1865.

Samuel E. Rankin, Washington county; elected October 9, 1866; term of office commenced January 7, 1867.

SUPERINTENDENTS OF PUBLIC INSTRUCTION.

Office created in 1847.

James Harlan, Henry county; elected April 5, 1847; †qualified June 5.

Thomas H. Benton, jr., Dubuque county; elected April 3, 1848; qualified May 23.

Thomas H. Benton, jr., Dubuque county; re-elected April 7, 1851; bond approved July 25.

James D. Eads, Lee county; elected April 4, 1854; bond approved June 7; suspended March 3, 1857.

Joseph C. Stone, Johnson county; appointed by the Governor and qualified March 4, 1857.

Maturin L. Fisher, Clayton county; elected April 1, 1857; qualified June 9.

Office abolished by act of the Board of Education passed December 24, 1858, the duties of the office to be performed by the Secretary of that Board.

SECRETARIES OF THE BOARD OF EDUCATION.

Office created by act of Board of Education, passed December 24, 1858.

Josiah T. Tubby, Polk county; acting as Secretary of the Board during its session which commenced December 6, 1858, and continuing after its adjournment as acting Secretary of the Board of Education, under resolution of December 24, until the Secretary elected by the Board should qualify. Mr. Tubby qualified December 29.

* The designation of this office was "Treasurer," under the Constitution of 1846.

† The Supreme Court decided (July term, 1847,) that the law creating the office of Superintendent of Public Instruction had not gone into effect when this election was held. A second election was accordingly held the following year.

Thomas H. Benton, jr., Pottawattamie county; elected by the Board of Education, December 21, 1858; qualified January 14, 1859.
Thomas H. Benton, jr., Pottawattamie county; re-elected December 21, 1859.
Thomas H. Benton, jr., Pottawattamie county; re-elected December 6, 1861; resigned in 1863.
Oran Faville, Mitchell county; appointed by the Governor and qualified January 1 1864.

Office abolished March 23, 1864, and duties devolved on Superintendent of Public Instruction.

SUPERINTENDENTS OF PUBLIC INSTRUCTION.

Office again created March 23, 1864.

Oran Faville, Mitchell county; elected by the General Assembly, March 26, 1864; qualified March 28.
Oran Faville, Mitchell county; re-elected, by the people, October 10, 1865; second term commenced January 1, 1866. Resigned March 1, 1867.
D. Franklin Wells, Johnson county; appointed by the Governor, March 4, 1867; qualified March 9; elected by the people October 8, 1867, for the balance of the term.
D. Franklin Wells, Johnson county; re-elected October 8, 1867; new term commences January 1, 1868.

REGISTERS OF THE STATE LAND OFFICE.

Anson Hart, Johnson county; elected April 2, 1855; bond approved May 5.
Theodore S. Parvin, Muscatine county; elected April 6, 1857; qualified May 13.
Amos B. Miller, Cerro Gordo county; elected October 12, 1858; term of office commenced January 3, 1859.
Amos B. Miller, Cerro Gordo county; re-elected November 6, 1860; second term commenced January 7, 1861. Appointed Captain Company B, Thirty-second Iowa Infantry, October 6, 1862.
Edwin Mitchell, Polk county; appointed by the Governor October 1862; qualified October 31.
Josiah A. Harvey, Fremont county; elected October 14, 1862; term of office commenced January 5, 1863.
Josiah A. Harvey, Fremont county; re-elected November 8, 1864; second term commenced January 2, 1865.
Cyrus C. Carpenter, Webster county; elected October 9, 1866; term of office commenced January 7, 1867.

STATE PRINTERS.

Office created January 3, 1849.

Garrett D. Palmer and George Paul, Johnson county; elected January 4, 1849; term commenced May 1.

Harrison Holt and Andrew Keesecker, Dubuque county; elected February 4, 1851; declined.

William H. Merritt, Dubuque county; appointed by Governor April 12, 1851; term of office commenced May 1, 1851.

William A. Hornish, Lee county; elected January 20, 1853; term commenced May 1; resignation accepted May 16.

Dennis A. Mahony and Joseph B. Dorr, Dubuque county; appointed May 16, 1853; qualified May 23.

Peter Moriarty, Jackson county; elected January 20, 1855; term of office commenced May 1.

John Teesdale, Johnson county; elected January 12, 1857; term commenced May 1.

John Teesdale; re-elected January 26, 1858; second term commenced May 1, 1859.

Francis W. Palmer, Dubuque county; elected January 25, 1860; term of office commenced May 1, 1861.

Francis W. Palmer; re-elected January 27, 1862; second term commenced May 1, 1863.

Francis W. Palmer; re elected January 16, 1864; third term commenced May 1, 1865.

Francis W. Palmer; re-elected March 10, 1866; fourth term commenced May 1, 1867.

STATE BINDERS.

Office created February 21, 1855.

William M. Coles, Scott county; appointed by the Governor March 16, 1855; term of office commenced May 1.

William M. Coles; elected by the General Assembly January 12, 1857; second term commenced May 1.

Frank M. Mills, Polk county; elected January 26, 1858; term of office commenced May 1, 1859.

Frank M. Mills; re-elected January 25, 1860; second term commenced May 1, 1861.

Frank M. Mills; re-elected January 27, 1862; third term commenced May 1, 1863.

Frank M. Mills; re-elected January 16, 1864; fourth term commenced May 1, 1865.

James S. Carter, Polk county; elected March 10, 1866; term commenced May 1, 1867.

THE JUDICIARY.

SUPREME COURT OF IOWA.

CHIEF JUSTICES.

*Charles Mason, Des Moines county; resigned in June, 1847.

Joseph Williams, Muscatine county; appointed by the Governor, June, 1847. Term expired January 25, 1848, by constitutional limitation.

S. Clinton Hastings, Muscatine county; appointed by the Governor, January 26, 1848. Term expired January 15, 1849.

Joseph Williams, Muscatine county; elected by the General Assembly December 7, 1848, and commissioned December 26, 1848, for six years—from January 15, 1849.

George G. Wright, Van Buren county; elected January 5, 1855; qualified January 11.

Ralph P. Lowe, Lee county; elected Judge October 11, 1859, with Caleb Baldwin and Lacon D. Stockton, and drawing the shortest term became Chief Justice; qualified January 12, 1860.

Caleb Baldwin, Pottawattamie county; elected as above, and drawing the second shortest term became Chief Justice January 1, 1862.

George G. Wright, Van Buren county; term commenced January 1, 1864.

Ralph P. Lowe, Lee county; term commenced January 1, 1866.

John F. Dillon, Scott county; term commences January 1, 1868.

ASSOCIATE JUDGES.

*Joseph Williams, Muscatine county. Appointed Chief Justice June, 1847.

*Thomas S. Wilson, Dubuque county. Resigned in October, 1847.

John F. Kinney, Lee county; appointed by the Governor June 12, 1847, and again January 26, 1848; elected by the General Assembly, and commissioned, December 8. Resignation accepted January 20, 1854, to take effect February 15.

George Greene, Dubuque county; appointed by the Governor November 1, 1847, and again January 26, 1848; elected by the General Assembly December, 7, 1848; term of office commenced January 15, 1849. Succeeded by W. G. Woodward.

Jonathan C. Hall, Des Moines county; appointed by the Governor January 20, 1854, to succeed Kinney, resigned. Succeeded by N. W. Isbell.

* Held over from territorial government, owing to failure of State Legislature to elect Judges. Their successors were appointed by the Governor, to hold office till the adjournment of the next session of the Legislature; when appointments were again made, as above.

William G. Woodward, Muscatine county; elected by the General Assembly January 5, 1855; qualified January 9.

Norman W. Isbell, Linn county; elected by the General Assembly January 6, 1855; qualified January 16. Resigned in 1856.

Lacon D. Stockton, Des Moines county; appointed by the Governor May 17, 1856, vice Isbell, resigned; qualified June 3; elected by the General Assembly January 12, 1857; re-elected by the people under the present Constitution October 11, 1859. Died June 9, 1860.

Caleb Baldwin, Pottawattamie county; elected by the people October 11, 1859 qualified January 11, 1860. Became Chief Justice January 1, 1862.

George G. Wright, Van Buren county; appointed by the Governor June 19, 1860, vice Stockton, deceased; qualified June 26; elected by the people November 6, 1860. Became Chief Justice January 1, 1864. Re-elected October 10, 1865; new term commenced January 1, 1866.

Ralph P. Lowe, Lee county; re-elected October 8, 1861; new term commenced January 1, 1862. Became Chief Justice January 1, 1866.

John F. Dillon, Scott county; elected October 13, 1863, vice Baldwin; term commenced January 1, 1864; becomes Chief Justice January 1, 1868.

Chester C. Cole, Polk county; appointed March 1, 1864, by the Governor, under the provisions of Chapter 23, Acts of 10th General Assembly, which took effect February 27, 1864; qualified same day; elected by the people November 8, 1864; term commenced January 1, 1865.

Joseph M. Beck, Lee county; elected by the people October 8, 1867; term commences January 1, 1868.

CLERKS OF THE SUPREME COURT.

George S. Hampton, Johnson county; appointed and bond approved July 6, 1867.
George S. Hampton, appointed February 2, 1848, for the 4th Judicial District.
James W. Woods, appointed 1848, for the 1st Judicial District.
Alexander D. Anderson, appointed 1848, for the 2d Judicial District.
Lewis J. Whitten, appointed ——, for the 5th Judicial District.
Thomas J. Given, appointed 1848, for the 3d Judicial District.
George S. Hampton, Johnson county; appointed 1853; bond approved March 5.
William Vandever; appointed and qualified June, 1855.

Lewis Kinsey, Wapello county; appointed November 3, 1856, and qualified November 14; re-appointed January 12, 1860.

Charles Linderman, Page county; elected by the people, October 9, 1866, for four years, under the provisions of Chapter 88, Acts of 11th General Assembly; term commenced January 7, 1867.

ATTORNEYS-GENERAL.

Office created February 9, 1853.

David C. Cloud, Muscatine county; elected by the people August 1, 1853; bond approved September 9; re-elected August 7, 1854.

Samuel A. Rice, Mahaska county; elected August 4, 1856; bond approved September 24; re-elected August 2, 1858.

Charles C. Nourse, Polk county; elected November 6, 1860; term commenced January 7, 1861; re-elected October 14, 1867.

Isaac L. Allen, Tama county; elected November 8, 1864; term commenced January 2, 1865. Resigned January 11, 1866.

Frederick E. Bissell, Dubuque county; appointed by the Governor and qualified January 12, 1866; elected by the people October 9, 1866; died June 12, 1867.
Henry O'Connor, Muscatine county; appointed by the Governor June 20, and qualified June 29, 1867; elected by the people October 8.

REPORTERS OF THE DECISIONS OF THE SUPREME COURT.

George Greene, Dubuque county, acting from 1847 to 1855.
The Attorney-General, *ex-officio*, from September 1853, under the law creating the office of Attorney-General. Mr. Cloud, Attorney-General, however, appears never to have acted, and Judge Greene continued to perform the duties of the office.
Wm. Penn Clarke, Johnson county; appointed by the Supreme Court, 1855.
Thomas F. Withrow, Polk county; appointed in 1860; qualified April 17; re-appointed in 1864.
Edward H. Stiles, Wapello county; elected by the people, October 9, 1866; term of office commenced January 7, 1867.

DISTRICT COURTS UNDER CONSTITUTION OF 1846.

FIRST DISTRICT.

[Composed of the counties of Des Moines, Henry, Lee, and Louisa. Washington county was at first a part of this district, but was detached and added to the Fourth District by Chapter 57, Acts 2d General Assembly, approved January 12, 1849.]

Created February 17, 1847.

JUDGES.

George H. Williams, Lee county; elected April 5, 1847, and commissioned April 27.
Ralph P. Lowe, Lee county; elected April 5, 1852. Resigned in 1857.
John W. Rankin, Lee county; appointed by the Governor April 9, 1857; qualified April 13.
Thomas W. Clagett, Lee county; elected April 6, 1857; qualified May 16.

SECOND DISTRICT.

[Originally composed of the counties of Buchanan, Cedar, Clayton, Clinton, Delaware, Dubuque, Fayette, Jackson, Jones, Muscatine, and Scott. To which were added: in 1847, Allamakee and Winneshiek; in 1851, Black Hawk, Bremer, Butler, and Grundy; and in 1853, Chickasaw and Howard. In 1853, the Eighth District was taken from the Second; and Butler and Grundy counties were added to the Fifth. In 1855, the new Tenth District took Allamakee, Chickasaw, Clayton, Fayette, Howard, and Winneshiek counties. In 1858, when the district was abolished, it consisted of the counties of Black Hawk, Bremer, Buchanan, Delaware, and Dubuque.]

Created February 17, 1847.

JUDGES.

James Grant, Scott county; elected April 5, 1847; commissioned November 15.
Thomas S. Wilson, Dubuque county; elected April 5, 1852; qualified May 8; re-elected April 6, 1857.

THIRD DISTRICT.

[Originally composed of the counties of Appanoose, Davis, Jefferson, Keokuk, Mahaska, Marion, Monroe, Van Buren, and Wapello, "and the counties west of the counties of Marion, Monroe, and Appanoose." In 1849, the new Fifth District took the counties of Appanoose, Marion, and Monroe, and the counties to the westward. Mahaska county was detached December 19, 1856, on the creation of the Eleventh District. When abolished in 1858, the district consisted of the counties of Davis, Jefferson, Keokuk, Van Buren, and Wapello.]

Created February 17, 1847.

JUDGES.

Cyrus Olney, Jefferson county; elected April 5, 1847; commissioned December 7. Resignation accepted March 15, 1851.
Joseph C. Knapp, Van Buren county; appointed by the Governor March 15, 1851.
William H. Seevers, Mahaska county; elected April 5, 1852; qualified May 7. Resigned; successor appointed January 10, 1856.
Caleb Baldwin, Jefferson county; appointed by the Governor and qualified January 10, 1856.
Henry B. Hendershott, Wapello county; elected April 7, 1856; qualified May 14, 1856.

FOURTH DISTRICT.

[Originally composed of the counties of Benton, Boone, Dallas, Iowa, Jasper, Johnson, Linn, Marshall, Polk, Poweshiek, Story, and Tama. In 1849, Washington county was annexed from the First District, and Boone, Dallas, Jasper, Marshall, Polk, and Story detached to the Fifth. In 1856, Poweshiek was detached to the new Eleventh District, and in 1857, Marshall and Story to the new Thirteenth. When abolished in 1858, the district consisted of Benton, Iowa, Johnson, Linn, Tama, and Washington counties.]

Created February 17, 1847.

JUDGES.

James P. Carleton, Johnson county; elected April 5, 1847; commissioned April 27; re-elected April 5, 1852. Resigned in 1853.

William Smyth, Linn county; appointed by the Governor October 6, 1853; qualified October 10; elected by the people April 3, 1854. Resigned.
Isaac Cook, Linn county; appointed by the Governor January 28, 1857; qualified March 20; elected by the people April 6.

FIFTH DISTRICT.

[Originally composed of the counties of Appanoose, Boone, Clarke, Dallas, Decatur, Fremont, Jasper, Lucas, Madison, Marion, Marshall, Monroe, Page, Polk, Ringgold, Story, Taylor, Warren, and Wayne. In February, 1851, the counties of Fremont, Page, Ringgold, and Taylor were made a part of the new Sixth District. On the 20th of the same month, the counties of Bancroft [now part of Kossuth], Emmett, Fox [now Calhoun], Greene, Guthrie, Hancock, Hardin, Humboldt, Kossuth, Palo Alto, Pocahontas, Risley [now Hamilton], Winnebago, Wright, and Yell [now Webster] were added to the district. On the 9th of February, 1853, the Ninth District was taken from the Fifth, and Guthrie county was added to the Sixth District; at the same time the district was increased by the addition of Butler, Cerro Gordo, Floyd, Franklin, Grundy, Mitchell, and Worth counties. In 1855, the counties of Cerro Gordo, Floyd, Mitchell, and Worth were made a part of the new Tenth District. On the 9th of December, 1856, the counties of Dallas, Jasper, Marion, and Polk were detached to the new Eleventh District. In the same year, by act approved January 27, 1857, the Thirteenth District was formed out of a portion of the Fifth. Guthrie county was reattached to the Fifth, February 26, 1857. On the 24th February, 1858, Webster county was detached, and annexed to the Thirteenth District. When abolished under the present Constitution, the district consisted of the following counties: Boone, Calhoun, Emmett, Greene, Guthrie, Hancock, Humboldt, Kossuth, Palo Alto, Pocahontas, and Winnebago.]

Created in 1849.

JUDGES.

William McKay, Polk county; elected April 2, 1849; commissioned April 27.
Phineas M. Casady, Polk county; elected April 3, 1854; qualified June 1. Resigned.
Charles J. McFarland, Boone county; appointed by the Governor May 7, 1854;* qualified in July.
William W. Williamson, Polk county; declared elected April 2, 1855; qualified April 11. This election was contested; and the contest was decided, January 10, 1856, against Judge Williamson, and in favor of
Charles J. McFarland, Boone county, who qualified January 10, 1856.

SIXTH DISTRICT.

[Originally composed of the counties of Adair, Adams, Audubon, Buena Vista, Buncombe [now Lyon], Carroll, Cass, Cherokee, Clay, Crawford, Dickinson, Fremont, Harrison, Ida, Mills, Monona, Montgomery, O'Brien, Osceola, Page, Plymouth, Pottawattamie, Ringgold, Sac, Shelby, Sioux, Taylor, Union, and Wahkaw [now Woodbury]. The 7th district was formed from a part of the 6th, on the 9th of February, 1853; at the same time Guthrie county was added to the 6th. Audubon and Cass counties were detached, and annexed

* According to the record; but it is evidently erroneous, as Judge Casady did not resign till June or July.

to the 7th district, December 26, 1856; Ringgold and Union were made a part of the 9th district, February 9, 1857; and Guthrie was attached to the 5th district, February 25. On the 3d of September, 1857, Mills county was added to the district by a special provision in the Constitution. When abolished under the new Constitution, the district therefore consisted of the following counties: Adair, Adams, Fremont, Mills, Montgomery, Page, and Taylor.]

Created February, 1851.

JUDGES.

James Sloan; elected April 7, 1851. Resignation accepted March 9, 1852.
Allen A. Bradford, Fremont county; appointed by the Governor, May 4, 1852; qualified May 24; elected by the people, April 4, 1853. Resigned.
E. H. Sears, Fremont county; appointed by the Governor, January 9, 1855; qualified February 1; elected by the people, April 2.

SEVENTH DISTRICT.

[Originally composed of the counties of Buena Vista, Buncombe [now Lyon], Carroll, Cherokee, Clay, Crawford, Dickinson, Harrison, Ida, Mills, Monona, O'Brien, Osceola, Plymouth, Pottawattamie, Sac, Shelby, Sioux, and Woodbury. On the 26th of December, 1856, the district was reduced by detaching all the counties except Harrison, Pottawattamie, and Shelby, to which were added Audubon and Cass counties. Mills county was unconnected formally with any district until September 3, 1857, when the new constitution took effect, which contained a special provision attaching Mills to the Sixth District. The other counties went to form the new Twelfth District, March 13, 1857.]

Created February 9, 1853.

JUDGE.

Samuel H. Riddle, Pottawattamie county; appointed by the Governor June 14, 1853; elected by the people April 3, 1854.

EIGHTH DISTRICT.

[Originally composed of the counties of Cedar, Clinton, Jackson, Jones, Muscatine, and Scott. On the 1st of March, 1857, the Fourteenth District was formed of a part of this district. At the time of its abolition, in 1858, it consisted therefore of the counties of Cedar, Jones, and Muscatine.]

Created February 9, 1853.

JUDGES.

William E. Leffingwell, Clinton county; elected April 4, 1853. Resigned.
John B. Booth, Jackson county; appointed by the Governor in 1854; qualified April 15.
William H. Tuthill, Cedar county; elected April 2, 1855; qualified May 3.

NINTH DISTRICT.

[Originally composed of the counties of Appanoose, Clarke, Decatur, Lucas, Madison, Monroe, Warren, and Wayne. Of these, Madison and Warren were detached, and made a part of the new Eleventh District, December 19, 1856. February 9, 1857, Ringgold and Union counties were added to the district from the Sixth. When abolished in 1858, the district consisted of the counties of Appanoose, Clarke, Decatur, Lucas, Monroe, Ringgold, Union, and Wayne.]

—

Created February 9, 1853.

—

JUDGE.

John S. Townsend, Monroe county; elected April 4, 1853.

TENTH DISTRICT.

[Composed of the counties of Allamakee, Cerro Gordo, Chickasaw, Clayton, Fayette, Floyd, Howard, Mitchell, Winneshiek, and Worth. These counties, with the exception of Cerro Gordo and Worth, and the addition of Bremer and Butler, became the Tenth Judicial District under the present Constitution in 1858.]

—

Created in 1855.

—

JUDGE.

Samuel Murdock, Clayton county; elected April 2, 1855; commissioned May 3.

ELEVENTH DISTRICT.

[Composed of the counties of Dallas, Jasper, Madison, Mahaska, Marion, Polk, Poweshiek, and Warren.]

—

Created December 19, 1856.

—

JUDGE.

William M. Stone, Marion county; elected April 6, 1857; commissioned April 23.

TWELFTH DISTRICT.

[Composed of the counties of Buncombe, [now Lyon], Buena Vista, Carroll, Cherokee, Clay, Crawford, Dickinson, Ida, Monona, O'Brien, Osceola, Plymouth, Sac, Sioux, and Woodbury.]

Created March 13, 1857.

JUDGE.

Marshall F. Moore, Woodbury county; elected April 6, 1857; commissioned September 5.

THIRTEENTH DISTRICT.

[Originally composed of the counties of Butler, Franklin, Grundy, Hamilton, Hardin, Marshall, Story, and Wright, to which Webster county was added February 24, 1858.]

Created March, 1857.

JUDGE.

James D. Thompson, Hardin county; elected April 6, 1857; commissioned July 1.

FOURTEENTH DISTRICT.

[Composed of the counties of Clinton, Jackson, and Scott.]

Created February 6, 1857.

JUDGES.

Gilbert C. R. Mitchell, Scott county; elected April 6, 1857; qualified May 20. Resigned.

Asahel H. Bennett, Scott county; appointed by the Governor October 19, 1857.

The above districts were superseded, in accordance with Article V. of the Constitution of 1857, by eleven new districts, the Judges and District-Attorneys of which entered upon their duties on the first day of January, 1859.

DISTRICT COURTS UNDER CONSTITUTION OF 1857.

FIRST JUDICIAL DISTRICT.

[Composed of the counties of Des Moines, Henry, Lee, and Louisa.]

JUDGE.

Francis Springer, Louisa county; elected October 12, 1858; re-elected October 14, 1862, and October 9, 1866.

DISTRICT-ATTORNEY.

Joshua Tracy, Des Moines county; elected October 12, 1858; re-elected October 14, 1862, and October 9, 1866.

SECOND JUDICIAL DISTRICT.

[Composed of the counties of Appanoose, Davis, Lucas, Monroe, Van Buren, Wapello, and Wayne.]

JUDGES.

John S. Townsend, Monroe county; elected October 12, 1858.
Henry H. Trimble, Davis county; elected October 14, 1862.
Harvey Tannehill, Appanoose county; elected October 9, 1866.

DISTRICT-ATTORNEYS.

Amos Harris, Appanoose county; elected October 12, 1858; re-elected October 14, 1862.
James B. Weaver, Davis county; elected October 9, 1866.

THIRD JUDICIAL DISTRICT.

[Originally composed of the counties of Adams, Cass, Clarke, Decatur, Fremont, Mills, Montgomery, Page, Pottawattamie, Ringgold, and Union. On the 27th of January, 1864, Cass county was detached, and annexed to the Fifth District.]

JUDGES.

E. H. Sears, Fremont county; elected October 12, 1858.
James G. Day, Fremont county; elected October 14, 1862; re-elected October 9, 1866.

DISTRICT-ATTORNEYS.

Robert B. Parrott, Clarke county; elected October 12, 1858.
Charles E. Millard, Mills county; elected October 14, 1862; re-elected October 9, 1866.

FOURTH JUDICIAL DISTRICT.

[Composed of the counties of Buena Vista, Calhoun, Cherokee, Clay, Crawford, Dickinson, Emmett, Harrison, Humboldt, Ida, Kossuth, Lyon, Monona, O'Brien, Osceola, Palo Alto, Plymouth, Pocahontas, Sac, Shelby, Sioux, and Woodbury.]

JUDGES.

Asahel W. Hubbard, Woodbury county; elected October 12, 1858.
Isaac Pendleton, Woodbury county; elected October 14, 1862.
Henry Ford, Harrison county; elected October 9, 1866.

DISTRICT-ATTORNEYS.

Orlando C. Howe; elected October 12, 1858.
Henry Ford, Harrison county; elected October 14, 1862.
Orson Rice, Dickinson county; elected October 9, 1866.

FIFTH JUDICIAL DISTRICT.

[Originally composed of the counties of Adair, Audubon, Carroll, Dallas, Greene, Guthrie, Madison, Warren, and Polk. The county of Cass was added January 27, 1864.]

JUDGES.

John H. Gray, Polk county; elected October 12, 1858; re-elected October 14, 1862. Died October 14, 1865.
Charles C. Nourse, Polk county; appointed by the Governor, October 16, 1865; qualified October 20. Resigned, to take effect August 1, 1866.
Hugh W. Maxwell, Warren county; appointed by the Governor, July 23, 1866, from August 1; elected by the people, October 9.

DISTRICT-ATTORNEYS.

P. Gad Bryan, Warren county; elected October 12, 1858.
John Leonard, Madison county; elected October 14, 1862; resigned January, 1864.
Benjamin F. Murray, Madison county; appointed January 23, 1864; qualified January 27.
Hugh W. Maxwell, Warren county; elected by the people November 8, 1864; qualified December 22; resigned July 3, 1866.
Samuel D. Nichols, Guthrie county; appointed by the Governor July 5, 1866; qualified July 9; elected by the people October 9.

SIXTH JUDICIAL DISTRICT.

[Composed of the counties of Jasper, Jefferson, Keokuk, Mahaska, Marion, Poweshiek, and Washington.]

JUDGES.

William M. Stone, Marion county; elected October 12, 1858. Commissioned as Captain of Company B, Third Iowa Infantry Volunteers, May 29, 1861.
William Loughridge, Mahaska county; appointed by the Governor September 5, 1851; elected by the people October 8, 1861; re-elected October 14, 1862.
Ezekiel S. Sampson, Keokuk county; elected October 9, 1866.

DISTRICT-ATTORNEYS.

George D. Woodin, Keokuk county; elected October 12, 1858.
Horace S. Winslow, Jasper county; elected October 14, 1862.
Moses A. McCoid, Jefferson county; elected October 9, 1866.

SEVENTH JUDICIAL DISTRICT.

[Composed of the counties of Clinton, Jackson, Muscatine, and Scott.]

JUDGES.

John F. Dillon, Scott county; elected October 12, 1858; re-elected October 14, 1862. Resigned to take effect December 25, 1863, having been elected Judge of the Snpreme Court.
J. Scott Richman, Muscatine county; appointed October 27, 1863, from December 25; elected by the people November 8, 1864; re-elected October 9, 1866.

DISTRICT-ATTORNEYS.

Henry O'Connor, Muscatine county; elected October 12, 1858.
Lyman A. Ellis, Clinton count elected Octobe 14 1862 re-elected October 1866.

EIGHTH JUDICIAL DISTRICT.

[Composed of the counties of Benton, Cedar, Iowa, Johnson, Jones, Linn, and Tama].

JUDGES.

William E. Miller, Johnson county; elected October 12, 1858; appointed Colonel, Twenty-eighth Iowa Infantry Volunteers, August 10, 1862.
Norman W. Isbell, Linn county; appointed by the Governor September 10, 1862; qualified September 15; elected by the people October 14. Resigned to take effect August 31, 1864.
Charles H. Conklin, Benton county; appointed by the Governor August 19, 1864, from August 31; elected by the people November 8. Resigned in 1865.
Nathaniel M. Hubbard, Linn county; appointed by the Governor November 15, 1865; qualified December 1.
James H. Rothrock, Cedar county; elected October 9, 1866.

DISTRICT-ATTORNEYS.

Isaac L. Allen, Tama county; elected October 12, 1858; re-elected October 14, 1862. Resignation accepted August 19, 1864, to take effect October 1.
C. R. Scott, Jones county; appointed by the Governor from October 1, 1864; elected by the people November 8; re-elected October 8, 1866.

NINTH JUDICIAL DISTRICT.

[Composed of the counties of Black Hawk, Buchanan, Delaware, Dubuque, and Grundy.]

JUDGES.

Thomas S. Wilson, Dubuque county; elected October 12, 1858.
James Burt, Dubuque county; elected October 14, 1862; re-elected October 9, 1866.

DISTRICT-ATTORNEYS.

Winslow T. Barker, Dubuque county; elected October 12, 1858.
George Wattson, Delaware county; elected October 14, 1862.
Matthew M. Trumbull, Black Hawk county; elected October 9, 1866.

TENTH JUDICIAL DISTRICT.

[Originally composed of the counties of Allamakee, Bremer, Butler, Clayton, Chickasaw, Fayette, Floyd, Howard, Mitchell, and Winneshiek. The counties of Bremer, Butler, Floyd, and Mitchell were detached in organizing the Twelfth Judicial District, July 4, 1864, but remained connected with this district, except for election purposes, till January 2, 1865.]

JUDGES.

Elias H. Williams, Clayton county; elected October 12, 1858; re-elected October 14, 1862.
Milo McGlathery, Fayette county; elected October 9, 1866.

ELEVENTH JUDICIAL DISTRICT.

[Originally composed of the counties of Boone, Cerro Gordo, Franklin, Hamilton, Hancock, Hardin, Marshall, Story, Webster, Winnebago, Worth, and Wright. July 4, 1864, the counties of Cerro Gordo, Hancock, Winnebago, and Worth were detached in organizing the Twelfth Judicial District, but remained connected with this district except for election purposes till January 2, 1865.]

JUDGES.

John Porter, Hardin county; elected October 12, 1858; re-elected October 14, 1862. Resigned.
Daniel D. Chase, Hamilton county; appointed by the Governor February 5, 1866; qualified February 10; elected by the people October 9.

DISTRICT-ATTORNEYS.

William P. Hepburn, Marshall county; elected October 12, 1858. Appointed Captain Company B, Second Iowa Cavalry Volunteers, August 14, 1861.
Daniel D. Chase, Hamilton county; elected October 8, 1861; qualified November 12; re-elected October 14, 1862. Appointed Judge of the District Court February 5, 1866.
John H. Bradley, Marshall county; appointed February 5, 1866; qualified February 8; elected by the people October 9.

TWELFTH JUDICIAL DISTRICT.

[Composed of the counties of Bremer, Butler, Cerro Gordo, Floyd, Hancock, Mitchell, Winnebago, and Worth.]

Created July 4, 1864; *the counties composing it to remain connected with their former districts* (*the Tenth and Eleventh*) *for purposes of holding court till Jannary* 1, 1865.

JUDGE.

William B. Fairfield, Floyd county; elected November 8, 1864; term commenced January 1, 1865.

DISTRICT-ATTORNEY.

John E. Burke, Bremer county; elected November 8, 1864.

NOTE.—The terms of office of the judges and district-attorneys under the present Constitution commence on the first day of January following their election, except when elected to fill vacancies, in which case they enter upon their duties immediately on qualification.

THE MILITIA.

ADJUTANTS-GENERAL.

Daniel S. Lee, Lee county; appointed April 3, 1851.
George W. McCleary, Louisa county; appointed May 16, 1855.
Elijah Sells, Muscatine county; appointed January 15, 1857.
Jesse Bowen, Johnson county; appointed January 18, 1858.

ADJUTANT AND INSPECTOR GENERAL.

Nathaniel B. Baker, Clinton county; appointed and qualified July 25, 1861; reappointed January 14, 1864.

ASSISTANT ADJUTANTS-GENERAL.

John Scott, Story county; appointed March 27, 1860.
John C. Culbertson, Johnson county; appointed October 10, 1861. Resigned January 1, 1862.
Philo E. Hall, Clinton county; appointed September 22, 1862. Resigned June 19, 1863.
Matthew M. Trumbull, Black Hawk county; appointed June 19, 1863. Appointed Colonel of the Ninth Iowa Cavalry Volunteers September 26, 1863.
John C. Culbertson, Johnson county; appointed October 5, 1863. Resigned November 30, 1864.
Francis H. Impey, Scott county; appointed December 1, 1864. Resigned October 31, 1865.
Edward E. Bassett, Scott county; appointed November 1, 1865.

Office abolished April 4, 1866.

QUARTERMASTERS-GENERAL.

Ezra Drown, Jefferson county; appointed April 16, 1851.
Nathaniel B. Baker (Adjutant-General); acting from July 25, 1861.

COMMISSARIES-GENERAL.

Thomas S. Epsy, Lee county; appointed April 16, 1851.
Charles B. Richards, Webster county; appointed February 5, 1858.
Duties devolved on Quartermaster-General from and after June 12, 1861.

PAYMASTERS-GENERAL.

Constantine Holtenbach, Dubuque county; appointed April 16, 1851.
Hiram Price, Scott county; commissioned October 28, 1861; to date from August 30.

Office abolished, and duties devolved on Adjutant-General, April 26, 1862. Duties discharged by Assistant Adjutant-General from and after October 2, 1862. Duties again devolved on Adjutant-General April 4, 1866.

JUDGE-ADVOCATE GENERAL.

H. M. Shelley, Van Buren county; appointed April 16, 1851.

Office vacated June 12, 1861.

SURGEONS-GENERAL.

John Kell, jr., Louisa county; appointed July 21, 1851.
Nathan Udell, Appanoose county; appointed March 27, 1860.
J. C. Hughes, Lee county; appointed in 1861.

Office abolished February 17, 1864.

ASSISTANT SURGEON-GENERAL.

John C. Bennett, Polk county; appointed March 27, 1860.

MILITARY SECRETARIES.

James Burt, Dubuque county; appointed April 16, 1851.
N. H. Brainerd, Johnson county; appointed in 1861.
George J. North, Polk county; appointed January 16, 1864. Relieved from duty January 12, 1866.

NOTE.—Chapter 17, Laws of Extra Session, Eighth General Assembly, approved May 28, 1861, which took effect June 12, 1861, annulled all prior commissions above the rank of Captain in the Iowa Militia, except those for the three regiments then recently organized for the service of the United States.

REPRESENTATION IN CONGRESS.

XXIXTH CONGRESS—1846 TO 1847.

U. S. SENATORS.	Dist.	REPRESENTATIVES.
First General Assembly failed to elect.	..	S. Clinton Hastings, Muscatine.... ..
	..	Shepherd Leffler, Burlington.........

XXXTH CONGRESS—1847 TO 1849.

U. S. SENATORS.	Dist.	REPRESENTATIVES.
Augustus C. Dodge, Burlington; elected December 7, 1848	1	William Thompson, Mt. Pleasant.....
	2	Shepherd Leffler, Burlington.........
George W. Jones, Dubuque; elected December 7, 1848.............. ...		

XXXIst CONGRESS—1849 to 1851.

U. S. SENATORS.	Dist.	REPRESENTATIVES.
George W. Jones, Dubuque..........	1	*First Session*—William Thompson, Mt. Pleasant; unseated by the House of Representatives on a contest, and the election remanded to the people....
Augustus C. Dodge, Burlington; re-elected January 10, 1849...........	1	*Second Session*—Daniel F. Miller, Fort Madison; elected September 4, 1850.
	2	Shepherd Leffler, Burlington.........

XXXIId CONGRESS—1851 to 1853.

U. S. SENATORS.	Dist.	REPRESENTATIVES.
George W. Jones, Dubuque..........	1	Bernhart Henn, Fairfield............
Augustus C. Dodge, Burlington.......	2	Lincoln Clark, Dubuque.............

XXXIIId CONGRESS—1853 to 1855.

U. S. SENATORS.	Dist.	REPRESENTATIVES.
Augustus C. Dodge, Burlington......	1	Bernhart Henn, Fairfield ....
George W. Jones, Dubuque; re-elected December 21, 1852.................	2	John P. Cook, Davenport............

XXXIVth CONGRESS—1855 to 1857.

U. S. SENATORS.	Dist.	REPRESENTATIVES.
George W. Jones, Dubuque..........	1	Augustus Hall, Keosauqua...........
James Harlan, Mt. Pleasant; elected Jan. 6, 1855, and Jan. 17, 1857*.....	2	James Thorington, Davenport ....

XXXVth CONGRESS—1857 to 1859.

U. S. SENATORS.	Dist.	REPRESENTATIVES.
George W. Jones, Dubuque..........	1	Samuel R. Curtis, Keokuk...........
James Harlan, Mt. Pleasant..........	2	Timothy Davis, Elkader.............

XXXVIth CONGRESS—1859 to 1861.

U. S. SENATORS.	Dist.	REPRESENTATIVES.
James Harlan, Mt. Pleasant..........	1	Samuel R. Curtis, Keokuk...........
James W. Grimes, Burlington; elected January 26, 1858..................	2	William Vandever, Dubuque.........

* Election declared illegal by the U. S. Senate, January 12, 1857; again elected as above.

XXXVIITH CONGRESS—1861 TO 1863.

U. S. SENATORS.	Dist.	REPRESENTATIVES.
James Harlan, Mount Pleasant; re-elected January 11, 1860...........	1	*First Session*—Samuel R. Curtis, Keokuk.*...........................
James W. Grimes, Burlington.........	1	*Second and Third Sessions*—James F. Wilson, Fairfield; elected October 8, 1861..........................
	2	William Vandever, Dubuque.........

* Vacated seat by acceptance of commission as Brigadier-General; and J. F. Wilson chosen his successor.

XXXVIIITH CONGRESS—1863 TO 1865.

U. S. SENATORS.	Dist.	REPRESENTATIVES.
James Harlan, Mt. Pleasant...........	1	James F. Wilson, Fairfield...........
James W. Grimes, Burlington	2	Hiram Price, Davenport............
	3	William B. Allison, Dubuque........
	4	Josiah B. Grinnell, Grinnell..........
	5	John A. Kasson, Des Moines........
	6	Asahel W. Hubbard, Sioux City. ...

XXXIXTH CONGRESS—1865 TO 1867.

U. S. SENATORS.	Dist.	REPRESENTATIVES.
James Harlan, Mt. Pleasant *....	1	James F. Wilson, Fairfield...........
James W. Grimes, Burlington.........	2	Hiram Price, Davenport ....
Samuel J. Kirkwood, Iowa City; elected January 13, 1866.........	3	William B. Allison, Dubuque........
	4	Josiah B. Grinnell, Grinnell..........
	5	John A. Kasson, Des Moines.........
	6	Asahel W. Hubbard, Sioux City......

* Became Secretary of the Interior May 1, 1865, and resigned his seat in the Senate. Samuel J. Kirkwood chosen his successor as above.

XLTH CONGRESS—1867 TO 1869.

U. S. SENATORS.	Dist.	REPRESENTATIVES.
James W. Grimes, Burlington.........	1	James F. Wilson, Fairfield...........
James Harlan, Mt. Pleasant; elected January 13, 1866..................	2	Hiram Price, Davenport.............
	3	William B. Allison, Dubuque... ...
	4	William Loughridge, Oskaloosa .. ..
	5	Grenville M. Dodge, Council Bluffs...
	6	Asahel W. Hubbard, Sioux City. ....

LEGISLATIVE.

FIRST GENERAL ASSEMBLY.

Convened at Iowa City, November 30, 1846. *Adjourned February* 25, 1847.
Convened in Extra Session, January 3, 1848. *Adjourned Jan.* 25, 1848.

SENATE.

COUNTIES REPRESENTED.	NAMES OF MEMBERS.
Lee	Jacob Huner, *James Sprott
Van Buren	John M. Whitaker, *John F. Sanford
Davis and Appanoose	John J. Selman
Wapello and Monroe	*James Davis
Marion, Polk, Dallas, Jasper	Thomas Baker
Des Moines	*Milton D. Browning, Samuel Fullinwider
Henry	*Evan Jay
Jefferson	†Robert Brown
Louisa and Washington	*Francis Springer
Keokuk and Mahaska	*R. R. Harbour
Muscatine, Johnson, and Iowa	Thomas Hughes
Scott and Clinton	*Loring Wheeler
Cedar, Linn, and Benton	Samuel A. Bissell
Jackson and Jones	*Philip B. Bradley
Dubuque, Delaware, Clayton, Fayette, Buchanan, and Black Hawk	*Theophilus Crawford, Thomas H. Benton, jr.

Thomas Baker, elected President December 1, 1846. Thomas Hughes, elected January 4, 1848.

John B. Russell, elected Secretary December 1, 1846, and January 5, 1848.

* Drew for the term of four years in the classification, December 4, 1846.
† In the extra session, John Howell represented Jefferson county.

HOUSE OF REPRESENTATIVES.

COUNTIES REPRESENTED.	NAMES OF MEMBERS.
Lee	Jesse B. Browne, William Steele, William J. Cochran, Josiah Clifton, Reuben Conlee, *Daniel S. Baker,
Van Buren	George Montague, Anderson McPherrin, Dudley Hardy, R. B. Willoughby
Davis and Appanoose	Andrew Leech
Wapello	A. B. Comstock
Monroe	Charles Anderson
Marion, Polk, Dallas, and Jasper	John N. Kinsman, Simeon Reynolds
Des Moines	Alfred Hebard, David E. Blair, †G. W. Bowie, Joshua Holland
Henry	John T. Morton, Abraham Updegraff, Thomas Wright
Jefferson	†Samuel Whitmore, James R. Bailey, William H. Lyons
Louisa	Wright Williams
Washington	Stewart Goodrell
Keokuk	Nelson King
Mahaska	†John W. Smith
Muscatine	Elijah Sells
Muscatine, Johnson, and Iowa	Irad C. Day
Johnson and Iowa	Smiley H. Bonham
Scott	James McManus
Clinton	William E. Leffingwell
Cedar	Nelson Rathbun
Linn and Benton	Robert Smyth
Jackson and Jones	Sylvester G. Matson, George F. Green
Dubuque, Delaware, Clayton, Fayette, Buchanan, and Black Hawk	Samuel B. Olmstead, Michael O'Brien

Jesse B. Brown, elected Speaker December 26, 1846, and January 4, 1848.

Silas A. Hudson, elected Chief Clerk December 26, 1846. J. Scott Richman elected January 4, 1848.

* Mr. Conlee died December 23, 1846, and the vacancy was filled by Daniel S. Baker from and after February 2, 1847, during the regular session.

† At the extra session, Josiah Kent filled the place of Baker from Lee; T. L. Sargeant, that of Bowie, from Des Moines; George Weyand, that of Whitmore from Jefferson; and William Edmundson, that of Smith from Mahaska.

SECOND GENERAL ASSEMBLY.

Convened at Iowa City, December 4, 1848. *Adjourned January* 15, 1849.

SENATE.

COUNTIES REPRESENTED.	NAMES OF MEMBERS.
Lee	James Sprott, *Thomas S. Espy
Van Buren	John F. Sanford, *George G. Wright
Davis and Appanoose	*John J. Selman
Wapello and Monroe	†Barney Royston
Marion, Polk, Dallas, Jasper	*Phineas M. Casady
Des Moines	Milton D. Browning, *Alfred S. Fear
Henry	Evan Jay
Jefferson	*John Howell
Louisa and Washington	Francis Springer
Keokuk and Mahaska	R. R. Harbour
Muscatine, Johnson, and Iowa	*Freeman Alger
Scott and Clinton	Loring Wheeler
Cedar, Linn, and Benton	*John P. Cook
Jackson and Jones	Philip B. Bradley
Dubuque, Clayton, Delaware, Fayette, Buchanan, and Black Hawk	Theophilus Crawford, *John G. Shields

John J. Selman, elected President December 5.
C. C. Rockwell, elected Secretary December 7.

* Elected at the general election of 1848 for four years.
† Elected to fill vacancy.

HOUSE OF REPRESENTATIVES.

COUNTIES REPRESENTED.	NAMES OF MEMBERS.
Lee	William C. Read, Cave J. McFarland, Michael H. Walker, Samuel Norton, Isaac W. Griffith
Van Buren	John Alexander, Josiah W. McManaman, Abner H. McCrary, Willard Elmer
Davis and Appanoose	Reuben Riggs
Wapello	Joseph H. Flint
Monroe	William M. Allison
Marion, Polk, Dallas, and Jasper	Lysander W. Babbitt, Manly Gifford
Des Moines	Thomas L. Sargeant, George Davidson, John Penny, John L. Corse
Henry	Samuel D. Woodworth, Mark Burroughs, H. R. Thompson
Jefferson	George Weyand, William Baker, Andrew Collins.
Louisa	Wright Williams
Washington	Stewart Goodrell
Keokuk	William Jacobs
Mahaska	
Muscatine	George D. Stephenson
Muscatine, Johnson, and Iowa	Joseph E. Harrison
Johnson and Iowa	Smiley H. Bonham
Scott	John D. Evans
Clinton	James D. Bourne
Cedar	Jeremiah C. Betts
Linn and Benton	Abraham Timmons
Jackson and Jones	Dennis A. Mahony, Nathan G. Sales
Dubuque, Delaware, Clayton, Fayette, Buchanan, and Black Hawk	Sidney Wood, James A. Langton

Smiley H. Bonham, elected Speaker December 5.
Wm. E. Leffingwell, elected Chief Clerk December 6.

THIRD GENERAL ASSEMBLY.

Convened at Iowa City, December 2, 1850. *Adjourned February* 5, 1851.

SENATE.

COUNTIES REPRESENTED.	NAMES OF MEMBERS.
Lee	Thomas S. Espy, *Nathan Baker
Van Buren	George G. Wright, *John B. Spees
Davis, Appanoose, and Wayne.	John J. Selman
Wapello, Monroe, and Lucas.	*Henry B. Hendershott.
Marion, Polk, Dallas, Jasper, Marshall, Story, Boone, Warren, and Madison	Phineas M. Casady
Des Moines	*George Hepner, †Enos Lowe
Henry	*John T. Morton
Jefferson	John Howell
Louisa and Washington	*Norman Everson
Mahaska, Keokuk, Poweshiek.	*Joseph Lowe
Muscatine, Johnson, and Iowa.	Freeman Alger
Scott and Clinton	*William E. Leffingwell
Cedar, Linn, Benton, and Tama	John P. Cook
Jackson and Jones	*Nathan G. Sales
Dubuque, Clayton, Delaware, Buchanan, Black Hawk, Winneshiek, and Allamakee	John G. Shields, *Warner Lewis

Enos Lowe, elected President December 3.

Philip B. Bradley, elected Secretary December 3.

* Elected at the general election, 1850, for four years.

† Elected to fill vacancy.

HOUSE OF REPRESENTATIVES.

COUNTIES REPRESENTED.	HOUSE OF REPRESENTATIVES.
Lee	E. S. McCulloch, John Thompson, R. P. Wilson, Smith Hamill, Adolphus Salmon
Van Buren	Abner H. McCrary, George C. Allender, Chauncey G. Dibble
Davis, Appanoose, and Wayne	Reuben Riggs, Samuel Riggs
Wapello	Joseph H. Flint, Andrew Major
Monroe and Lucas	N. B. Preston
Marion, Polk, Dallas, Jasper, Marshall, Story, Boone, Warren, and Madison	Lysander W. Babbitt, Edwin R. Guiberson
Des Moines	William Harper, George Temple, Moses W. Robinson
Henry	Peyton Wilson, Abraham Updegraff
Jefferson	Charles Negus, Thomas McCulloch, Hiram D. Gibson
Louisa	Andrew Gamble
Washington	David Bunker
Mahaska, Keokuk, and Poweshiek	William Jacobs, R. R. Harbour
Muscatine	John A. Parvin
Johnson and Iowa	Gilman Folsom
Scott	Laurel Summers
Clinton	William G. Haun
Cedar	Goodwin Taylor
Linn, Benton, and Tama	Isaac M. Preston
Jackson and Jones	Richard B. Wyckoff, John E. Goodenow
Dubuque, Delaware, Buchanan, and Black Hawk.	Theophilus Crawford, Hugh V. Gildea, A. K. Eaton
Clayton, Fayette, Winneshiek, and Allamakee	Eliphalet Price

George Temple, elected Speaker December 3.
C. C. Rockwell, elected Chief Clerk December 3.

FOURTH GENERAL ASSEMBLY.

Convened at Iowa City, December 6, 1852. *Adjourned January* 24, 1853.

SENATE.

COUNTIES REPRESENTED.	NAMES OF MEMBERS.
Lee	‖Calvin J. Price, *James M. Love, †Salmon Cowles
Des Moines	*Milton D. Browning, George Hepner
Van Buren	John B. Spees, *George Schramm
Jefferson	*William G. Coop, ‖John Park
Henry	†Archibald McKinney
Wapello	‖John W. Hedrick
Wapello, Monroe, Lucas, Clarke	Henry B. Hendershott
Davis	‖Samuel G. McAchran
Davis, Appanoose, Wayne, and Decatur	*Amos Harris
Pottawattamie	‖Hadley D. Johnson
Mills, Montgomery, Adams, Union, Ringgold, Taylor, Page, and Fremont	‖George W. Lucas
Louisa and Washington	Norman Everson
Keokuk	Joseph Lowe
Mahaska	‖John R. Needham
Marion, Warren, and Madison	*Jefferson D. Hillis
Scott	‖Eli S. Wing
Muscatine	‖Jonathan E. Fletcher
Cedar and Clinton	William E. Leffingwell
Johnson, Iowa, and Poweshiek	*George D. Crosthwait
Jasper, Polk, Dallas, Guthrie, Greene, Boone, Story, Marshall, Hardin, Risley, Yell, Fox, Pocahontas, Humboldt, Wright, Franklin, Cerro Gordo, Hancock, Kossuth, Palo Alto, Emmett, Bancroft, Winnebago, Worth	‖Andrew Y. Hull
Jackson	‖Elisha F. Clark
Jackson and Jones	Nathan G. Sales
Linn, Benton, and Tama	*Isaac M. Preston
Dubuque, Delaware, Buchanan, Black Hawk, Grundy, Butler, Bremer, Clayton, Fayette, Allamakee, Winneshiek, Howard, Mitchell, Floyd, and Chickasaw.	‖John G. Shields, Warner Lewis, *Maturin L. Fisher.

William E. Leffingwell, elected President December 7.
T. B. Cuming, elected Secretary December 7.

* Elected at the general election, 1852, for four years.
† Elected to fill vacancy.
‖ Elected at the general election, 1852, to fill original vacancies, and in the classification Messrs. Clark, Lewis, Needham, McAchran, Park, and Shields drew the long term.

HOUSE OF REPRESENTATIVES.

COUNTIES REPRESENTED.	NAMES OF MEMBERS.
Lee	S. G. Wright, H. Washburn, J. S. Gilmore, J. M. Anderson, F. Hesser, S. W. Sears
Des Moines	James W. Grimes, Justus Clark, W. Seymour, J. Wilson Williams
Van Buren	Anderson McPherrin, Lewis Fordyce, Jacob Ream, Robert Russell
Jefferson	Samuel Whitmore, W. T. Rogers, H. B. Mitchell.
Henry	Robert Caulk, James C. Green, Levi Jessup.
Wapello	*Robert Cock, James C. Ramsey
Wapello, Monroe, Lucas, and Clarke	Henry Allen
Monroe, Lucas, and Clarke	John S. Townsend.
Davis	Albert Duckworth, John A. Drake
Davis, Appanoose, Wayne, and Decatur	Abraham Putman
Appanoose, Wayne, Decatur	Harvey B. Duncan
Pottawattamie	A. S. Bryant
Mills, Montgomery, Adams, Union, Ringgold, Taylor, Page, and Fremont	William C. Means
Pottawattamie, Mills, Fremont, Page, Taylor, Ringgold, Union, Adams, Montgomery, Cass, Adair, Audubon, Shelby, Harrison, Monona, Crawford, Carroll, Sac, Ida, Wahkaw, Plymouth, Cherokee, Buena Vista, Sioux, O'Brien, Clay, Dickinson, Osceola, and Buncombe	Joseph L. Sharp
Louisa	Micajah Reeder, John Cleaves
Washington	David Bunker, Horace H. Wilson
Keokuk	Harvey Stevens
Mahaska	William R. Ross
Keokuk and Mahaska	Samuel Coffin.
Marion, Warren, and Madison	P. Gad Bryan, James M. Walters, Napoleon B. Allison
Scott	James Grant, Le Roy Dodge
Muscatine	Elijah Sells, Freeman Alger
Cedar	Amos Witter.
Clinton	William G. Haun
Johnson	Gilman Folsom
Johnson, Iowa, and Poweshiek	Robert M. Hutchinson
Jasper, Polk, Dallas, Guthrie, Greene, Boone, Story, Marshall, Hardin, Risley, Yell, Fox, Pocahontas, Humboldt, Wright, Franklin, Cerro Gordo, Hancock, Kossuth, Palo Alto, Emmett, Bancroft, Winnebago, and Worth	J. F. Rice, Joseph C. Goodson, Benjamin Green.
Jackson	George F. Green, L. Wasson
Jones	John Taylor
Linn, Benton, and Tama	A. F. Stedman, John McArthur
Dubuque, Delaware, Buchanan,	A. K. Eaton, A. D. Anderson, Richard Bonson,

* Name changed to "Coles" by Chapter 39, Acts 4th General Assembly, which took effect January 20, 1853.

Black Hawk, Grundy, Butler, and Bremer.	Lyman Dillon
Clayton, Fayette, Allamakee, Winneshiek, Howard, Mitchell, Floyd, and Chickasaw...	Edwin Montgomery, John Garber

James Grant, elected Speaker December 7.
J. Smith Hooton, elected Chief Clerk December 7.

FIFTH GENERAL ASSEMBLY.

Convened at Iowa City, December 4, 1854. *Adjourned January* 26, 1855.
Convened in Extra Session, July 2, 1856. *Adjourned July* 16, 1856.

SENATE.

COUNTIES REPRESENTED.	NAMES OF MEMBERS.
Lee	*James M. Love, †E. S. McCulloch, †W. A. Thurston
Des Moines	Milton D. Browning, †William F. Coolbaugh
Van Buren	George Schramm, †Abner H. McCrary
Jefferson	William G. Coop, John Park
Henry	†Alvin Saunders
Wapello	†James C. Ramsey
Wapello, Monroe, Lucas, and Clarke	†Dan. Anderson
Davis	Samuel G. McAchran
Davis, Appanoose, Wayne, and Decatur	‡Nathan Udell
Pottawattamie	†James D. Test
Mills, Montgomery, Adams, Union, Ringgold, Taylor, Page and Fremont	George W. Lucas
Louisa and Washington	†H. T. Cleaver
Keokuk	†James L. Hogin
Mahaska	John R. Needham
Marion, Warren, and Madison	Jefferson D. Hillis
Scott	†Ambrose C. Fulton
Muscatine	†George W. Wilkinson
Cedar and Clinton	†Julius J. Matthews
Johnson, Iowa, and Poweshiek	‡Samuel Workman
Jasper, Polk, Dallas, Guthrie, Greene, Boone, Story, Marshall, Hardin, Risley, Yell, Fox, Pocahontas, Humboldt, Wright, Franklin, Cerro Gordo, Hancock, Kossuth, Palo Alto, Emmett, Bancroft, Winnebago, and Worth	†Theophilus Bryan, §James C. Jordan

* At the extra session, David T. Brigham filled the place of James M. Love, of Lee county, appointed Judge of the United States District Court.

† Elected at the general election, 1854, for four years. ‡ Elected to fill vacancies.

§ The seat of Theophilus Bryan was contested by James Jordan, and the contest was decided in favor of Jordan, January 8, 1856.

Jackson	Elisha F. Clark
Jackson and Jones	*Joseph Birge
Linn, Benton, and Tama	Isaac M. Preston
Dubuque, Delaware, Buchanan, Black Hawk, Grundy, Butler, Bremer, Clayton, Fayette, Allamakee, Winneshiek, Howard, Mitchell, Floyd, and Chickasaw.	*Wm. W. Hamilton, Maturin L. Fisher, John G. Shields

Maturin L. Fisher, elected President December 7.
P. B. Rankin, elected Secretary December 8.

HOUSE OF REPRESENTATIVES.

Dis.	COUNTIES.	NAMES OF MEMBERS.
1	Allamakee and Winneshiek	James D. McKay
2	Clayton	Reuben Noble, Lafayette Bigelow
3	Fayette, Chickasaw, Butler, Bremer, Black Hawk, Grundy, Franklin, Cerro Gordo, Floyd, Howard, Mitchell, and Worth	Jacob W. Rogers
4	Delaware and Buchanan	Thomas E. Turner
5	Dubuque	Richard Bonson, John M. Moore, Ben M. Samuels, William S. Hall
6	Jackson	James P. Edie, Thomas S. Smith
7	Jones	William H. Holmes
8	Jackson and Jones	David Kinert
9	Cedar	Allen D. Graham
10	Clinton	Joseph A. Brown
11	Scott	Amos Witter, Andrew J. Hyde
12	Cedar, Clinton, and Scott	George Smith
13	Washington	Samuel A. Russell
14	Louisa	John C. Lockwood
15	Washington and Louisa	James N. Young
16	Muscatine	Reasin Pritchard, John H. Pigman
17	Des Moines	Thomas L. Sargeant, John L. Corse, Joshua Tracy, George S. Albright
18	Henry	Willet Dorland, Francis White, Samuel McFarland
19	Lee	George Newsam, William Damon, Josiah Hinkle, Horace Dewey, Samuel Boyles, Robert P. Creel
20	Linn	John P. Conkey, Robert Holmes
21	Johnson	Samuel H. McCrory
22	Johnson and Iowa	Rolla Johnson
23	Poweshiek, Jasper, Benton, and Tama	John Connell
24	Van Buren	George N. Rosser, Joseph Barker, Robert Meek, Henry Weatherington
25	Jefferson	James Wamsley, Edmund Meachem, Robert Stephenson
26	Davis	O. D. Tisdale, D. C. Greenleaf.
27	Wapello	Samuel K. Creamer, Nimrod Poston
28	Wapello and Keokuk	Cyrus Franklin
29	Keokuk	W. F. Morgan

*Elected at the general election, 1854, for four years.

30	Appanoose	William Monroe
31	Monroe	Matthew A. Goodfellow
32	Wayne, Decatur, Lucas, Clarke	S. P. Yeomans
33	Mahaska	Samuel Coffin, Micajah Williams
34	Marion	*James M. Walters, Green T. Clark
35	Marion, Warren, and Madison	P. Gad Bryan, Jairus E. Neal
36	Polk	Alfred M. Lyon
37	Polk, Dallas, and Guthrie	Ezra Vanfossen
38	Greene, Boone, Story, Hardin, Webster, Yell, Fox, Pocahontas, Humboldt, Wright, Hancock, Kossuth, Palo Alto, Emmett, Bancroft, Winnebago, and Marshall	Samuel B. McCall
39	Fremont, Page, Taylor, and Ringgold	William Dewey
40	Mills, Montgomery, Adams, Union, Adair, Audubon, and Cass	†Richard Tutt
41	Pottawattamie	Daniel S. Jackson, John T. Baldwin
42	Harrison, Shelby, Carroll, Crawford, Monona, Woodbury, Ida, Sac, Buena Vista, Cherokee, Plymouth, Sioux, O'Brien, Clay, Dickinson, Osceola, and Buncombe	*Thomas B. Neely

Reuben Noble, elected Speaker December 5.
Charles C. Nourse, elected Chief Clerk December 5.

* Seat contested by Green T. Clark, and contest decided in favor of Mr. Clark, January 4.
† Died December 22, 1854, never having qualified. His seat remained vacant during the regular session.
NOTE.—At the extra session, Lewis Kinsey filled the place of Mr. Lockwood of Louisa county; J. Scott Richman, that of Mr. Pritchard of Muscatine; John S. Hamilton, that of Mr. Damon of Lee; S. J. Reid, that of Mr. Hinkle of Lee; W. F. B. Lynch, that of Mr. Dewey of Lee; J. M. Anderson, that of Mr. Boyles of Lee; William Beckford, that of Mr. Wamsley of Jefferson; C. E. Noble, that of Mr. Meachem of Jefferson; and Joseph W. Russell, that of Mr. Tutt of the 40th district.

SIXTH GENERAL ASSEMBLY.

Convened at Iowa City, December 1, 1856. Adjourned January 29, 1857.

SENATE.

Dis.	COUNTIES.	NAMES OF MEMBERS.
1	Lee	E. S. McCulloch, William A. Thurston
2	Lee and Van Buren	*David T. Brigham
3	Van Buren	Abner H. McCrary
4	Des Moines	William F. Coolbaugh, *Lyman Cook
5	Davis	*Henry H. Trimble

* Elected at the general election, 1856, for four years.

6	Jefferson	*William M. Reid
7	Henry	Alvin Saunders
8	Wapello	James C. Ramsey
9	Monroe, Lucas, and Clark	Dan. Anderson
10	Appanoose, Wayne, Decatur	*John W. Warner
11	Fremont, Mills, Page, Taylor, Montgomery, Ringgold, Adams, and Union	*Samuel Dale
12	Pottawattamie, Harrison, Shelby, Woodbury, Monona, Audubon, Crawford, Calhoun, Sac, Ida, Cherokee, Buena Vista, Pocahontas, Palo Alto, Emmett, Clay, Dickinson, Osceola, O'Brien, Plymouth, Sioux, and Buncombe	James D. Test
13	Louisa	H. T. Cleaver
14	Washington	*Charles Foster
15	Keokuk	James L. Hogin
16	Mahaska	*William Loughridge
17	Marion	*Jairus E. Neal
18	Warren, Madison, Adair, and Cass	*M. L. McPherson
19	Muscatine	George W. Wilkinson
20	Johnson and Iowa	*Samuel J. Kirkwood
21	Scott	†Nicholas J. Rusch
22	Cedar	*Jonathan W. Cattell
23	Clinton	Julius J. Matthews
24	Linn	*William G. Thompson
25	Linn, Benton, Black Hawk, and Buchanan	*George McCoy
26	Poweshiek, Jasper, Marshall, and Tama	*Josiah B. Grinnell
27	Polk, Dallas, and Guthrie	James C. Jordan
28	Jackson	*Jeremiah W. Jenkins
29	Jackson and Jones	Joseph Birge
30	Dubuque	*William G. Stewart
31	Dubuque and Delaware	William W. Hamilton
32	Clayton	*Henry B. Carter
33	Fayette, Bremer, Butler, Franklin, Grundy, Hardin, Wright, Webster, Boone, Story, Greene, and Humboldt	*Aaron Brown
34	Allamakee, Winneshiek, Howard, Chickasaw, Mitchell, Floyd, Worth, Cerro Gordo, Hancock, Winnebago, Bancroft, and Kossuth	*Jeremiah T. Atkins

William W. Hamilton, elected President December 2.
Charles C. Nourse, elected Secretary December 2.

* Elected at the general election, 1856, for four years.
† Elected to fill vacancy.

HOUSE OF REPRESENTATIVES.

Dis.	COUNTIES.	NAMES OF MEMBERS.
1	Lee	Joseph Van Valkenburgh, Thomas Sawyer, J. B. Pease, J. H. Sullivan, W. H. Griswold
2	Des Moines	Thomas J. R. Perry, J. Wilson Williams, E. D. Rand.
3	Van Buren	David Doud, jr., R. H. McDow, Dudley Hardy.
4	Davis	Barnett Milliser, David Mendenhall
5	Jefferson	Charles O. Stanton, W. H. Copeland, Lewis Reeder
6	Henry	Willet Dorland, Samuel McFarland
7	Wapello.	Cyrus Franklin, S. G. Finney
8	Wapello and Keokuk	Morrison F. Bottorf
9	Monroe	Samuel Gossage
10	Lucas, Clarke, and Union	D. W. Scoville
11	Appanoose	James Galbraith
12	Wayne and Decatur	Thomas M. Bowen
13	Fremont	William Kelsey
14	Mills, Taylor, Page, Montgomery, Ringgold, and Adams	Samuel H. Moer
15	Pottawattamie	A. V. Larimer
16	Harrison, Shelby, Woodbury, Monona, Audubon, Crawford, Carroll, Calhoun, Sac, Ida, Cherokee, Buena Vista, Pocahontas, Palo Alto, Emmett, Clay, Dickinson, Osceola, O'Brien, Plymouth, Sioux, and Buncombe	N. G. Wyatt
17	Louisa	N. W. Burris
18	Washington	William B. Lewis
19	Louisa and Washington	Andrew J. Kirkpatrick
20	Keokuk	Abraham C. Price
21	Mahaska	R. M. Wilson, John H. Fry
22	Marion	Green T. Clark, Miles Jordan
23	Warren	C. B. Jones
24	Madison, Adair, and Cass	Benjamin F. Roberts
25	Muscatine	David C. Cloud, J. A. Mills
26	Johnson	George D. Woodin
27	Johnson and Iowa	Phineas Inskeep
28	Scott	Eli S. Wing, Horatio G. Barner, Robert H. Rogers
29	Cedar	Ed Wright
30	Clinton	Charles H. Toll
31	Clinton and Cedar	*E. M. Wright
32	Linn	John E. Kurtz, Daniel Lothian
33	Poweshiek and Jasper	David Edmundson
34	Benton, Tama, and Marshall.	Delos Arnold
35	Polk	William P. Davis
36	Polk, Dallas, and Guthrie	Benjamin Green
37	Jackson	William Mordan, Jacob K. Hershberger
38	Jones	William H. Holmes
39	Jackson and Jones	William Thomas
40	Delaware	James M. Noble
41	Black Hawk and Buchanan	Morrison Bailey
42	Dubuque	John M. Moore, Winslow T. Barker, Thomas Hardie, Daniel Cort
43	Clayton	La Fayette Bigelow, Francis Rodman

* E. M. Wright died about the time the session convened, and the vacancy was not filled.

44	Boone, Webster, Story, Hardin, Greene, Franklin, Wright, and Humboldt	Walter C. Wilson
45	Allamakee	James Bryson
46	Winneshiek, Howard, Mitchell, Worth, Winnebago, and Bancroft	Claus L. Clausen
47	Fayette	Robert A. Richardson
48	Bremer, Chickasaw, Butler, Floyd, Cerro Gordo, Hancock, Kossuth, and Grundy.	E. R. Gillett

Samuel McFarland, elected Speaker December 2.
J. W. Logan, elected Chief Clerk December 2.

THIRD CONSTITUTIONAL CONVENTION.

Convened at Iowa City, January 19, 1857. *Adjourned March* 5, 1857.

Dis.	COUNTIES.	NAMES OF MEMBERS.
1	Lee	Edward Johnston, William Patterson
2	Lee and Van Buren	Squire Ayers
3	Van Buren	Timothy Day
4	Des Moines	Jonathan C. Hall, Moses W. Robinson
5	Davis	David P. Palmer
6	Jefferson	James F. Wilson
7	Henry	Rufus L. B. Clarke
8	Wapello	George Gillaspy
9	Monroe, Lucas, and Clarke	John Edwards
10	Appanoose, Wayne, Decatur	Amos Harris
11	Fremont, Mills, Page, Taylor, Montgomery, Ringgold, Adams, and Union	Daniel H. Solomon
12	Pottawattamie, Harrison, Shelby, Woodbury, Monona, Audubon, Crawford, Carroll, Calhoun, Sac, Ida, Cherokee, Buena Vista, Pocahontas, Palo Alto, Emmett, Clay, Dickinson, Osceola, O'Brien, Plymouth, Sioux, Buncombe.	Daniel W. Price
13	Louisa	Francis Springer
14	Washington	David Bunker
15	Keokuk	Jeremiah Hollingsworth
16	Mahaska	James A. Young
17	Marion	Hiram D. Gibson
18	Warren, Madison, Adair, Cass.	Lewis Todhunter
19	Muscatine	John A. Parvin
20	Johnson and Jones	William Penn Clarke
21	Scott	George W. Ells
22	Cedar	Robert Gower
23	Clinton	Aylett R. Cotton

24	Linn	Hosea W. Gray
25	Linn, Benton, Black Hawk, and Buchanan	James C. Traer.
26	Poweshiek, Jasper, Marshall, and Tama	Harvey J. Skiff.
27	Polk, Dallas, and Guthrie	Thomas Seely
28	Jackson	William A. Warren
29	Jackson and Jones	Albert H. Marvin
30	Dubuque	John H. Emerson
31	Dubuque and Delaware	John H. Peters
32	Clayton	Alpheus Scott
33	Fayette, Bremer, Butler, Franklin, Grundy, Hardin, Wright, Webster, Boone, Story, Greene Allamakee, Winneshiek, and Humboldt	Sheldon G. Winchester
34	Howard, Chickasaw, Mitchell, Floyd, Worth, Cerro Gordo, Hancock, Winnebago, Bancroft, and Kossuth	John T. Clark

Francis Springer, elected President January 20.

Thomas J. Saunders, elected Secretary January 20.

The Constitution adopted by this Convention was sanctioned by the people at an election held on the 3d day of August, 1857, there being 40,311 votes cast "For the Constitution," and 38,681 votes cast "Against the Constitution," and took effect by proclamation of the Governor September 3d, 1857.

SEVENTH GENERAL ASSEMBLY.

Convened at Des Moines, January 11, 1858. *Adjourned March* 23, 1858.

SENATE.

Dis.	COUNTIES.	NAMES OF MEMBERS.
1	Lee	*John R. Allen, *John W. Rankin
2	Lee and Van Buren	David T. Brigham
3	Van Buren.	*Gideon S. Bailey
4	Des Moines	*William F. Coolbaugh, Lyman Cook
5	Davis	Henry H. Trimble
6	Jefferson	William M. Reid
7	Henry	*Alvin Saunders
8	Wapello	John A. Johnson
9	Monroe, Lucas, and Clarke	*Dan. Anderson
10	Appanoose, Wayne, and Decatur	John W. Warner
11	Fremont, Mills, Page, Taylor, Montgomery, Ringgold, Union, and Adams	Samuel Dale

* Elected at the general election in 1857 for four years.

12	Pottawattamie, Harrison, Shelby, Woodbury, Monona, Audubon, Crawford, Calhoun, Sac, Ida, Cherokee, Buena Vista, Pocahontas, Palo Alto, Emmett, Clay, Dickinson, Osceola, O'Brien, Plymouth, Sioux, and Buncombe....	*W. H. M. Pusey
13	Louisa	*Samuel Reiner
14	Washington	Charles Foster
15	Keokuk	*O. P. Sharradan
16	Mahaska	William Loughridge
17	Marion	Jairus E. Neal
18	Warren, Madison, Adair, and Cass	M. L. McPherson
19	Muscatine	*A. O. Patterson
20	Johnson and Iowa	Samuel J. Kirkwood
21	Scott	*Nicholas J. Rusch
22	Cedar	Jonathan W. Cattell
23	Clinton	*George M. Davis
24	Linn	William G. Thompson
25	Linn, Benton, Black Hawk, and Buchanan	George McCoy
26	Poweshiek, Jasper, Marshall, and Tama	Josiah B. Grinnell
27	Polk, Dallas, and Guthrie	*William P. Davis
28	Jackson	Jeremiah W. Jenkins
29	Jackson and Jones	*Joseph Mann
30	Dubuque	William G. Stewart
31	Dubuque and Delaware	*David S. Wilson
32	Clayton	Henry B. Carter
33	Fayette, Bremer, Butler, Franklin, Grundy, Hardin, Wright, Webster, Boone, Story, Greene, and Humboldt	Aaron Brown
34	Allamakee, Winneshiek, Howard, Chickasaw, Mitchell, Floyd, Worth, Cerro Gordo, Hancock, Winnebago, Bancroft, and Kossuth	Jeremiah T. Atkins

President—Oran Faville, Lieutenant-Governor; inaugurated January 15.
Secretary—George E. Spencer; elected January 12.

HOUSE OF REPRESENTATIVES.

Dis.	COUNTIES.	NAMES OF MEMBERS.
1	Allamakee	George W. Gray
2	Winneshiek	E. E. Cooley
3	Fayette	Robert A. Richardson
4	Clayton	L. G. Collins, W. H. Sterns
5	Buchanan and Fayette	J. S. Woodward
6	Black Hawk	Zimri Streeter
7	Dubuque	Theophilus Crawford, Lincoln Clark, Dennis A. Mahony
8	Delaware	Joseph Grimes
9	Dubuque, Jones, and Clayton	W. S. Johnson

* Elected at the general election in 1857 for four years.

10	Benton	Thomas Drummond
11	Howard, Chickasaw, Bremer	W. P. Harmon
12	Mitchell, Floyd, and Butler	Matthew M. Trumbull
13	Worth, Cerro Gordo, Franklin, Wright, Hancock, Winnebago, Kossuth, Webster, Hamilton, Calhoun, Pocahontas, Palo Alto, Sac, Buena Vista, Clay, Dickinson, and Emmett	Cyrus C. Carpenter
14	Pottawattamie, Harrison, Shelby, Monona, Crawford, Woodbury, Ida, Plymouth, Cherokee, O'Brien, Osceola, and Buncombe	Samuel H. Casady
15	Guthrie, Dallas, Cass, and Adair	Leroy Lambert
16	Boone, Greene, Carroll, Audubon	Cornelius Beal
17	Hardin, Grundy, and Story	John L. Dana
18	Tama and Marshall	T. Walter Jackson
19	Polk	Thomas Mitchell
20	Jasper	Stephen B Shelledy
21	Iowa, Poweshiek, and Mahaska	William H. Seevers
22	Johnson	John Clark, J. Cavanaugh
23	Linn	E. D. Waln, Ellsworth N. Bates
24	Jones	H. Steward
25	Cedar	Ed Wright
26	Jackson	Philip B. Bradley, T. Millsap
27	Clinton	Horace Anthony, Thomas Watts,
28	Scott	John W. Thompson, Benjamin F. Gue, Robert Scott
29	Muscatine	Freeman Alger
30	Muscatine and Cedar	William Lundy
31	Louisa	Royal Prentiss
32	Des Moines	Justus Clark, Wm. H. Clune
33	Des Moines and Louisa	D. N. Sprague
34	Washington	Samuel E. Rankin
35	Keokuk	Theron A. Morgan
36	Washington and Keokuk	W. McGrew
37	Iowa and Poweshiek	C. J. L. Foster
38	Mahaska	A. M. Cassiday
39	Marion	Israel C. Curtis, Martin B. Bennett
40	Warren	Charles E. Millard
41	Madison	Edwin R. Guiberson
42	Lucas and ——	John Edwards
43	Fremont, Mills, and Montgomery	James M. Dews
44	Adams, Union, Page, Taylor, and Ringgold	W. B. Davis
45	Decatur	W. J. Laney
46	Davis	Barnett Milliser
47	Wayne, Appanoose, and Davis.	Alonzo W. Sharp
48	Appanoose	J. A. Pierson
49	Van Buren	Squire Ayers, J. J. Cassady
50	Monroe	John Reitzel
51	Wapello	William Campbell, William McCormick
52	Jefferson	James F. Wilson, T. Moorman
53	Henry	Lauren Dewey, J. F. Randolph
54	Lee	C. C. Bauder, J. A. Casey, William W. Belknap.
55	Lee, Henry, and Van Buren	George W. McCrary

Stephen B. Shelledy, elected Speaker January 12.

Benjamin Franklin Jones, elected Chief Clerk January 12. Resigned January 18, and William P. Hepburn elected to fill the vacancy.

EIGHTH GENERAL ASSEMBLY.

Convened at Des Moines, January 8, 1860. *Adjourned April* 3, 1860.
Convened in Extra Session May 15, 1861. *Adjourned May* 29, 1861.

SENATE.

Dsi.	COUNTIES.	NAMES OF MEMBERS.
1	Lee	John W. Rankin, †Valentine Buechel
2	Van Buren	Gideon S. Bailey
3	Davis	*Cyrus Bussey
4	Appanoose	*Nathan Udell
5	Wayne and Decatur	*William E. Taylor
6	Ringgold, Taylor, Adams, Union, and Clarke	*J. C. Hagans
7	Page, Fremont, Mills, and Montgomery	*Harvey W. English
8	Des Moines	William F. Coolbaugh
9	Henry	Alvin Saunders
10	Jefferson	*James F. Wilson
11	Wapello	John A. Johnson
12	Monroe and Lucas	Dan. Anderson
13	Louisa	Samuel Reiner
14	Muscatine	A. O. Patterson
15	Washington	*William B. Lewis
16	Keokuk	O. P. Sharradan
17	Mahaska	*H. H. Williams
18	Marion	*Jairus E. Neal
19	Scott	†John W. Thompson
20	Clinton	George M. Davis
21	Cedar	*James M. Kent
22	Johnson	*Jesse Bowen
23	Polk	William P. Davis
24	Jackson	*George F. Green
25	Jones	Joseph Mann
26	Linn	*H. G. Angle
27	Dubuque	David S. Wilson, *George W. Trumbull
28	Clayton	*D. Hammer
29	Warren	*Paris P. Henderson
30	Madison, Dallas, and Adair	*M. L. McPherson
31	Pottawattamie, Cass, Harrison, Shelby, Audubon, and Guthrie	W. H. M. Pusey
32	Monona, Crawford, Carroll, Greene, Woodbury, Sac, Ida, Calhoun, Webster, Humboldt, Pocahontas, Buena Vista, Cherokee, Plymouth, Sioux, O'Brien, Clay, Palo Alto, Kossuth, Emmett, Dickinson, Osceola, and Buncombe	*John F. Duncombe
33	Iowa and Poweshiek	*J. J. Watson
34	Jasper and Marshall	*A. M. Pattison

*Elected at the general election, 1857, for four years.
†Elected to fill vacancies.

35	Benton and Tama	*Thomas Drummond
36	Grundy, Black Hawk, Butler, and Franklin	*A. F. Brown
37	Delaware and Buchanan	*David C. Hastings
38	Fayette and Bremer	*Lucian L. Ainsworth
39	Allamakee and Winneshiek	*George W. Gray
40	Howard, Chickasaw, Mitchell, Floyd, Cerro Gordo, Worth, Hancock, Winnebago, and Wright	*Julius H. Powers
41	Story, Boone, Hardin, and Hamilton	*John Scott

President—Nicholas J. Rusch, Lieutenant-Governor; inaugurated January 12.
Secretary—James H. Sanders; elected January 10.

HOUSE OF REPRESENTATIVES.

Dis.	COUNTIES.	NAMES OF MEMBERS.
1	Lee	E. S. McCulloch, Calvin J. Price, Nathaniel G. Hedges, Thomas W. Clagett
2	Van Buren	John M. Whitaker, Henry Clay Caldwell
3	Davis	Harvey Dunlavy, Marvin Hotchkiss
4	Appanoose	Frederick A. Stephens
5	Wayne	Hartley Bracewell
6	Decatur	Racine D. Kellogg
7	Ringgold and Taylor	Reuben A. Moser
8	Page and Fremont	Reuben F. Conner
9	Des Moines	Justus Clark, Moses W. Robinson, Jonathan C. Hall
10	Henry	Alvah H. Bereman, A. J. Withrow
11	Jefferson	Matthew Clark, W. W. Cottle
12	Wapello	Jonathan C. Mitchell, James Doggett
13	Monroe	L. O. Haskall
14	Lucas	John Edwards
15	Clarke	John L. Millard
16	Union, Adams, Adair, and Cass	K. W. Macomber
17	Montgomery and Mills	Washington Darling
18	Louisa	John H. Williamson
19	Muscatine	Michael Price, George C. Shipman
20	Washington	Matthew Morehead, Robert Glasgow
21	Keokuk	H. Campbell, George P. Ellis
22	Mahaska	Mahlon Stanton, Thomas N. Barnes
23	Marion	Martin B. Bennett, Israel C. Curtis
24	Warren	James E. Williamson
25	Madison	Thomas D. Jones
26	Pottawattamie	Samuel H. Riddle
27	Scott	Benjamin F. Gue, James Quinn, William H. F. Gurley
28	Clinton	Nathaniel B. Baker, George W. Parker
29	Cedar	Ed Wright
30	Johnson	Rush Clark, George T. Davis
31	Iowa	Hugh B. Lynch
32	Poweshiek	A. M. Cowing
33	Jasper	C. M. Davis
34	Polk	Stewart Goodrell
35	Dallas	Leroy Lambert
36	Guthrie, Audubon, Shelby, and Harrison	Daniel M. Harris

* Elected at the general election, 1857, for four years.

37	Jackson	Benjamin McCullough, William H. Reed
38	Jones	John Taylor
39	Linn	Amos Witter, Jennings Crawford
40	Benton	James McQuinn
41	Tama	Abraham Tompkins
42	Marshall	William Bremner
43	Story and Hamilton	S. B. Rosenkrans
44	Boone	Cornelius Beal
45	Crawford, Monona, Carroll, and Greene	J. W. Denison
46	Dubuque	Francis A. Gniffke, James H. Williams, F. Mangold, John D. Jennings
47	Delaware	John W. LeLacheur
48	Buchanan	George W. Bemis
49	Black Hawk	Zimri Streeter
50	Hardin	David Hunt
51	Humboldt, Webster, Pocahontas, and Calhoun	Samuel Rees
52	Clayton	S. R. Peet, Samuel Merrill
53	Fayette	Leander C. Noble
54	Bremer and Chickasaw	George W. Ruddick
55	Franklin, Wright, Butler, and Grundy	Chauncey Gillett
56	Allamakee	Charles Paulk
57	Winneshiek	Amos Hoag
58	Cerro Gordo, Worth, Winnebago, and Floyd, also Hancock	Elbridge G. Bowdoin
59	Mitchell and Howard	D. D. Sabin
60	Woodbury, Ida, Plymouth, Cherokee, also Sioux, O'Brien, Buncombe, and Osceola	Patrick Robb
61	Dickinson, Sac, Buena Vista, Kossuth, also Emmett, Clay, and Palo Alto	John E. Blackford

John Edwards, elected Speaker January 10.

Charles Aldrich, elected Chief Clerk January 10, 1860. William Thompson, elected May 15, 1861.

NINTH GENERAL ASSEMBLY.

Convened at Des Moines, January 13, 1862. *Adjourned April* 8, 1862.
Convened in Extra Session, September 3, 1862. *Adjourned September* 11, 1862.

SENATE.

Dis.	COUNTIES.	NAMES OF MEMBERS.
1	Lee	*Frederick Hesser, *George W. McCrary
2	Van Buren	*Abner H. McCrary
3	Davis	†James Pollard; qualified February 8
4	Appanoose	Nathan Udell
5	Wayne and Decatur	†E. F. Esteb; qualified February 19
6	Ringgold, Taylor, Page, Union, Adams, and Montgomery	J. C. Hagans
7	Fremont, Mills, and Pottawattamie	Harvey W. English
8	Des Moines	*John G. Foote
9	Henry	*Theron W. Woolson
10	Jefferson	†J. Monroe Shaffer
11	Wapello	*J. W. Dixon
12	Monroe and Lucas	*Warren S. Dungan
13	Louisa	*James S. Hurley
14	Muscatine	*William G. Woodward
15	Washington	William B. Lewis
16	Keokuk	*I. P. Teter
17	Mahaska	H H. Williams
18	Marion	Jairus E. Neal
19	Scott	*Benjamin F. Gue, *Joseph B. Leake
20	Clinton	*Norman Boardman
21	Cedar	James M. Kent
22	Johnson	Jesse Bowen
23	Polk	*Josiah H. Hatch
24	Jackson	George F. Green
25	Jones	*William H. Holmes
26	Linn	H. G. Angle
27	Dubuque	George W. Trumbull, *John D. Jennings
28	Clayton	D. Hammer
29	Warren	John Kern; qualified February 15
30	Madison and Clarke	M. L. McPherson
31	Adair, Cass, Dallas, Guthrie, Andubon, and Shelby	*James Redfield
32	Harrison, Monona, Crawford, Carroll, Woodbury, Sac, Ida, Calhoun,, Webster, Humboldt, Pocahontas, Buena Vista, Cherokee, Plymouth, Sioux, O'Brien, Clay, Palo Alto, Kossuth, Emmett, Dickinson, Osceola, and Buncombe	John F. Duncombe

* Elected at the general election, 1861, for four years.
† Elected to fill vacancy.

33	Iowa and Poweshiek	J. J. Watson
34	Marshall, Hardin, and Grundy	A. M. Pattison
35	Benton and Tama	†Joseph Dysart
36	Black Hawk, Butler and Franklin	A. F. Brown D. C. Hastings
37	Delaware	
38	Fayette and Bremer	Lucian L. Ainsworth
39	Allamakee	George W. Gray
40	Chickasaw, Howard, Mitchell, Winnebago. Hancock, Floyd, Worth, Cerro Gordo, and Wright	†George W. Howard; qualified March 21
41	Story, Boone, Hamilton, and Greene	†Edwin B. Potter; qualified February 19
42	Winneshiek	*Martin V. Burdick
43	Jasper	*Sherman G Smith

President—John R. Needham, Lieutenant-Governor; inaugurated January 15.
Secretary—William F. Davis, elected January 14.

HOUSE OF REPRESENTATIVES.

Dis.	COUNTIES.	NAMES OF MEMBERS.
1	Lee	Charles W. Lowrie, T. G. Stevenson, Martin Thompson, Godfrey Eichorn
2	Van Buren	George Schramm, Joshua Glanville
3	Davis	Harvey Dunlavy, David Ferguson
4	Appanoose	George B. Stewart, Edward J. Gault
5	Wayne	Hartley Bracewell
6	Decatur	Racine D. Kellogg
7	Des Moines	J. Wilson Williams, Franklin Wilcox, Calvin J. Jackson
8	Henry	W. C. Woodworth, John P. West
9	Jefferson	Peter Walker, Abial R. Pierce
10	Wapello	Joseph H. Flint, Thomas D. McGlothlen
11	Monroe	Oliver P. Rowles
12	Lucas	John D. Sarver
13	Clarke	William M. Calfee
14	Fremont	James L Mitchell
15	Mills	Appler R. Wright
16	Louisa	John Cleves
17	Washington	Thaddeus H. Stanton, John W. Quinn
18	Keokuk	John Wasson, Louis Hollingsworth
19	Mahaska	Micajah T. Williams, Samuel G. Castor
20	Marion	Hiram D. Gibson, W. E. Wetherall
21	Warren	Newton Guthrie
22	Madison	Alfred Hood
23	Pottawattamie	W. W. Wilson
24	Muscatine	George C. Shipman, Michael Price
25	Johnson	Rush Clark, Samuel H. Fairall
26	Iowa	Henry M. Martin
27	Poweshiek	Thomas Holyoke
28	Jasper	John Meyer
29	Polk	John Mitchell
30	Dallas	Peter T. Russell
31	Scott	James T. Lane, Jos. R. Porter, Jos. H. White.

* Elected at the general election, 1861, for four years.
† Elected to fill vacancies.

32	Clinton	George W. Parker, John S. Maxwell
33	Cedar	H. C. Loomis, James H. Rothrock.
34	Jackson	Ebenezer Dorr, Joseph P. Eaton
35	Jones	Otis Whittemore, John Russell
36	Linn	Joseph B. Young, Isaac Milburn
37	Benton	James McQuinn
38	Tama	Leander Clark
39	Marshall	Thomas Mercer
40	Story	Thomas C. McCall
41	Boone	Alfred L. Speer
42	Dubuque	Thomas Hardie, William McLennan, F. M. Knoll, Christian Denlinger
43	Delaware	Salue G. Van Anda
44	Buchanan	Jed Lake
45	Black Hawk	Warner H. Curtiss
46	Hardin	W. J. Moir
47	Clayton	George L. Bass, D. W. Chase
48	Fayette	W. B. Lakin, Levi Fuller
49	Bremer	Joseph O. Hudnutt
50	Chickasaw	J. F. Wilson
51	Allamakee	Joseph Burton
52	Winneshiek	William H. Baker, Ole Nelson
53	Howard and Mitchell	D. G. Frisbie
54	Floyd, Cerro Gordo, Worth, and Winnebago	Elbridge G. Bowdoin
55	Butler, Grundy, and Franklin.	Alonzo Converse
56	Hancock, Kossuth, Emmett, and Palo Alto	J. E. Blackford
57	Humboldt, Wright, Hamilton, and Webster	Lewis H. Cutler
58	Dickinson, Clay, Buena Vista, and Pocahontas	Charles C. Smeltzer
59	Plymouth, Cherokee, Ida, and Woodbury	Isaac Pendleton
60	Sac, Calhoun, Carroll, and Greene.	George S. Walton
61	Audubon, Guthrie, Cass, and Adair	Samuel L. Lorah
62	Taylor, Ringgold, and Union	Reuben A. Moser.
63	Adams, Montgomery, and Page	George A. Gordon
64	Shelby, Harrison, Monona, and Crawford	William W. Fuller

Rush Clark, elected Speaker January 14.
Charles Aldrich, elected Chief Clerk January 14.

TENTH GENERAL ASSEMBLY.

Convened at Des Moines, January 11, 1864. *Adjourned March* 29, 1864.

SENATE.

Dis.	COUNTIES.	NAMES OF MEMBERS.
1	Lee	Frederick Hesser, George W. McCrary
2	Van Buren	Abner H. McCrary
3	Davis	*Samuel A. Moore
4	Appanoose	*Nathan Udell
5	Wayne, Lucas, and Clarke	†Ziba Brown
6	Decatur	*C. G. Bridges
7	Ringgold, Taylor, Page, Union, Adams, and Montgomery	*L. W. Hillyer
8	Fremont, Mills, Cass, and Pottawattamie	*Lewis W. Ross
9	Des Moines	John G. Foote
10	Henry	Theron W. Woolson
11	Jefferson	*D. P. Stubbs
12	Wapello	J. W. Dixon
13	Monroe	*William C. Shippen
14	Louisa	James S. Hurley
15	Muscatine	†John A. Parvin
16	Washington	*J. F. McJunkin
17	Keokuk	†John C. Hogin
18	Mahaska	*J. A. L. Crookham
19	Marion	*Thomas McMillan
20	Warren	*Philo G. C. Merrill
21	Madison, Dallas, Guthrie, and Adair	†Benjamin F. Roberts
22	Scott	Benjamin F. Gue, †Thomas J. Saunders
23	Clinton	Norman Boardman
24	Cedar	*Henry Wharton
25	Johnson	*Ezekiel Clark
26	Iowa and Poweshiek	*M. E. Cutts
27	Jasper	†Elisha Flaugh
28	Polk	Josiah H. Hatch
29	Jackson	*John Hilsinger
30	Jones	†Ezekiel Cutler; qualified February 6
31	Linn	*Joseph B. Young
32	Benton and Tama	*William B. King
33	Marshall, Story, Boone, Hamilton, and Greene	*Henry C. Henderson
34	Dubuque	John D. Jennings, *F. M. Knoll
35	Delaware	*John M. Brayton
36	Buchanan and Bremer	*L. W. Hart
37	Clayton	*Benjamin T. Hunt
38	Fayette	*Harvey S. Brunson
39	Hardin, Grundy, Black Hawk, Butler, and Franklin	*Coker F. Clarkson
40	Allamakee	*George W. Gray

* Elected in 1863 for four years.
† Elected to fill vacancies.

41	Winneshiek	Martin V. Burdick
42	Howard, Mitchell, Worth, Cerro Gordo, Floyd and Chickasaw	*John G. Patterson
43	Harrison, Shelby, Audubon, Monona, Crawford, Carroll, Woodbury, Ida, Sac, Calhoun, Webster, Plymouth, Cherokee, Buena Vista, Winnebago, Hancock, Wright, Pocahontas, Humboldt, Sioux, O'Brien, Clay, Palo Alto, Kossuth, Emmett, Dickinson, Osceola, and Buncombe	George W. Bassett

President—Enoch W. Eastman, Lieutenant-Governor; inaugurated January 14.
Secretary—William F. Davis; elected January 12.

HOUSE OF REPRESENTATIVES.

Dis.	COUNTIES.	NAMES OF MEMBERS.
1	Lee	Ferdinand Meissner, B. S. Merriam, Washington Galland
2	Van Buren	William C. Garrett, James W. Latham
3	Davis	F. H. Cary, Dennis A. Hurst
4	Appanoose	Edward F. Morton
5	Wayne	Elijah Glendenning
6	Decatur	John R. Andrews
7	Des Moines	Joseph J. McMakin, James Bruce
8	Henry	H. R. Lyons, Alvah H. Bereman
9	Jefferson	George C. Fry, Owen Bromley
10	Wapello	Peter Knox, Edward H. Stiles
11	Monroe	John Clark
12	Lucas	H. H. Day
13	Clarke	Calvin R. Johnson
14	Page	N. L. Van Sandt
15	Fremont	T. L. Buckham
16	Mills	William Hale
17	Louisa	Enoch Potter
18	Washington	Samuel A. Russell, Nathan Littler
19	Keokuk	Joseph Andrews, R. S. Mills
20	Mahaska	J. N. H. Campbell, Ephraim Munsell
21	Marion	John L. McCormack, Stephen Y. Gose
22	Warren	Samuel B. Lindsay
23	Madison	John E. Darby
24	Pottawattamie	Andrew J. Bell
25	Muscatine	Jacob Butler, Samuel McNutt
26	Johnson	Robert S. Finkbine, Warner Spurrier
27	Iowa	Silas G. Sweet
28	Poweshiek	Reuben Sears
29	Jasper	Salem Jeffries
30	Polk	Nicholas Baylies
31	Dallas	Elwood Lindley
32	Scott	Hugh M. Thomson, Hugh M. G. Skiles, William Sanderson
33	Clinton	George W. Parker, Samuel G. Magill

* Elected in 1863 for four years.

34	Cedar	John W. Stanton, William P. Wolf
35	Jackson	Henry Green, Ebenezer Dorr
36	Jones	John Russell, J. H. Fuller
37	Linn	John P. Carbee, Charles Weare
38	Benton	Alexander Runyon
39	Tama	Phineas Helm
40	Marshall	Oliver F. Hixson
41	Dubuque	Daniel Cort, Benjamin B. Richards, John Christoph, D. O'Brien
42	Delaware	Joseph W. Simpson
43	Buchanan	Dilazon D. Holdridge
44	Black Hawk	Cicero Close
45	Hardin	William J. Moir
46	Clayton	William J. Gilchrist, Henry White
47	Fayette	P. F. Sturgis
48	Bremer	John E. Burke
49	Chickasaw	Henry C. Vinton
50	Allamakee	Charles Paulk
51	Winneshiek	Ole Nelson, James H. Brown
52	Howard and Mitchell	Thomas R. Perry
53	Butler, Franklin, and Grundy	Willis A. Lathrop
54	Cerro Gordo and Floyd	A. B. F. Hildreth
55	Hamilton and Story	George M. Maxwell
56	Boone and Greene	Samuel B. McCall
57	Wright, Hancock, Winnebago, and Worth	Charles D. Pritchard
58	Emmett, Humboldt, Kossuth, and Palo Alto	Edward McKnight
59	Clay, Dickinson, O'Brien, and Sioux	John Smith
60	Buena Vista, Calhoun, Pocahontas, and Webster	James W. Logan
61	Cherokee, Ida, Plymouth, and Woodbury	William L. Joy
62	Carroll, Crawford, Monona, and Sac	Addison Oliver
63	Harrison and Shelby	Stephen King
64	Adair, Audubon, Cass, and Guthrie	Elbridge B. Fenn
65	Adams, Montgomery, Union	W. B. Davis
66	Ringgold and Taylor	William Elliott

Jacob Butler, elected Speaker January 12.
Jacob Rich, elected Chief Clerk January 12.

ELEVENTH GENERAL ASSEMBLY.

Convened at Des Moines, January 8, 1866. *Adjourned April* 3, 1866.

SENATE.

Dis.	COUNTIES.	NAMES OF MEMBERS.
1	Lee	*Nathaniel G. Hedges, *Joseph Holman
2	Van Buren	*Eliab Doud
3	Davis	†Samuel A. Moore
4	Appanoose	Nathan Udell
5	Lucas, Clark, and Wayne	Edward E. Edwards
6	Ringgold and Decatur	C. G. Bridges
7	Taylor, Page, Union, Adams, and Montgomery	L. W. Hillyer
8	Fremont, Mills, Cass, and Pottawattamie	Lewis W. Ross
9	Des Moines	*Fitz Henry Warren
10	Henry	*Theron W. Woolson
11	Jefferson	D. P. Stubbs
12	Wapello	*Edward H. Stiles
13	Monroe	William C. Shippen
14	Louisa	*James M. Robertson
15	Muscatine	*John A. Parvin
16	Washington	J. F. McJunkin
17	Keokuk	*Ezekiel S. Sampson
18	Mahaska	J. A. L. Crookham
19	Marion	Thomas McMillan
20	Warren	†William M. Marshman
21	Madison, Dallas, Adair, and Guthrie	*Joseph R. Reed
22	Scott	*Joseph B. Leake, *Andrew M. Larimer
23	Clinton	*John Henry Smith
24	Cedar	Henry Wharton
25	Johnson	Ezekiel Clark
26	Iowa and Poweshiek	M. E. Cutts
27	Jasper	*John Meyer
28	Polk	*Jonathan W. Cattell
29	Jackson	John Hilsinger
30	Jones	*Sewell S. Farwell
31	Linn	†Joseph B. Young; admitted February 22.
32	Benton and Tama	William B. King
33	Marshall, Story, and Boone	Henry C. Henderson
34	Dubuque	F. M. Knoll, *Benjamin B. Richards
35	Delaware	John M. Brayton
36	Buchanan and Bremer	L. W. Hart
37	Clayton	Benjamin T. Hunt
38	Fayette	†William B. Lakin
39	Hardin, Grundy, and Hamilton	Coker F. Clarkson
40	Black Hawk and Butler	*James B. Powers
41	Allamakee	†Charles Paulk

* Elected in 1865 for four years.
† Elected to fill vacancies.

42	Winneshiek	*H. C. Bulis
43	Howard, Mitchell, Floyd, and Chickasaw	John G. Patterson
44	Worth, Winnebago, Kossuth, Emmett, Dickinson, Clay, Palo Alto, Hancock, Cerro Gordo, Wright, Humboldt, Pocahontas, Buena Vista, Sac, Calhoun, Webster, and Franklin	George W. Bassett
45	Harrison, Shelby, Audubon, Carroll, Greene, Crawford, Monona, Woodbury, Ida, Cherokee, Plymouth, Sioux, O'Brien, Osceola, and Lyon	*Addison Oliver

President—Benjamin F. Gue, Lieutenant-Governor; inaugurated January 11.
Secretary—J. W. Dixon; elected January 9.

* Elected in 1865 for four years.

HOUSE OF REPRESENTATIVES.

Dis.	COUNTIES.	NAMES OF MEMBERS.
1	Lee	Webster Ballinger, William G. Buck, Peter M. Lowden
2	Van Buren	Joel Brown, Jonathan Thatcher
3	Davis	J. M. Garrett, Henry C. Traverse
4	Appanoose	Madison M. Walden
5	Wayne	Samuel L. Glasgow
6	Decatur	Thomas H. Brown
7	Des Moines	J. Wilson Williams, Charles Ben Darwin, Samuel A. Flanders
8	Henry	John P. West, Thomas A. Bereman
9	Jefferson	George C. Fry, John T. McCullough
10	Wapello	Peter Knox, Charles Dudley
11	Monroe	Henry L. Dashiell
12	Lucas	A. B. Conaway
13	Clarke	John F. Landes
14	Page	Charles Linderman
15	Fremont	William C. Sipple
16	Mills	William Hale
17	Louisa	*N. T. Brown
18	Washington	Granville G. Bennett, Howard M. Holden
19	Keokuk	Theron A. Morgan, †David A. Stockman
20	Mahaska	Thomas N. Barnes, Simon G. Gary
21	Marion	B. F. Van Leuven, James D. Gamble
22	Warren	George E. Griffith
23	Madison	Joseph M. Browne
24	Pottawattamie	William F. Sapp
25	Muscatine	Samuel McNutt, R. M. Burnett
26	Johnson	G. E. DeForest, Robert S. Finkbine
27	Iowa	John R. Serrin
28	Poweshiek	David H. Emery
29	Jasper	David Ryan
30	Polk	Hoyt Sherman, George Lute Godfrey
31	Dallas	W. S. M. Abbott

* Died April 1. † Died February 7th.

32	Scott	Hugh M. Thomson, M. J. Rohlfs, John N. Rogers
33	Clinton	B. R. Palmer, G. W. Thorne
34	Cedar	Ed Wright, John G. Safely
35	Jackson	John Wilson, Alva McLaughlin
36	Jones	John Russell, John McKean
37	Linn	John B. Carbee, A. Sydney Belt
38	Benton	Alexander Runyan
39	Tama	Leander Clark
40	Marshall	Thomas J. Wilson
41	Dubuque	D. O'Brien, Winslow T. Barker, Thomas S. Wilson, Andrew Bahl
42	Delaware	Albert Boomer
43	Buchanan	Phineas C. Wilcox
44	Black Hawk	Cicero Close
45	Hardin	Thomas B. Knapp
46	Clayton	John Garber, P. P. Olmsted, Douglas Leffingwell
47	Fayette	Alonzo Abernethy, D. G. Goodrich
48	Bremer	Allen E. Holmes
49	Chickasaw	Gilbert J. Tisdale
50	Allamakee	P. G. Wright, L. E. Fellows
51	Winneshiek	James H. Brown, Horace B. Williams
52	Boone	W. C. Martin
53	Story	George M. Maxwell
54	Howard and Mitchell	D. W. Poindexter
55	Butler and Grundy	Lorenzo D. Tracy
56	Floyd and Cerro Gordo	Wilberforce P. Gaylord
57	Webster, Pocahontas, Buena Vista, and Clay	Robert Alcorn
58	Worth, Winnebago, Kossuth, and Hancock	L. Dwelle
59	Humboldt, Wright, Franklin, and Hamilton	G. W. Hand
60	Dickinson, Palo Alto, Emmett, and O'Brien, also, Osceola and Lyon	Howard Graves
61	Woodbury, Plymouth, Cherokee, and Sioux	William L. Joy
62	Monona, Crawford, Ida, Sac	S. J. Comfort
63	Harrison and Shelby	L. R. Bolter
64	Calhoun, Greene, Carroll, and Audubon	Azor R. Mills
65	Guthrie, Adair, and Cass	Abraham L. McPherson
66	Montgomery, Adams, Union	A. K. Crawford
67	Taylor and Ringgold	Alexander Z. Huggins

Ed Wright, elected Speaker January 9.
Charles Aldrich, elected Chief Clerk January 9.

RECAPITULATION OF LEGISLATIVE AND GENERAL ASSEMBLIES.

Names of the Presidents and Secretaries of the Council and Senate, and Speakers and Chief Clerks of the House of Representatives, of the several sessions of the Legislative and General Assemblies of the Territory and State of Iowa, from 1838 to 1866, also the place and date of meeting and of adjourning.

TERRITORIAL ORGANIZATION.

No. of Session.	Date of Convening.	Date of Adjourning.	Place of Meeting.	Name of President of Council.	Name of Speaker House of Representatives.	Name of Secretary of Council.	Name of Chief Clerk of House of Representatives.
1st	Nov. 12, 1838	Jan. 25, 1839	Burlington	Jesse B. Brown	William H. Wallace	B. F. Wallace	Joseph T. Fales
2d	Nov. 4, 1839	Jan. 17, 1840	"	Stephen Hempstead	Edward Johnston	B. F. Wallace	Joseph T. Fales
2d, Extra	July 13, 1840	Aug. 1, 1840	"	James M. Clark	Edward Johnston	B. F. Wallace	Joseph T. Fales
3d	Nov. 2, 1840	Jan. 15, 1841	"	M. Bainbridge	Thomas Cox	B. F. Wallace	Joseph T. Fales
4th	Dec. 6, 1841	Feb. 18, 1842	Iowa City	Jonathan W. Parker	Warner Lewis	J. W. Woods	Joseph T. Fales
5th	Dec. 5, 1842	Feb. 17, 1843	"	John D. Elbert	James M. Morgan	Joseph T. Fales	B. F. Wallace
6th	Dec. 4, 1843	Feb. 16, 1844	"	*Thomas Cox	James P. Carleton	B. F. Wallace	Joseph T. Fales
6th, Extra	June 16, 1844	....	"	Francis Gehon	John Foley	Charles Maderd	Joseph T. Fales
7th	May 5, 1845	June 11, 1845	"	S. Clinton Hastings	James M. Morgan	John F. Kinney	William Thompson
8th	Dec. 1, 1845	Jan. 19, 1846	"	Stephen Hempstead	George W. McCleary	John F. Kinney	William Thompson

*Elected January 11, 1844, Francis Springer acting as President *pro tem.* till that date.

STATE ORGANIZATION.

No. of Session.	Date of Convening.	Date of Adjourning.	Place of Meeting.	Name of President of Senate.	Name of Speaker of the House of Representatives.	Name of Secretary of the Senate.	Name of Chief Clerk of the House of Representatives.
1st	Nov. 30, 1846	Feb. 25, 1847	Iowa City	Thomas Baker	Jesse B. Browne	John B. Russell	Silas A. Hudson
1st, Extra	Jan. 3, 1848	Jan. 25, 1848	"	Thomas Hughes	Jesse B. Browne	John B. Russell	J. Scott Richman
2d	Dec. 4, 1848	Jan. 15, 1849	"	John J. Selman	Smiley H. Bonham	C. C. Rockwell	Wm. E. Leffingwell
3d	Dec. 2, 1850	Feb. 5, 1851	"	Enos Lowe	George Temple	Philip B. Bradley	C. C. Rockwell
4th	Dec. 6, 1852	Jan. 24, 1853	"	Wm. E. Leffingwell	James Grant	T. B. Cuming	J. Smith Hooton
5th	Dec. 4, 1854	Jan. 26, 1855	"	Maturin L. Fisher	Reuben Noble	P. B. Rankin	Charles C. Nourse
5th, Extra	July 2, 1856	July 16, 1856	"	Maturin L. Fisher	Reuben Noble	Philip B. Bradley	Charles C. Nourse
6th	Dec. 1, 1856	Jan. 29, 1857	"	Wm. W. Hamilton	Samuel McFarland	Charles C. Nourse	J. W. Logan
7th	Jan. 11, 1858	Mar. 23, 1858	Des Moines	Oran Faville, Lieut.-Gov.	Stephen B. Shelledy	Geo. E. Spencer	W. P. Hepburn
8th	Jan. 9, 1860	Apr. 3, 1860	"	N. J. Rusch, Lieut.-Gov.	John Edwards	J. H. Sanders	Charles Aldrich
8th, Extra	May 15, 1861	May 29, 1861	"	Jas. F. Wilson (*pro tem.*)	John Edwards	J. H. Sanders	William Thompson
9th	Jan. 13, 1862	Apr. 8, 1862	"	Jno. R. Needham, Lt.-Gov.	Rush Clark	Wm. F. Davis	Charles Aldrich
9th, Extra	Sept. 3, 1862	Sept. 11, 1862	"	Jno. R. Needham, Lt.-Gov.	Rush Clark	Wm. F. Davis	Charles Aldrich
10th	Jan. 11, 1864	Mar. 29, 1864	"	E. W. Eastman, Lt.-Gov.	Jacob Butler	Wm. F. Davis	Jacob Rich
11th	Jan. 8, 1866	Apr. 3, 1866	"	Benj. F. Gue, Lt. Gov.	Ed Wright	J. W. Dixon	Charles Aldrich
12th	Jan. 13, 1868		"	John Scott, Lt.-Gov.			

EDUCATIONAL.

FIRST BOARD OF EDUCATION.

Convened at Des Moines, December 6, 1858. *Adjourned December* 25.
Convened December 5, 1859. *Adjourned December* 24.

NAMES OF MEMBERS.

Ralph P. Lowe, Governor; *ex-officio.*
1st Judicial District—*Charles Mason; elected October 12, 1858.
2d " " —T. B. Perry; elected October 12, 1858.
3d " " —†George P. Kimball; elected October 12, 1858.
4th " " —D. E. Brainard; elected October 12, 1858.
5th " " —Dan Mills; elected October 12, 1858.
6th " " —†Samuel F. Cooper; elected October 12, 1858.
7th " " —†Thomas H. Canfield; elected October 12, 1858.
8th " " —Frank M. Connelly; elected October 12, 1858.
9th " " —†O. H. P. Roszell; elected October 12, 1858.
10th " " —A. B. F. Hildreth; elected October 12, 1858.
11th " " —†Isaac J. Mitchell; elected October 12, 1858.

President—Oran Faville, Lieutenant-Governor.
Secretary—Josiah T. Tubby, acting from December 6, 1858. Thomas H. Benton, jr.; elected December 21; qualified January 14, 1859; re-elected December 21.

* In the second session, Philip Viele filled the place of Charles Mason.
† In the classification drew the short term.

SECOND BOARD OF EDUCATION.

Convened December 2, 1861. *Adjourned December* 20.

NAMES OF MEMBERS.

Samuel J. Kirkwood, Governor; *ex-officio.*
1st Judicial District—Philip Viele; elected October 11, 1859.
2d " " —T. B. Perry; elected October 12, 1858.
3d " " —Dexter C. Bloomer; elected November 6, 1860.
4th " " —D. E. Brainard; elected October 12, 1858.
5th " " —Dan Mills; elected October 12, 1858.
6th " " —Samuel F. Cooper; re-elected November 6, 1860.
7th " " —Daniel W. Ellis; elected November 6, 1860.
8th " " —Frank M. Connelly; elected October 12, 1858.
9th " " —Lyman N. Ingalls; elected November 6, 1860.
10th " " —A. B. F. Hildreth; elected October 12, 1858.
11th " " —Daniel D. Chase; elected November 6, 1860.

President—Nicholas J. Rusch, Lieutenant-Governor.
Secretary—Thomas H. Benton, jr.; re-elected December 6.

THIRD BOARD OF EDUCATION.

NAMES OF MEMBERS.

Samuel J. Kirkwood, Governor; *ex-officio.*
1st Judicial District—Henry K. Edson; elected October 14, 1862.
2d " " —Samuel M. Moore; elected October 14, 1862.
3d " " —Dexter C. Bloomer; elected November 6, 1860.
4th " " —William J. Wagoner; elected October 14, 1862.
5th " " —S. C. Vance; elected October 14, 1862.
6th " " —Reuben Mickel; elected October 14, 1862, to fill vacancy.
7th " " —Daniel W. Ellis; elected November 6, 1860.
8th " " —*William Reynolds; elected 14, 1862.
9th " " —Lyman N. Ingalls; elected November 6, 1860.
10th " " —G. H. Stevens; elected October 14, 1862.
11th " " —J. M. Brainard; elected October 14, 1862, to fill vacancy.

President—John R. Needham, Lieutenant-Governor.
Secretary—Thomas H. Benton, jr.; resigned in 1863. H. A. Wiltse, acting during a part of 1863, before Col. Benton's resignation. Oran Faville, appointed by the Governor January 1, 1864.

NOTE.—The Board of Education was abolished March 23, 1864, never having met since December, 1861.

* Samuel Storrs Howe was elected in place of Mr. Reynolds, October 13, 1863.

MISCELLANEOUS.

DES MOINES RIVER IMPROVEMENT.

BOARD OF PUBLIC WORKS.

—

Hugh W. Sample, Jefferson county, President; elected August 2, 1847; bond approved September 7.
Charles Corkery, Dubuque county, Secretary; elected August 2, 1847; bond approved September 7.
Paul Brattain, Van Buren county, Treasurer; elected August 2, 1847, bond approved September 7.

—

William Patterson, Lee county, President; elected August 6, 1849, for three years; qualified September 14.
Jesse Williams, Johnson county, Secretary; elected August 6, 1849, for two years; qualified September 15.
George Gillaspy, Marion county (subsequently of Wapello county), Treasurer; elected August 6, 1849, for one year; bond approved October 12; re-elected August 5, 1850, for three years.

—

NOTE.—The Board of Public Works, which had been established for the improvement of the navigation of the Des Moines river by Chapter 103, Acts First General Assembly, approved February 24, 1847, was abolished by Chapter 58, Acts Third General Assembly, approved February 5, 1851, and taking effect February 17, 1851; which act created the offices of Commissioner and Register of the Des Moines River Improvement, to be appointed by the Governor and Senate for two years from February 1, 1851. Chapter 103, Laws Fourth General Assembly, approved January 24, 1853, which took effect February 10, 1853, so far modified the law of 1851 as to provide for the election of Commissioner and Register by the people.

COMMISSIONERS OF THE DES MOINES RIVER IMPROVEMENT.

—

Ver Planck Van Antwerp, Lee county; appointed February 22, 1851; bond approved March 7.
Ver Planck Van Antwerp, appointed January 24, 1853.
Josiah H. Bonney, Van Buren county; elected April 4, 1853; bond approved May 18.
William McKay, Polk county; elected April 2, 1855; bond approved May 19. Resigned November 3, 1856.
Edwin Manning, Van Buren county; appointed by Governor November 17, 1856; bond approved December 1; elected April 6, 1857.
William C. Drake, Wayne county; elected October 12, 1858; term commenced January 3, 1859.
Office abolished March 16, 1860.

REGISTERS OF THE DES MOINES RIVER IMPROVEMENT.

George Gillaspy, Wapello county; appointed February 22, 1851; bond approved March 7.
Paul C. Jeffries, Wapello county; appointed January 24, 1853; bond approved February 7.
George Gillaspy, Wapello county; elected April 4, 1853; bond approved May 21.
John C. Lockwood, Louisa county; elected April 2, 1855; bond approved May 11.

Office abolished February 23, 1857, and duties devolved on Register of State Land office.

REVISION OF LAWS.

COMMITTEE TO DRAFT, REVISE, AND PREPARE A CODE OF LAWS FOR THE STATE OF IOWA.

Appointment took effect February 9, 1848.

Charles Mason, Des Moines county; qualified May 25.
William G. Woodward, Muscatine county; qualified February 4.
Stephen Hempstead, Dubuque county; qualified February 17.

NOTE.—The above Committee prepared what is known as the Code of 1851.

COMMISSIONERS TO REVISE AND IMPROVE THE SCHOOL LAWS OF IOWA.

Authorized July 31, 1856.

Horace Mann, of Ohio.
Frederick E. Bissell, Dubuque county.
Amos Dean, President of the State University.

COMMISSIONERS TO PREPARE A CODE OF CIVIL AND CRIMINAL PROCEDURE, AND REVISE AND CODIFY THE LAWS.

Under a Joint Resolution, and Chapter 40 *of the Acts, of the Seventh General Assembly*, 1858.

William Smyth, Linn county.
Winslow T. Barker, Dubuque county.
*Charles Ben Darwin, Des Moines county.

NOTE.—The "Revision of 1860" was prepared by these Commissioners.

COMMISSIONERS OF LEGAL INQUIRY.

Charles Ben Darwin, Des Moines county; appointed by the Governor and Senate, 1860.
William Smyth, Linn County; appointed by the Governor and Senate, 1860.
Winslow T. Barker, Dubuque county; appointed by the Governor and Senate, 1860.

Charles Ben Darwin, Des Moines county; appointed April 2, 1866.
Frederick E. Bissell, Dubuque county; appointed April 2, 1866. Died June 12, 1867.
William H. Seevers, Mahaska county; appointed April 2, 1866.
Jacob Butler, Muscatine county; appointed by the Governor September 13, 1866, vice Darwin.

SEAT OF GOVERNMENT.

COMMISSIONERS TO LOCATE THE CAPITAL AT MONROE CITY.

Under Chapter 71, *Acts of First General Assembly, approved February* 22, 1847.

John Brown, Lee county.
Joseph D. Hoag, Henry county.
John Taylor, Jones county.

Functions terminated by Chapter 120, Acts of Second General Assembly, approved January 15, 1849, which repealed former law.

*Charles Ben Darwin was also appointed April 21, 1860, to revise the General Laws of the Eighth General Assembly with the Revision.

COMMISSIONERS TO LOCATE THE CAPITAL AT FORT DES MOINES.

Under Chapter 72, *Acts of Fifth General Assembly.*

Lincoln Clark, Dubuque county; appointed March 3, 1856. Declined.
Guy Wells, Lee county; appointed March 3, 1856.
Stewart Goodrell, Washington county; appointed March 3, 1856.
J. A. L. Crookham, Mahaska county; appointed March 3, 1856.
Benjamin R. Pegram, Pottawattamie county; appointed March 3, 1856.
J. H. D. Street; appointed March 16, 1856, vice Clark.

GEOLOGICAL AND MINERALOGICAL SURVEY.

Authorized January 31, 1855.

James Hall, of New York, State Geologist; appointed in 1855; nominated by the Governor, and confirmed by the Senate, January 7, 1857.
J. D. Whitney, of Massachusetts, Chemical Assistant; appointed in 1855.

Again ordered April 2, 1866.

Charles A. White, Johnson county, State Geologist; appointed April 2, 1866.
Gustavus Hinrichs, Johnson county, Chemist; appointed April 6, 1866.
C. Child, Dubuque county, Assistant Geologist; appointed in 1866.
O. H. St. John, Black Hawk county, Assistant Geologist; appointed March 15, 1867, vice Child.

COMMISSIONER OF IMMIGRATION.

Office created April 11, 1860.

Nicholas J. Rusch, Scott county; appointed by the Governor and Senate April 12, 1860, for two years from May 1, 1860, under Chapter 81, Acts 8th General Assembly.

Office abolished at the expiration of Mr. Rusch's term, under Chapter 11, Acts 9th General Assembly.

REGISTER OF FEDERAL OFFICERS FOR THE TERRITORY AND STATE.*

JUDGES OF THE UNITED STATES CIRCUIT COURT.

Samuel F. Miller, Keokuk, Associate Justice of the Supreme Court of the United States; appointed in 1862.
James M. Love, United States District Judge.

JUDGES OF THE UNITED STATES DISTRICT COURT.

John J. Dyer, Dubuque; appointed in 1846. Died in 1856.
James M. Love, Keokuk (now of Ottumwa); appointed in 1856.

CLERK OF THE UNITED STATES CIRCUIT COURT.

William G. Woodward, Muscatine; appointed May, 1862.

CLERKS OF THE UNITED STATES DISTRICT COURT.

Theodore S. Parvin, Muscatine; appointed in 1846.
John C. Burns, Dubuque; appointed in 1856.

UNITED STATES DISTRICT-ATTORNEYS.

Isaac Van Allen; appointed 1838.
Charles Weston; appointed 1840.
John G. Deshler; appointed 1843.
Edward Johnston, Fort Madison; appointed 1845 and 1846.
Isaac M. Preston, Marion; appointed 1848.
Stephen Whicher, Muscatine; appointed 1849.

* The data for the information contained under this caption are from unofficial sources.

Joseph C. Knapp, Keosauqua; appointed 1853 and 1858.
William H. F. Gurley, Davenport; appointed 1861.
Caleb Baldwin, Council Bluffs; appointed 1865.
Milton D. Browning, Burlington; appointed 1867.

MARSHALS.

Francis Gehon; appointed 1838.
Thomas Johnson; appointed 1841.
Isaac Leffler; appointed 1842.
Gideon S. Bailey, Van Buren county; appointed 1845 and 1846.
Stephen B. Shelledy; appointed 1849.
Laurel Summers, Le Claire; appointed 1853 and 1858.
Herbert M. Hoxie, Des Moines; appointed 1861.
Peter Melendy, Cedar Falls; appointed 1865.
Joel M. Walker, Des Moines; appointed 1866.
George W. Clark, Indianola; appointed 1867.

SURVEYORS-GENERAL (Iowa and Wisconsin).

Albert G. Ellis; appointed 1838.
George W. Jones; appointed 1840.
James Wilson; appointed 1841.
George W. Jones; appointed 1845.
Warner Lewis, Dubuque; appointed 1848.
George B. Sargent, Davenport; appointed 1850.
Warner Lewis, Dubuque; appointed 1853 and 1858.
——— Townsend, of Wisconsin; appointed 1861. Died in 1863.
H. A. Wiltse, Dubuque; appointed 1863.

GENERAL ELECTION OF 1867.

Abstract of votes cast in the several counties of the State of Iowa, for Judge of the Supreme Court, Attorney-General, and Superintendent of Public Instruction of said State, at the General Election held on the 8th day of October, 1867:

COUNTIES.	For Judge of Supreme Court.		For Attorney-General.		For Sup't of Public Instruction.		For Sup't to fill vacancy.	
	Joseph M. Beck.	John H. Craig.	Henry O'Connor.	W. T. Barker.	D. Franklin Wells.	Maturin L. Fisher.	D. Franklin Wells.	Maturn L. Fisher.
Adair	237	108	237	.....	203	108	237	.....
Adams	310	135	309	136	310	115	188	6
Allamakee	1213	1311	1207	1311	1212	1312	985	187
Appanoose	1345	1164	1343	1163	1344	1163	1344	1163
Audubon	79	92	79	92	74	92	.....	.....
Benton	1510	762	1515	756	1512	762	1232	.....
Black Hawk	1405	612	1401	619	1408	612	1409	612
Boone	1082	876	1079	875	1082	876	.....	.....
Bremer	999	483	996	486	1000	484	577	245
Buchanan	1395	825	1393	818	1395	825	1194	714
Buena Vista	6	2	6	2	6	2	6	2
Butler	513	307	673	312	531	311	361	231
Calhoun	83	51	83	51	83	51	44	.....
Carroll	113	46	113	46	113	46	113	46
Cass	305	190	303	191	305	190	293	.....
Cedar	1837	1033	1832	1036	1841	1033	1841	1033
Cerro Gordo	344	52	344	52	.....	52	.....	.....
Cherokee	40	14	40	14	39	14	40	14
Chickasaw	758	331	759	330	760	328	651	205
Clarke	740	326	739	326	741	324	599	234
Clay	61	6	61	6	61	6	61	6
Clayton	2553	1709	2538	1718	2547	1773	2546	1788
Clinton	2133	1662	2104	.....	2127	1680	.....	.....
Crawford	134	119	135	118	134	118	111	63
Dallas	820	446	820	.....	820	446	820	....
Davis	1326	1221	1324	1221	1327	1223	1327	1223
Decatur	863	876	864	....	862	876	862	.....
Delaware	1508	890	1506	893	1489	891	.....	233
Des Moines	2173	1880	2142	2067	2165	1880	1498	.....
Dickinson	102	4	102	...	102	5	102	5
Dubuque	*3340	1940	1865	3405	.....	2435	.....	3337
Emmett	112	19	112	19	112	19	111	19
Fayette	2101	965	2122	965	1856	862	2129	967
Floyd	773	292	767	298	774	292	774	292
Franklin	397	55	392	55	397	55	397	.....

*As officially returned from the county. It is evidently an error. The figures for Messrs. Beck and Craig should be reversed.

ABSTRACT OF VOTES, 1867—CONTINUED.

COUNTIES.	For Judge of Supreme Court.		For Attorney-General.		For Sup't of Public Instruction.		For Sup't to fill vacancy.	
	Joseph M. Beck.	John H. Craig.	Henry O'Connor.	W. T. Barker.	D. Franklin Wells.	Maturin L. Fisher.	D. Franklin Wells.	Maturin L. Fisher.
Fremont	799	859	799	859	799	860	376	.....
Greene	303	214	301	215	288	214	234	.....
Grundy	277	7	277	7	277	7	37	.....
Guthrie	455	399	456	399	456	399	.....	....
Hamilton	465	120	464	.....	465	120	12	1
Hancock	64	24	63	24	64	24	4	.....
Hardin	1078	399	1076	369	1017	369	633	351
Harrison	694	588	695	599	694	603	.....	.....
Henry	2349	860	2339	859	2352	854	1882	.....
Howard	616	337	616	337	616	337	255	72
Humboldt	248	71	247	71	242	70	224	27
Ida	15	1	15	1	15	1	.....	.....
Iowa	1189	992	1186	968	1167	972	493	13
Jackson	1730	1859	1717	1854	1679	1782	1732	1851
Jasper	1814	681	1810	.....	1815	663	1811	682
Jefferson	1790	1311	1786	1315	1787	1315	1209	.....
Johnson	1928	.....	1928	2040	1920	2047	1924	2044
Jones	1753	1198	1746	1200	1753	1198	1459	971
Keokuk	1472	1312	1456	1358	858	853	1475	1313
Kossuth	217	13	217	13	217	13	217	13
Lee	2587	3078	2577	3094	2583	3095	2583	3095
Linn	2631	1169	2627	1173	2601	1171	2063	1091
Louisa	1344	698	1334	691	1344	697	1344	.....
Lucas	788	668	783	670	.....	668	.....	.....
Madison	1185	744	1184	744	1185	744	1056	.....
Makaska	2064	1340	2057	.....	2064	1340	2064	967
Marion	2064	1975	2054	1980	2060	1976	1642	1033
Marshall	1388	.....	1386	448	1389	446	1388	447
Mills	631	516	631	.....	627	516	498	.....
Mitchell	717	.....	711	165	714	165	672	.....
Monona	268	134	268	.....	269	133	189	24
Monroe	1096	753	1099	750	1095	754	1095	.....
Montgomery	261	189	260	189	261	189	178	.....
Muscatine	2071	1468	2051	1468	2060	1283	2072	300
O'Brien	6	3	6	3	6	3	6	3
Page	....	399	674	71	674	399	604	51
Palo Alto	39	56	39	56	38	42	38	36
Plymouth	50	5	50	5	50	5	50	5
Pocahontas	82	18	83	17	82	17	14	5

ABSTRACT OF VOTES, 1867—CONTINUED.

COUNTIES.	For Judge of Supreme Court.		For Attorney-General.		For Sup't of Public Instruction.		For Sup't to fill vacancy.	
	Joseph M. Beck.	John H. Craig.	Henry O'Connor.	W. T. Barker.	D. Franklin Wells.	Maturin L. Fisher.	D. Franklin Wells.	Maturin L. Fisher.
Polk	2162	1659	2153	1632	2157	1657	1932	.....
Pottawattamie	816	942	No	ret.	811	965	692	....
Poweshiek	1049	553	1048	562	1049	561	1049	561
Ringgold	436	204	436	205	436	205	436	205
Sac	111	34	111	34	111	34	111	34
Scott	1846	1737	1817	2447	1844	1777	1652	1642
Shelby	107	109	107	109	107	108	107	.....
Sioux	No	retu	rn.	.....	.....	.....	.....	.....
Story	769	405	764	405	770	407	665	.....
Tama	938	413	938	447	938	448	569	.....
Taylor	540	228	539	.....	540	202	511	142
Union	363	301	363	301	363	301	363	301
Van Buren	1881	1515	1884	1514	1885	1512	1885	.....
Wapello	1837	1790	1832	.....	1837	1789	1595	.....
Warren	1320	670	1323	667	1319	670	1150	589
Washington	1824	1024	1806	1024	1812	1024	1500	88
Wayne	863	619	855	617	862	615	862	.....
Webster	598	480	597	481	598	480	598	480
Winnebago	147	1	147	1	147	1	....	.....
Winneshiek	1319	528	1318	528	1319	527	1319	.....
Woodbury	254	238	254	238	254	238	241	227
Worth	180	36	180	36	180	36	180	36
Wright	191	62	190	.....	191	62	....	.....
Total	90789	58880	89035	54641	85845	61224	70902	31325

SCATTERING VOTES.

For Judge of the Supreme Court.

John L. Craig—Johnson county, 2043; Tama, 34. Total, 2077.
James M. Beck—Butler county, 165; Page, 675. Total, 840.
John M. Craig—Marshall county, 447; Mitchell, 164. Total, 611.
Joseph H. Beck—Fayette county, 27.
William P. Parker—Pottawattamie county, 25.
Henry O'Connor—Pottawattamie county, 17; Clinton, 1. Total, 18.
H. Thayer—Chickasaw county, 1.
E. H. Williams—Floyd county, 1.

ABSTRACT OF VOTES, 1867—CONTINUED.

For Attorney-General.

W. F. Barker—Mills, 516; Taylor, 175; Wapello, 1787; Wright, 62. Total, 2540.
W. T. Barker—Dickinson, 5; Jasper 681; Mahaska, 1340. Total, 2026.
William T. Barker—Adair county, 108; Clinton, 1685; Monona, 134. Total, 1927.
W. L. Barker—Decatur, 875.
W. T. Barker—Dallas, 447.
W. P. Barker—Page, 269; Taylor, 52. Total, 321.
W. D. Barker—Hamilton, 120.
W. J. Barker—Page 59.
W. P. Barlor—Taylor, 1.

For Superintendent of Public Instruction.

Franklin Wells—Dubuque, 1626.
B. F. Wells—Butler, 151; Lucas, 788. Total, 939.
F. D. Wells—Cerro Gordo, 343.
George Walker—Van Buren, 1.

For Superintendent of Public Instruction, to fill Vacancy.

Franklin Wells—Dubuque, 1944.
F. D. Wells—Cerro Gordo, 285.
B. F. Wells—Butler, 7.

NOTE.—Sioux county, the returns of which were received at the office of the Secretary of State subsequent to the official canvass, gave 8 votes for Joseph M. Beck, Henry O'Connor, and D. Franklin Wells for both terms, respectively, for the offices for which they were severally candidates.

—

The following is the state of the vote for the several candidates, giving each the vote evidently intended for him.

For Judge of the Supreme Court.

Joseph M. Beck	90,797	
James M. Beck	840	
Joseph H. Beck	27	—91,664
Deduct for error in Dubuque county		1,400
Total for Beck		90,264
John H. Craig	58,880	
John L. Craig	2,077	
John M. Craig	611	
Add for error in Dubuque county	1,400	—62,968
Scattering		45
Total vote		153,277
Beck over Craig	27,296	

For Attorney-General.

Henry O'Connor		89,043
W. T. Barker	54,641	
W. F. Barker	2,540	
William T. Barker	1,927	
W. T. Baker	2,026	
W. L. Barker	875	
W. T. Parker	447	
W. P. Barker	321	
W. D. Barker	120	
W. J. Barker	59	
W. P. Barlor	1	—62,957
Total vote		152,000
O'Connor's majority	26,086	

ABSTRACT OF VOTES, 1867—Continued.

For Superintendent of Public Instruction.

D. Franklin Wells	85,853	
Franklin Wells	1,626	
B. F. Wells	939	
F. D. Wells	343	—88,761
Maturin L. Fisher		61,224
Scattering		1
Total		149,986
Wells over Fisher	27,537	

For Superintendent of Public Instruction, to fill vacancy.

D. Franklin Wells	70,910	
Franklin Wells	1,944	
F. D. Wells	285	
B. F. Wells	7	—73,146
Maturin L. Fisher		31,325
Total vote		104,471
Wells's majority	41,821	

ABSTRACT

OF THE VOTE IN THE SEVERAL COUNTIES OF THE STATE OF IOWA, AT THE GENERAL ELECTIONS HELD IN THE YEARS **1846, 1850, 1854, 1857, 1859, 1861, 1863,** AND **1865**, FOR THE OFFICE OF GOVERNOR OF THE STATE.

COUNTIES.	Oc.26,'46.		August 5, 1850.			Aug. 7,1854.		October 13, 1857.			Oct.11,1859.		October 8, 1861.			Oct.13,1863.		Oct.10,1865.	
	Ansel Briggs.	Thomas McKnight.	Stephen Hempstead.	James L. Thompson.	Wm. Penn Clarke.	James W. Grimes.	Curtis Bates.	Ralph P. Lowe.	Ben M. Samuels.	W. T. Henry.	Samuel J. Kirkwood.	Augustus C. Dodge.	Samuel J. Kirkwood.	William H. Merritt.	Ben M. Samuels.	William M. Stone.	James M. Tuttle.	William M. Stone.	Thomas H. Benton, jr.
Adair	....	....	....	....	....	7	8	40	25	....	120	76	132	60	....	119	60	162	95
Adams	....	....	....	....	....	11	29	90	65	....	177	123	212	88	2	197	93	184	111
Allamakee	....	....	30	27	....	299	197	543	574	....	743	1025	955	990	....	997	1343	1004	1290
Appanoose	42	8	263	176	6	373	507	296	584	4	627	985	687	1044	16	867	1131	1096	986
Audubon	....	....	....	....	....	....	....	36	44	....	58	60	36	68	....	43	45	52	66
Benton	13	28	58	46	....	208	191	359	556	....	914	732	641	514	88	1024	656	1054	512
Black Hawk	....	....	....	....	....	191	153	476	309	....	815	550	1077	457	....	1137	432	1240	373
Boone	....	....	79	14	....	89	181	213	334	2	298	413	327	417	....	341	457	566	668
Bremer	....	....	....	....	....	64	101	307	228	....	417	438	562	340	....	669	308	725	217
Buchanan	....	....	28	35	5	216	146	560	327	....	816	570	791	461	9	992	587	947	583
Buena Vista	....	....	....	....	....	....	....	....	....	....	2	6	9	10	...	3	4	....	....
Butler	....	....	....	....	....	....	....	196	150	....	474	246	438	159	13	495	245	454	232
Calhoun	...	...	....	....	....	....	....	16	16	....	17	17	14	18	....	14	26	18	41
Carroll	....	....	....	....	....	....	....	18	26	....	30	30	13	45	....	28	29	38	54
Cass	....	....	....	....	....	22	53	79	91	....	179	152	172	171	....	194	113	203	171
Cedar	221	212	330	256	18	600	430	918	694	3	1152	1002	1313	394	513	1562	958	1551	760
Cerro Gordo	....	....	....	....	....	....	....	81	32	....	117	72	215	2	....	158	24	242	17
Cherokee	....	....	....	....	....	....	....	....	....	....	12	7	8	3	....	6	1	14	8

Chickasaw	...	...	...	...	...	38	29	332	180	3	439	308	497	114	5	549	283	501	419
Clarke	...	...	...	...	...	86	73	405	320	...	462	351	594	130	128	665	290	559	359
Clay	...	...	...	...	...	...	...	...	...	...	3	9	3	19	...	11	4	27	...
Clayton	163	144	315	221	14	687	332	949	719	11	1630	1429	1861	990	1	2022	1704	1633	1529
Clinton	163	157	245	138	...	443	465	1157	991	...	1605	1521	1429	693	734	1909	1398	1708	1091
Crawford	...	...	...	...	...	...	...	46	27	...	45	55	47	...	...	50	35	56	56
Dallas	...	...	70	59	...	202	189	418	380	...	530	448	549	404	...	615	347	662	402
Davis	...	...	513	446	...	690	711	250	687	413	715	1142	691	1457	...	994	1331	1185	1072
Decatur	...	...	70	59	...	110	253	240	494	4	390	771	465	681	...	673	801	667	824
Delaware	*76	*69	124	130	3	382	299	523	399	...	844	894	1185	542	1	1305	721	1182	704
Des Moines	769	894	812	682	...	1045	1213	1162	1405	181	1704	1923	1823	1313	...	2070	1788	1871	1609
Dickinson	...	...	...	...	...	...	...	9	9	...	31	15	46	4	...	31	1	52	2
Dubuque	490	492	721	353	...	669	1101	999	2482	...	1751	3153	1987	2750	...	2064	3280	1552	2842
Emmett	...	...	...	...	...	...	...	...	...	...	18	5	23	...	...	23	2	35	2
Fayette	...	...	38	63	1	352	225	592	344	27	1102	849	1151	682	...	1339	813	1145	740
Floyd	...	...	...	...	...	72	4	344	211	...	495	281	492	153	...	568	206	571	233
Franklin	...	...	...	...	...	...	...	70	32	...	201	51	237	30	...	193	63	243	85
Fremont	...	...	77	78	...	179	186	223	273	14	293	504	344	556	3	519	396	542	776
Greene	...	...	...	...	...	...	...	51	119	...	126	146	59	83	...	131	102	198	97
Grundy	...	...	...	...	...	...	...	59	4	...	110	17	142	2	...	168	27	134	24
Guthrie	...	...	...	...	...	37	113	168	192	...	257	263	283	284	...	295	266	329	275
Hamilton	...	...	...	...	...	...	...	149	92	...	192	105	214	106	...	198	78	283	79
Hancock	...	...	...	...	...	...	...	...	...	...	19	14	34	14	...	27	19	57	14
Hardin	...	...	...	...	...	65	100	435	289	...	645	458	552	253	...	681	307	772	334
Harrison	...	...	...	...	...	78	93	150	198	...	297	351	406	...	255	332	319	357	437
Henry	370	614	467	669	142	1164	530	1632	829	44	1596	998	1723	802	13	2036	880	1885	828
Howard	...	...	...	...	...	...	...	189	127	...	336	279	316	251	...	413	244	353	283
Humboldt	...	...	...	...	...	...	...	66	10	...	49	29	46	16	...	51	30	96	31
Ida	...	...	...	...	...	...	...	...	...	...	4	3	9	5	...	6	3	9	3
Iowa	31	13	76	39	1	228	129	466	360	...	765	549	687	729	...	764	742	840	734

*Includes the vote of Buchanan county.

ABSTRACT OF VOTES FOR GOVERNOR—Continued.

COUNTIES.	Oc.26,'46.		August 5, 1850.			Aug.7,1854.		October 13, 1857.			Oct.11,1859.		October 8, 1861.			Oct.13,1863.		Oct.10,1865.	
	Ansel Briggs.	Thomas McKnight.	Stephen Hempstead.	James L. Thompson.	Wm. Penn Clarke.	James W. Grimes.	Curtis Bates.	Ralph P. Lowe.	Ben M. Samuels.	W. T. Henry.	Samuel J. Kirkwood.	Augustus C. Dodge.	Samuel J. Kirkwood.	William H. Merritt.	Ben M. Samuels.	William M. Stone.	James M. Tuttle.	William M. Stone.	Thomas H. Benton, jr.
Jackson	357	222	523	337	1	618	717	872	1019	....	1273	1477	1338	1280	22	1598	1726	1587	1525
Jasper	27	15	98	93	....	279	73	727	424	....	946	705	1006	669	9	1120	688	1304	1027
Jefferson	516	421	733	674	19	967	774	1151	960	8	1282	1199	1379	403	716	1378	1199	1478	1086
Johnson	300	254	396	268	7	699	560	1163	1193	59	1602	1395	1675	1472	52	1546	1569	1547	1509
Jones	71	89	213	165	14	438	440	787	708	...	1161	1153	1309	457	....	1427	1002	1463	839
Keokuk	202	164	400	307	2	507	519	879	780	....	1025	1043	1211	898	242	1215	1098	1306	1197
Kossuth	...	....	....	....	....	....	....	70	45	....	75	37	71	3	2	54	15	138	12
Lee	1040	767	1473	931	103	1425	1676	....	....	...	2159	2392	1657	2197	1	2473	2489	2289	2865
Linn	272	197	436	380	26	835	610	1214	998	89	1771	1345	1715	1308	....	2070	1147	2095	1230
Louisa	291	356	299	352	21	645	459	559	669	....	956	679	1097	559	1	1237	631	1114	832
Lucas	....	....	46	41	....	101	124	399	396	5	521	457	549	474	....	580	481	553	516
Lyon (unorganized)	....	....	....	....	....	....	....	....	....	....	....	....	....	....	....	....	....	....	....
Madison	....	....	100	62	....	159	202	491	533	....	651	729	705	666	....	777	624	976	562
Mahaska	251	300	484	518	....	887	568	1027	846	2	1212	1137	1488	1113	2	1733	1167	1820	1188
Marion	128	104	367	268	3	493	649	809	1131	7	1256	1438	1441	1402	4	1365	1534	1634	1804
Marshall	....	....	24	11	....	110	114	416	142	26	795	442	735	390	....	960	492	1002	375
Mills	....	....	....	....	....	177	155	183	213	...	262	245	364	74	119	407	284	432	243
Mitchell	....	....	....	....	....	32	....	437	416	...	516	204	597	132	....	574	169	606	119
Monona	....	....	....	....	....	25	7	49	85	...	105	105	135	86	....	99	95	115	138
Monroe	79	49	282	181	11	360	358	610	548	1	749	665	762	681	45	806	790	880	654

Montgomery	....	....	....	....	....	10	16	69	56	....	125	115	148	79	...	141	90	174	113
Muscatine	348	361	430	394	....	739	619	1140	1105	....	1457	1364	1689	1318	1	1721	1354	1678	1481
O'Brien	....	....	....	....	....	....	....	....	....	....	....	....	1	18	....	4	4	2	5
Osceola (unorg'zed)	....	....	....	....	....	....	....	....	....	....	....	....	....	....	....	....	....	....	...
Page	....	....	....	....	....	....	....	128	206	....	377	333	410	243	13	434	241	397	298
Palo Alto	....	....	....	....	....	61	93	....	....	..	3	44	2	21	17	.....	29	6	48
Plymouth	....	....	....	....	....	....	....	....	....	....	24	11	30	8	....	22	5	23	.....
Pocahontas	....	....	....	....	....	....	....	....	....	....	16	17	10	17	...	17	12	43	10
Polk	78	74	358	312	....	450	450	1115	879	...	1078	1048	1146	1182	11	1420	1243	1689	1468
Pottawattamie	....	....	82	446	....	....	....	205	463	7	295	600	406	189	186	463	317	490	435
Poweshiek	....	....	47	59	...	217	215	473	296	....	595	411	676	374	48	722	526	805	393
Ringgold	....	....	....	....	....	....	....	90	43	....	260	135	307	77	....	353	114	336	152
Sac	....	....	....	....	....	....	....	8	43	....	28	37	5	43	....	21	19	36	40
Scott	285	337	418	352	4	773	583	1717	1399	3	2208	1625	1785	1511	187	2613	1315	2081	1648
Shelby	....	....	....	....	....	19	23	38	33	....	78	96	99	.....	6	80	82	73	74
Sioux	....	....	....	....	....	....	....	....	....	....	....	....	8	....	....	....	4	....	....
Story	....	....	....	....	....	61	51	217	243	....	395	358	412	317	....	453	342	539	439
Tama	....	....	....	....	....	117	37	303	174	4	600	295	649	270	1	818	418	863	479
Taylor	....	...	....	....	....	11	65	222	168	.. .	304	257	363	186	1	381	170	382	271
Union	....	....	....	...	....	8	26	88	115	....	151	193	209	186	....	213	187	233	179
Van Buren	820	732	930	815	52	1067	1026	1035	1116	16	1397	1402	1434	1367	1	1619	1272	1565	1202
Wapello	....	....	702	567	....	823	857	856	1153	20	1016	1260	1295	1604	....	1401	1464	1544	1446
Warren	....	....	40	61	....	63	281	696	394	8	937	609	961	739	....	1122	758	1172	756
Washington	223	306	289	358	122	815	499	1124	775	42	1208	946	1381	508	403	1587	1107	1600	988
Wayne	....	....	....	....	....	127	100	210	314	....	416	535	449	.....	3	500	575	599	529
Webster	....	....	....	....	....	22	104	269	358	....	252	333	245	263	....	299	264	396	432
Winnebago	....	....	....	....	....	....	....	....	....	....	11	24	49	....	....	29	18	83	....
Winneshiek	....	....	....	....	....	185	76	525	229	....	1022	771	1055	.....	621	1400	863	1144	668

ABSTRACT OF VOTES FOR GOVERNOR—Continued.

COUNTIES.	Oc.26,'46.		August 5, 1850.			Aug. 7,1854.		October 13, 1857.			Oct.11,1859.		October 8, 1861.			Oct.13,1863.		Oct.10,1865.	
	Ansel Briggs.	Thomas McKnight.	Stephen Hempstead.	James L. Thompson.	Wm. Penn Clarke.	James W. Grimes.	Curtis Bates.	Ralph P. Lowe.	Ben. M. Samuels.	W. T. Henry.	Samuel J. Kirkwood.	Augustus C. Dodge.	Samuel J. Kirkwood.	William H. Merritt.	Ben M. Samuels.	William M. Stone.	James M. Tuttle.	William M. Stone.	Thomas H. Benton, jr.
Woodbury........	....	....	....	....	...	....	23	125	144	1	132	163	137	111	....	122	107	112	87
Worth	....	....	....	....	....	....	....	....	....	....	98	26	126	3	....	120	35	143	6
Wright	....	....	....	....	....	....	....	60	49	....	80	52	93	35	....	75	43	124	45
Soldiers' vote......	....	....	....	....	....	....	....	....	....	....	....	....	....	....	....	17001	3000	736	607
Total	7626	7379	13486	11403	575	23312	21192	38498	36088	1004	56532	53332	59853	43245	4492	86122	57948	70445	54070
			Scattering....... 11			Scattering.. 10							Henry Clay Dean 463 Charles Mason.. 119 Lincoln Clark... 50 Scattering......, 25			Scattering.. 25		Scattering. 350	

INDEX.

30

ERRATA.

Page 11.—In line 13, third column, after "McGregor," insert "city of."

Page 16.—The blank in the last line, third column, which was caused by type dropping from the "form," should be filled with "Jackson."

Page 64.—The total white population of Cass county is 2,477, instead of 12,477, and of Cedar county 16,035, instead of 6,035.

Page 115.—For the name of the State Librarian, read "Lewis I. Coulter," instead of "Lewis J. Coulter."

Page 131.—For the name of the County Superintendent of Buena Vista, read "O. H. Stala," instead of "O. H. Starle."

Page 133.—The names of the County Superintendents of Linn, Marion, and Pocahontas counties, are severally "Zarah *V.* Ellsberry," "*D. F. Bonner*," and "James J. *Bruce*."

Page 159.—Correct the name of the member of the House of Representatives from Clinton county, to "Shubael Coy."

Page 160.—In the names of members of the House of Representatives from Lee county, for "Jacob Hunter," read "Jacob Huner"; and from Wapello county, read "Flint" instead of "Flink."

Page 165.—Insert, under head "Registers of the State Land Office," "Office created February 9, 1855."

Page 170.—Under the head of "Fourth District," omit, from fifth and sixth lines, the words, "and in 1857, Marshall and Story to the new Thirteenth."

Page 171.—Under the sub-head "Judges," (Fifth District,) for "Charles J. McFarland," read "Cave J. McFarland," in both places.

Page 176.—Charles E. Millard was re-elected District-Attorney of the Third Judicial District "October 9," 1866. Hugh W. Maxwell was appointed by the Governor Judge of the Fifth Judicial District "July 23, 1866," to take effect August 1.

Page 198.—An asterisk (*) should have been prefixed to the name of "John A. Johnson," Senator from Wapello county.

Page 201.—In first foot-note, for "1857", read "1859".

Page 208.—An asterisk (*) should have been prefixed to the name of "George W. Bassett," Senator from District 43.

CHANGES AND CORRECTIONS IN POST-OFFICES.

Allamakee County.—P. 4—Omit "Hardin."

Winneshiek County.—P. 61—Omit "Conover"; after "Springwater," in the same line, insert "Locust Lane"; insert "Twin Springs" in the same line with "Plymouth Rock"; omit "Woodville," "Burr Oak Springs," and "Locust Lane" (Pleasant township); and read "New Alba" for "Festina."

Alphabetical List.—Pages 106-114—Omit the following: "Burr Oak Springs, Winneshiek;" "Clayton Center, Clayton;" "Conover, Winneshiek;" "Festina, Winneshiek;" "North McGregor, Clayton;" "Sawana, Clayton;" "Sigel, Clayton;" and "Woodville, Winneshiek." Insert the following: "Littleport, Clayton; "New Alba, Winneshiek;" "Read, Clayton;" and "Twin Springs, Winneshiek."

Page 109.—The county in which Hardin post-office is situated is "Clayton," not "Allamakee."

Page 111.—"Milpine" should read "Melpine."

The following are corrected lists of post-offices received since the foregoing pages were printed:

BREMER COUNTY.

NO. TP.	NO. RANGE.	CIVIL TOWNSHIP.	POST-OFFICES.
92	11	Dayton	Buck Creek (§ 92)
93	13	Douglas	Frederika (§ 13)
91	11	Franklin	Eagle Hill (§ 22), Grove Hill (§ 11)
93	12	Frederika	Tripoli (§ 33)
92	12	Fremont	None
91	13 14	Jackson	Janesville (§ 35, R. 14)
91	13	Jefferson	Denver (§ 24)
92	14	Lafayette	Spring Lake (§ 17)
93	11	Le Roy	None
93	12	Le Roy	Mentor (§ 1), Leroy (§ 13)
91	12	Maxfield	Maxfield (§ 4)
93	14	Polk	Horton (§ 26), Syracuse (§ 30)
93	11	Sumner	None
93	12	Sumner	Sumner (§ 10), Dayton (§ 34)
92	13	Warren	None
91	13	Washington	None
91	14	Washington	Waverly
92	14	Washington	None

CLAYTON COUNTY.

NO. TP.	NO. R.	CIVIL TOWNSHIP.	POST-OFFICES.
93	5	Boardman	Elkader
91	1	Buena Vista	None
91	6	Cass	Strawberry Point
93	2	Clayton	None
pt. 93, 94	3	Clayton	Clayton
92	5	Cox Creek	Cox Creek, Littleport
91	4	Elk	None
94	4	Farmersburg	Farmersburg, National
pt. 93	3, 4	Garnavillo	Ceres, Garnavillo, (R. 3)
95	4	Giard	Council Hill, Giard
95	6	Grand Meadow	None
In 92	2	Guttenberg, city	Guttenberg
93	6	Highland	Highland
pt. 92, 93	2, 3	Jefferson, exc. of Guttenberg	None
91	5	Lodomillo	Yankee Settlement
In 95	3	McGregor, city of	McGregor
91	3	Mallory	None
94	6	Marion	Gem
95 pt. 94	3	Mendon, exc. of McGregor	None
91	2	Millville	Millville
95	5	Monona	Monona, Hardin
pt. 93	4	Read	Read
92	6	Sperry	Volga City
92	4 pt. 3	Volga	Elkport, (R. 4)
94	5	Wagner	Wagner, Communia

NEWSPAPERS.—Pages 139-143.—The following are names of newspapers and periodicals reported since the foregoing pages were printed:

Dubuque County.—"The Evergreen," Dubuque, monthly, Masonic.

Mahaska County.—"The Evangelist," Oskaloosa, monthly, religious (Disciples'). "Business Expositor and College Advocate," Oskaloosa; published "in the interest of Oskaloosa College."

Wapello County.—"Weekly Irish Harp," Ottumwa, Fenian.

Winnebago County.—"Winnebago Press," Forest City, Weekly, Republican.

www.ingramcontent.com/pod-product-compliance
Lightning Source LLC
LaVergne TN
LVHW010255110826
845151LV00004B/1475
* 9 7 8 1 4 2 5 5 2 2 1 1 7 *